Eyewitness Memory

Theoretical and Applied Perspectives

EYEWITNESS MEMORY

Theoretical and Applied Perspectives

Edited by

Charles P. Thompson
Kansas State University

Douglas J. Herrmann
Indiana State University

J. Don Read
University of Lethbridge

Darryl Bruce
St. Mary's University

David G. Payne
State University of New York, Binghamton

Michael P. Toglia
State University of New York, Cortland

Ψ **Psychology Press**
Taylor & Francis Group

NEW YORK AND LONDON

First published 1998 by Lawrence Erlbaum Associates, Inc.

Published 2014 by Psychology Press
711 Third Avenue, New York, NY 10017

and by Psychology Press
27 Church Road, Hove, East Sussex, BN3 2FA, UK
First issued in paperback 2014

*Psychology Press is an imprint of the Taylor & Francis Group, an
informa business*

Copyright © 1998 by Lawrence Erlbaum Associates, Inc.

Cover design by Kathryn Houghtaling

Library of Congress Cataloging-in-Publication Data

Eyewitness memory : theoretical and applied perspectives / edited by Charles P. Thompson ... [et al.].
     p. cm
    Companion volume to: Autobiographical memory
    Includes bibliographical references and indexes.
    ISBN 978-0-8058-2794-1 (hbk)
    ISBN 978-1-138-00297-5 (pbk)
    ISBN 978-0-8058-2795-8 (set)
    1. Memory in children. 2. Recollection (Psychol-
ogy). 3. Child witnesses. I. Thompson, Charles P.
BF723.M4E94 1997
153.1'2—dc21   97-8625
                                       CIP

Contents

Preface

The first meeting of the Society for Applied Research in Memory and Cognition (SARMAC) was held in Vancouver in July 1995. Over 175 people attended the meeting, which featured more than 60 research presentations, major invited addresses by Steve Ceci and Dave Rubin, and presentations by SARMAC Chair Doug Herrmann and Chair-elect Chuck Thompson. We wanted to capture some of the excitement of the meeting with a book consisting of elaborations of some of the presentations. However, there were too many excellent presentations with the result that a single book would have been too lengthy and too expensive. Thus, we decided to publish companion volumes around the two related themes of autobiographical memory and eyewitness testimony. We hope that the chapters included in this book will give the reader a feeling for what was a focused and exciting meeting.

ACKNOWLEDGMENTS

Many people deserve credit for making that first meeting possible. Don Read was the chair of the Conference Organizing Committee and deserves the highest praise for his work. Darryl Bruce and Don Read organized special sessions on autobiographical memory and eyewitness testimony, respectively. David Payne and Mike Toglia co-chaired the program committee. Finally, John Yuille was the on-site organizer whose able assistant, Melissa Nisbet, seemed to be able to handle any emergency!

The 1995 meeting was a good kick-off for SARMAC. It is an energetic and growing organization that encourages participation by all those interested in practical applications of memory and cognition. If your research interests include (or have implications for) practical applications, contact Darryl Bruce, Don Read, Chuck Thompson, or Mike Toglia to get information on the Society for Applied Research in Memory and Cognition. My e-mail is chuckt@ksu.edu and I welcome your inquiries.

We hope you enjoy the book!

—Charles P. Thompson

I

Overview

1

Eyewitness Memory:
Themes and Variations[1]

J. Don Read
University of Lethbridge

Darryl Bruce
Saint Mary's University

The organization of the first SARMAC conference around only two specifically identifiable research topics—autobiographical memory and eyewitness memory—may, at first blush, seem puzzling. The two areas, longtime staples on the menu of investigators of memory in more natural settings, differ on a variety of dimensions, perhaps most notably on their specific goals for scientific inquiry and application.

Yet these differences should not be exaggerated. For many questions about memory and cognition of interest to scientific psychology, there have been historical as well as rather arbitrary reasons for their assignment to the autobiographical or eyewitness memory fields. Both fields are highly active, are represented by substantial numbers of scientists, and continue to grow in size. In both areas, several separate scientific meetings dedicated to their respective interests have been held, numerous monographs published, and overlapping yet somewhat different journals established. To a significant extent, however, research in one area often serves as the basis for research

---

[1]As noted in the preface, some of the papers presented at the first Society for Applied Research in Memory and Cognition (SARMAC) conference in Vancouver in 1995 were revised and extended for chapters in these companion volumes on autobiographical memory and eyewitness memory. The two volumes are closely related, and this chapter describes how the same themes are expressed in both volumes. This chapter occurs in both volumes with slight changes in the title and text to make it appropriate for the volume in which it appears. Because it was truly coauthored, the order of authors also is reversed in the two volumes.

in the other. Most typically, work by eyewitness memory researchers has been stimulated by investigations of a more basic and theoretical nature in autobiographical memory.

Perhaps as a result of differing historical orientations, the seven chapters in the companion autobiographical memory volume generally focus on the qualities or types of recall from research participants, whereas the seven chapters in this volume generally focus on the quantity (a concern for completeness) and accuracy of recall. This interest in the ultimate end product and its application within the legal process in general encourages eyewitness memory investigators to modify their testing procedures continually in an attempt to gain even more information from participants about an event. Indeed, several of the chapters presented here reflect such attempts.

The types of events to be recalled by participants in the two research environments also have traditionally differed: Eyewitness memory participants have usually recalled very brief, recently witnessed, public (or staged) events, whereas individuals participating in autobiographical memory research have generally recalled private, personally significant, and personally selected events from remote memory, events for which accurate or complete public records have rarely existed. It is therefore not surprising that investigators of autobiographical memory have usually concentrated more on the quality than the quantity or veridicality of such reports.

In our view, research over the last decade has changed in such a way as to reflect more commonalties than differences between the two areas: For example, eyewitness researchers, prompted perhaps by the fact that a public record exists, have explored the recall of events that are both personal and autobiographically significant to the participants. Chapter 3 by Parker, Bahrick, Lundy, Fivush, and Levitt on children's recall of Hurricane Andrew well reflects this orientation. Investigation by Yuille and Daylen (chap. 8, this volume) of the recall of single or repeated instances of traumatic experiences, even though not in the public domain or documented, also shows the long-standing concern of traditional eyewitness researchers for the remembering of events of personal importance, a matter that for methodological and ethical reasons has been difficult to study. Both of these chapters could just as easily fit within the field of autobiographical memory, but because the events described are either public or their recollection has legal implications, they find themselves on the eyewitness side of the ledger.

Similarly, the companion autobiographical memory volume contains contributions that, if not central to the topic of eyewitness memory, at least have considerable relevance to it. For example, Bahrick (chap. 5, companion volume) deals with the problem of distortions of memory, an issue of enormous moment to those concerned about recollections made in legal and clinical situations. Likewise, the observations described in Pillemer, Ebanks, and Desrochers (chap. 9, companion volume) on verb tense shifts have implications for the authenticity of experiences reported in personal narratives and should thus be of interest to those working in clinical and legal contexts. Finally, Fivush's (chap. 6, companion volume) research shows the close relation between the qualitative characteristics of autobiographical memory and their relevance to matters of eyewitness testimony.

THEMES AND VARIATIONS

From our perusal of the autobiographical memory and eyewitness memory volumes, it appears that each featured one or more of the following six themes: accuracy, affect, imagery, development, methods, and theory. We emphasize that we developed these themes after the fact; other readers may develop other themes. Nevertheless, they permit us to provide the reader with a framework for organizing the information to come and to introduce the chapters themselves. Here, then is an indication of how the six themes or threads crop up in the various chapters.

Accuracy and Distortions of Memory in Children and Adults

Accuracy in remembering is a prominent these in a number of chapters. Three in the companion autobiographical memory volume touch on the problem. Bahrick's (chap. 5, companion volume) particular interest is the basis for distortion in the recollection of one's grades in high school. If they are not accurately recalled, errors are usually inflations of the actual grades. The contribution by Pillemer et al. (chap. 9, companion volume) examines shifts from the past to the present tense that sometimes occur in the recounting of a personal narrative. Such shifts may be an indicator of accuracy; that is, they may suggest that an individual is reporting something that was actually experienced rather than known secondhand or even fabricated. In his highly original essay, Larsen (chap. 10, companion volume) explores the phenomenal qualities of memories and notes that assessing memory accuracy is really a matter of comparing one's original experience (not the objective event itself) with one's later recollection. The problem, as Larsen points out, lies in what we can know of our initial experience.

Four of the chapters on eyewitness memory examine accuracy in the recollections of both children and adults. The exploration of the subject with children reflects an interest in cognitive development as well as the interface between psychology and the law. What is recalled by a child about a personally significant (and sometimes criminal) event is often critical to the legal process. For Ceci, Crossman, Gilstrap, and Scullin (chap. 2, this volume), the question is related to developmental differences in suggestibility between younger and older children across very different types of information, including bodily touching. For Walker and Hunt (chap. 4, this volume), on the other hand, the primary question is how we can better obtain from young children more complete recall of their experiences. Walker and Hunt point to a variety of specific interview techniques that psychologists have recommended for use with children as methods for bolstering recall. But when evidence of their use is sought within actual forensic interviews with children, their presence is very rare indeed.

Concerning adults, Yarmey (chap. 7, this volume) and Read, Lindsay, and Nicholls (chap. 6, this volume) describe recent data concerned with accuracy of person identification following brief interactions between research participants and a target individual. Yarmey's chapter focuses on a number of specific identification techniques (e.g., showups) and bases of identification (e.g., faces, voices, and bodily movements), whereas Read et al.'s chapter evaluates the controversial relation between the accuracy of a participant's identification decision and the subjective confidence expressed in that decision. The results of the latter chapter demonstrate that the association between accuracy and confidence can be very strong. They also suggest that eyewitness memory research has generally been unsuccessful at incorporating those characteristics of real-world identifications that may set the stage for the observation of a substantial link between accuracy and confidence.

Affect, Emotion, and Memory

The relation of affect and emotion to memory is complex and any attempt on our part to summarize the situation would be well beyond the scope and purpose of our introductory chapter. Bahrick (chap. 5, companion volume) provides a useful review of some of the relevant literature as well as some pitfalls in conducting and interpreting research in the area. Bahrick proposes a number of ideas of his discussion, a chief one being that reconstructive memory processes lead to erros of recollection that engender positive affect.

A number of the chapters in the companion autobiographical memory volume report intriguing effects concerning emotion and memory. Pillemer et al. (chap. 9, companion volume) show that a narrator's shift from the past to the present tense in recounting a past experience typically tends to occur at an emotional high point in the story. Fivush (chap. 6, companion volume) notes certain adult gender differences in autobiographical memory reports (e.g., women's are generally more emotional than men's), and asks whether they might originate in differences in the way that mothers and fathers reminisce with their children over the preschool years. One of her many findings is that both parents used substantially more emotion words in reminiscing with their daughters than with their sons. Larsen (chap. 10, companion volume) describes the results of an investigation of memory for emotional experiences. A particularly intriguing outcome was that when the focus of an emotion was an internal state (e.g., being joyful), the accompanying imagery was more somatic; when the focus was an external event (e.g., a holiday breakfast), the accompanying imagery was more visual. In a more theoretical vein, Rubin (chap. 4, companion volume) sees affect as one of the major components of the process of autobiographical recollection.

Some of the contributions in this volume also bear on the relation of affect and memory. One possibility is that it depends critically on the valence of the affect. When events generate positive affect, the relation is positive; when they generate negative affect, the relation is reversed. That is, it has often been argued that life events accompanied by strong negative affect or emotion are recalled with much greater difficulty than events accompanied by less emotional intensity. Consistent with the latter position are reports of "recovered" memories by individuals of events claimed to have been completely forgotten for several years, even decades. Parker et al. (chap. 3, this volume) point to the complexity of the association between affect and memory and, in so doing, finds support for both positions: Recall of a hurricane and its aftermath by children reflected a curvilinear, Yerkes–Dodson relation between emotion and recall. In a related way, Ceci et al. (chap. 2, this volume) suggest that children are less willing to develop false beliefs about events that have negative rather than positive valence, although the effects of suggestive questioning in general were seen in the accounts of preschool and older children and across different domains of inquiry.

Like Parker et al., Yuille and Daylen (chap. 8, this volume) are also concerned with events accompanied by negative emotion. They emphasize what they refer to as events of impact, and they restrict their interest to a subset of those that are traumatic. The authors make the important point that at this stage of our knowledge, in both eyewitness memory and autobiographical memory, the consequences of emotional events may be so idiosyncratic as to preclude the possibility of any generalizations about the relation between emotion and memory. Yuille and Daylen describe a variety of hypothetical patterns relating trauma to memory that may well provide useful direction to future researchers.

Imagery and Memory

If anything can be considered a defining aspect of autobiographical memory, it is imagery, especially visual imagery. Larsen's (chap. 10, companion volume) investigation, referred to earlier, yields helpful amplifying information. First, the imagery accopanying a personal recollection appears to be based at least partly on the original experience and not simply generated at the time of retrieval. Second, imagery of a visual nature is indeed prominent in autobiographical remembering, but if an internal emotion is being retrieved, then somatic imagery can be strongly in evidence. Pillemer et al.'s (chap. 9, companion volume) analysis of changes from the past to the present tense in relating an episode from one's past may likewise underscore the central role of imagery in autobiographical memory. They suggest that such shifts may occur partly because the episode has a strong sensory representation in memory, and that the past is being perceived again. But whatever the implications of the findings of Larsen and Pillemer et al., Rubin (chap. 4, companion volume) considers imagery, especially visual imagery, as a key component in recollecting one's personal past.

Within a series of five experiments designed to assess the boundary conditions and ages, if any, at which suggestive effects of misleading information occur with children, Ceci et al. (chap 2, this volume) also emphasize the centrality of visual imagery (or of repeatedly imagining an event) in the formation and retention of autobiographical memories, albeit false ones. For example, the children in Ceci et al.'s investigations were sometimes encouraged to develop a memory of an unusual (and nonexperienced) event by generating on 10 occasions a visual image of the event and their involvement with it. Although explanations other than the production of vivid imagery exist for the construction of what appear to some firmly entrenched false autobiographical memories following successive applications of the researchers' instructions, imagination and imagery do seem likely candidates.

The potentially misleading consequences of mental imagery are also seen in Yarmey's (chap. 7, this volume) study of participants whose estimates of the duration of their brief interactions with a target person were preceded by brief periods of mental rehearsal. As it turned out, the rehearsal manipulation reduced confidence ratings of the duration estimates, but an explanation for the effect is not obvious at this time. Finally, Yuille and Daylen (chap. 8, this volume) suggest that the quality of the verbal report following a traumatic incident, including access to detailed imagery, is a joint function of the type of event experienced and the locus of a witness' attention (internal or external) during the event. Taken together, the eyewitness memory chapters frequently do consider imagery (visual or otherwise) as an important moderator and indicator of events in autobiographical memory, but the focus seems more on the measurement of imagery than on its function.

Development of Memory

A number of the authors in the companion autobiographical memory volume are concerned to varying degree with the development of memory. Fivush (chap. 6, companion volume) concentrates on the preschool years and looks for variations in reminiscences during that period between daughters and sons on the one hand and mothers and fathers on the other. She finds that gender differences appear early on in autobiographical narratives. In comparison with boys, girls recalled more information, referred more to emotions (as mentioned earlier), and included more orientations (linkages to other events) and evaluations in their narratives. Fivush believes that parents may be contributing to this pattern because in conversing with their daughters, both mothers and fathers elaborated and confirmed more and used more emotion words.

Cohen (chap. 7, companion volume) focuses on the later years of life and considers the changes that occur in both the character and function of autobiographical memories. One such change is that personal memories of older people sometimes become overgeneral. At other times, however, they retain their vivid and detailed nature, perhaps because they are personally important and are rehearsed. Cohen speculates that such memories maintain the individual's self-concept and sense of personal identity.

An important developmental question in the chapter by Robinson and Taylor (chap. 8, companion volume) is whether a reminiscence bump (heightened recall of autobiographical memories from the period spanning 10–30 years of age) would be obtained when participants—here, middle-aged women—gave narrative accounts of their lives. The authors observed such heightened recall, but more for experiences from, the childhood and preadolescent years than from the adolescent years, suggesting that "the reminiscence bump reflects a feature of autobiographical memory at all levels of its hierarchical structure" (p. 132).

The chapters in this volume by Ceci et al. (chap. 2) and Walker and Hunt (chap. 4) easily fit with the developmental concerns of the autobiographical memory authors, albeit from a different perspective. For Ceci et al., the primary issue is whether a child's autobiographical memory can be substantially altered through suggestive techniques and whether, as some have suggested, there is an age beyond which children are less at risk. Further, Ceci and his associates explore the long-term fate of information suggested to and accepted by a child.

Walker and Hunt, on the other hand, take as a given the need to tailor interview practices acording to the age of a child in recognition of the developmental differences between children and adult eyewitnesses in the recollection of description of autobiographical events. That is, the accurate and complete description of a witnessed event, like all autobiographical memories studied by both groups of researchers, results from an interaction between questioner and respondent and assumes their common under-standing of the ground rules, language, and goals of the interview. Unfortunately, as Walker and Hunt demonstrate, although the goals may be common, age-appropriate language and rules were not evident in the majority of professional interviews they analyzed. Perhaps this lack best demonstrates the need for the application of research on cognition and memory to problems in the world beyond the laboratory.

Methods

Several chapters in the companion autobiographical memory volume have implications for the methods used to investigate memory. Bahrick (chap. 5, companion volume) not only raises several methodological problems in studying the influence of affect on memory; he recommends research strategies for combatting them. In studying autobiographical memory in the aged person, Cohen (chap. 7, companion volume) notes that the picture varies depending on whether such memories are self-selected (e.g., obtained by cuing with a word) or experimenter designated (e.g., asking the participant to recall a flashbulb memory event): Experimenter-designated memories show aging effects (less detail and accuracy in reports by older individuals) for self-selected memories, the general pattern is that there are no age differences in vividness and detail.

Three of the autobiographical memory chapters have the methodological commonality of asking individuals to give some kind of narrative account of their personal pasts. In this respect, they represent something of a departure from the more typical methods used to study autobiographical memory (see Cohen's chap. 7 in the companion volume for an overview). The most extensive use of the approach is by Robinson and Taylor (chap. 8, companion volume). They obtained life narratives from the middle-aged participants in their study. The findings provide a wealth of information on the interplay between narrative forms and the reconstruction of one's past. Pillemer et al. (chap. 9, companion volume), as we have previously indicated, emphasize the verb tense shifts that are sometimes a feature of the narrative structure of autobiographical recollections. Fivish (chap. 6, companion volume) also focuses on narrative structure, but as it develops in preschoolers. She reports gender differences in the use of various narrative devices that show up very early in conversations between children and their parents. The investigations by Robinson and Taylor, Pillemer et al., and Fivush may make it more obvious to the reader why Rubin (chap. 4, companion volume) holds narrative structure to be one of five essential components of autobiographical remembering.

An emphasis on methodology is also evident in the eyewitness memory chapters of Köhnken (chap. 5, this volume) and of Walker and Hunt (chap. 4, this volume). Both stress that for children and adults, respectively, interview techniques should enhance the accuracy and utility of testimony about life events. In Köhnken's case, the procedures are intended to be prescriptive and, for many specific components, are based on empirical work with the cognitive interview technique. For Walker and Hunt, the goals of accuracy and completeness are the same, but specific techniques are recommended as a means of reducing the possibility of contamination of child witness accounts by interviews and other sources. One feature for which there is agreement across these two chapters is that an opportunity for the interviewee (whether adult or child) to provide at the outset an unstructured narrative account of the event or events in question is central to a complete and accurate recollection.

Theory

The most theoretical of the autobiographical memory volume's chapters is by Rubin (chap. 4, companion volume), who describes a theory of autobiographical recollection. Taking Proust's classic autobiographical recollections as prototypical, Rubin presents an account of remembering one's past that starts with an initial cue and then moves on to a slow search process that retrieves and integrates narrative, visual imagery, and affect components. Rubin also explores the underlying neurophysiological processing that may be involved.

Although no other chapter is as much concerned with theory as Rubin's, many have significant theoretical implications. Larsen (chap. 10, companion volume), for example, would have us pay more attention to the phenomenal qualities of remembering—the subjective conscious experience associated with memory and recollection. He sets forth a framework that distinguishes three kinds of qualities: (a) content qualities, which are about the past experience itself; (b) appearance qualities, which have to do with the present experience and evaluation of the content qualities; and (c) process qualities, which concern how content and appearance qualities are cognitively produced.

At least three of the volume's chapters have implications for the structure of autobiographical memory: Robinson and Taylor's (chap. 8, companion volume) consideration of self-narratives convinces them that autobiographical memory is organized at several levels, with self-narratives themselves perhaps being one type of organization. Pillemer et al. (chap 9, companion volume) argue that verb tense shifts also suggest multiple levels of representation, among them, personal memories that are expressed through images or emotions and those expressed via a narrative memory system. Cohen's (chap. 7, companion volume) general explanation for the prevalence in older people of overgeneral autobiographical memories — ones that are imprecise and lacking in detail — is that autobiographical memory is hierarchically organized and that overgeneral memories are due to truncated retrieval at a level in the hierarchy that is too high for the retrieval of specific details.

With the exception of Yuille and Daylen (chap. 8, this volume), the eyewitness memory authors have not concerned themselves with the construction of broad models of memory. This is not the say that the chapters are atheoretical: Several have hypothetical general relations between variables as their general concern. For example, for Read et al. (chap. 6, this volume), the relation is between accuracy and confidence; for Ceci et al. (chap. 2, this volume), between age and susceptibility to different types of misleading information; and for Parker et al. (chap. 3, this volume), between level of arousal and recall memory. Of the autobiographical memory chapters, we believe the theoretical discussion provided by Larsen (chap. 10, companion volume) to be most readily applicable to the eyewitness domain. In particular, it bears on questions concerning the assessment of the credibility of witnesses' statements.

CONCLUSIONS

Beyond the specific contributions of each chapter to the literature on autobiographical and eyewitness memory, what do we hope that the reader will come away with in general concerning the many basic and applied investigations of remembering discussed herein? At the very least, that the autobiographical and eyewitness memory fields are thriving; that they are likely to remain center stage in the further investigation of memory in natural contexts; that although the autobiographical and eyewitness memory chapters have been segregated in these two volumes, the separation is often more arbitrary than real and that connections between the two areas abound; that the two research traditions are entirely mindful of fundamental laboratory methods, research, and theory, sometimes drawing their research inspirations from that quarter; and, perhaps finally, that the two fields, although driven largely by everyday memory concerns, can contribute to a more basic understanding of memory at both an empirical and a theoretical level.

II

Eyewitness Memory

2

Social and Cognitive Factors in Children's Testimony

Stephen J. Ceci
Angela M. Crossman
Livia L. Gilstrap
Matthew H. Scullin
Cornell University

By now it has been well established that there are significant age-related differences in suggestibility, with the youngest preschoolers being disproportionately more suggestible than older children and adults (Ceci & Bruck, 1993). Of the more than 20 studies that have contrasted preschoolers with older age groups, all but two have reported that preschoolers are more suggestible. In this chapter, we ask whether there are important constraints on this age-related trend; particularly, whether there are certain boundaries beyond which the suggestibility effect disappears or is greatly attenuated. Thus, in this chapter we examine both age- and event-related parameters on suggestibility.

For instance, a number of writers have suggested that, although younger children are more suggestible about peripheral and unimportant events, there is little evidence that they are suggestible about central, bodily acts (e.g., Pope & Brown, 1996). Some authors have gone so far as to propose a quasi-evolutionary mechanism through which children should be more adept at encoding events that are important to their survival, such as bodily touching: "Survival of the species requires that we learn—quickly and with lasting impact—to avoid danger and sustain life. . . . Recent research suggests that nature wisely provided us with a physiological mechanism to consolidate memory for personally significant events rapidly" (Goodman, Rudy, Bottoms, & Aman, 1990, p. 251) Many researchers have reported that younger children's suggestibility is greatly reduced for bodily touching

15

(e.g., Goodman & Clarke-Stewart, 1991; Myers, 1995). But how true is this claim and what does the most recent research indicate?

In what follows, we review five classes of research that address different boundaries beyond which it is alleged that children are not suggestible. In the first experiment, we examined whether the age differences in suggestibility were diminished when children were repeatedly asked about the behavior of others. Experiment 2 examined whether age differences were reduced when events were actually experienced as opposed to merely being imagined. In Experiments 3 and 4 we examined whether age differences occur for events that involve either pain or embarrassment (inoculation and genital touching by a pediatrician). In Experiment 5 we studied the effect of an interviewer's confirmatory bias on the accuracy of children's recollections. Finally, in the last experiment we examined conditions that tilt suggestibility in the opposite direction, causing older children to become more suggestible than younger ones.

EXPERIMENT 1: CHILDREN'S MEMORIES FOR EVENTS ABOUT OTHERS

In an effort to better understand children's reactions to repeated questioning about the behavior of another person, Leichtman and Ceci (1995) tested the impact of repeated suggestions and stereotypes on children's memory reports. Why study the effects of repeated suggestions and stereotypes on children's reports? Because there are frequent examples of the operation of both in actual court cases. A particularly moving example of this can be seen in the case of a child witness recanting her testimony in a death row case:

> When I first saw Fred with red stuff on his shirt, I didn't think it was that important. At first, I didn't really know if it was blood or chili. Later, when I saw Fred had a gun or a knife, it caught my attention, and I thought that it must be blood. Because different people asked me so many different questions about what I saw, I became confused. I thought I might have seen something that would be helpful to the police. I didn't realize that it would become so important. I thought they wanted me to be certain, so I said I was certain even though I wasn't. Originally, I think I told the police just what I saw. But the more questions I was asked, the more confused I became. I answered questions I wasn't certain about because I wanted to help the adults. (*State v. Macias*, 1987; subscribed and sworn before Regina Jarius, Notary, on the 13th day of August 1988)

Several years prior to this recantation, a man was convicted of murder based mainly on this child's claim that she had seen him with blood on his shirt and a weapon in his hand. Not only was the child interviewed repeatedly, in a series of highly suggestive interviews spanning an extended period of time, but she also possessed a strong negative stereotype about the defendant prior to the event (her mother repeatedly warned her that he was a bad man with whom she should not be friendly). Thus, in this case, a child was suggestively interviewed repeatedly about the actions and appearance of another person, a person about whom she possessed a negative stereotype. This is the situation Leichtman and Ceci (1995) attempted to replicate and examine with the Sam Stone study.

In this experiment, a stranger named Sam Stone paid a 2-minute visit to preschoolers (3–6 years old) in their day-care center. Following his visit, the children were asked for details about the visit on four separate occasions over a 10-week period. Children in the control condition received no information about Sam Stone prior to his visit and during the four subsequent interviews they were simply asked questions about what Sam Stone had done during his visit. They were given no suggestions about the nature of the visit or Sam Stone's activities. One month after the fourth interview (i.e., 3 months following Sam Stone's visit), children were interviewed a fifth time by a new interviewer. This interviewer first elicited a free narrative about Sam Stone's visit and then, using probes, asked about two "nonevents" that involved San Stone doing something to a teddy bear and a book. In reality, he never touched either item.

No child in the control group made false reports of any kind during the free narrative, and in response to the question regarding the nonevents, "Did Sam Stone do anything to a book or a teddy bear?" most of the children in the control group accurately replied "No." Only 10% of the youngest (3- to 4-year-old) children's claims contained assertions that Sam Stone did anything to a book or teddy bear. When asked if the children actually saw the misdeeds (as opposed to thinking or hearing he did something), only 5% of their answers continued to contain claims that anything occurred. Finally, when gently challenged ("You didn't really see him do anything to the book/teddy bear, did you?"), only 2.5% of the youngest children still insisted that the fictitious misdeeds had occurred. None of the older (5- to 6-year-old) children claimed that they had seen Sam Stone do anything with either object. These data are shown in Fig. 2.1.

A second group of children received a good deal of information about Sam Stone's personality prior to his visit. They were told a total of 12 stories, three per week for 1 month prior to his visit, depicting Sam Stone as a kind, but very clumsy person. For example,

You'll never guess who visited me last night [pause] That's right. Sam Stone! And guess what he did this time? He asked to borrow my Barbie and when he was carrying her down the stairs, he tripped and fell and broke her arm. That Sam Stone is always getting into accidents and breaking things!

Following Sam Stone's visit, these children were also interviewed four times over a 10-week period. However, each interview contained erroneous

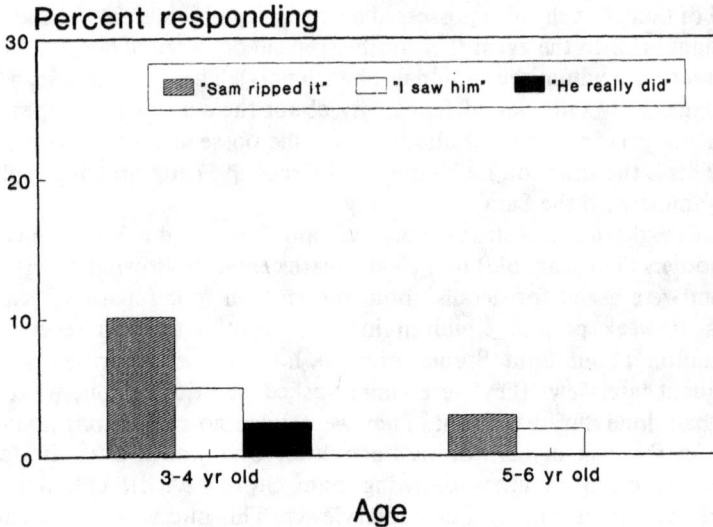

FIG. 2.1. The percentage of children in the control condition (no suggestion; no stereotype) responding to fictitious events. See the text for a description of the various levels of responding.

suggestions built into the questions, such as "When Sam Stone ripped that book, was he being silly or was he angry?" During the fifth interview (which was identical to the interview for the control group), 46% of the youngest and 30% of the oldest preschoolers spontaneously reported that Sam Stone had committed one or both misdeeds during their free narratives. Further, in response to specific questions, 72% of the youngest children claimed that Sam Stone did one or both of the misdeeds. Nearly half (44%) stated that they actually saw him do these things, and 21% continued to insist that he did them even when they were gently challenged. Although they were more accurate, a full 11% of older preschoolers also insisted that they had seen Sam Stone perform the misdeeds when gently challenged. The data for that group are presented in Fig. 2.2.

Obviously, then, even the youngest of child witnesses are capable of accurately reporting the behaviors of others when they are allowed to deliver their reports with little interference or misguidance from adult interviewers. Yet, when faced with both suggestive questioning and a negative stereotype about an individual, it seems that preschoolers are much less resistant than older children to misleading information regarding the behavior and appearance of other people. Whether this degree of suggestibility is seen with personally experienced or imagined events, however, is a question we address later.

Percent responding

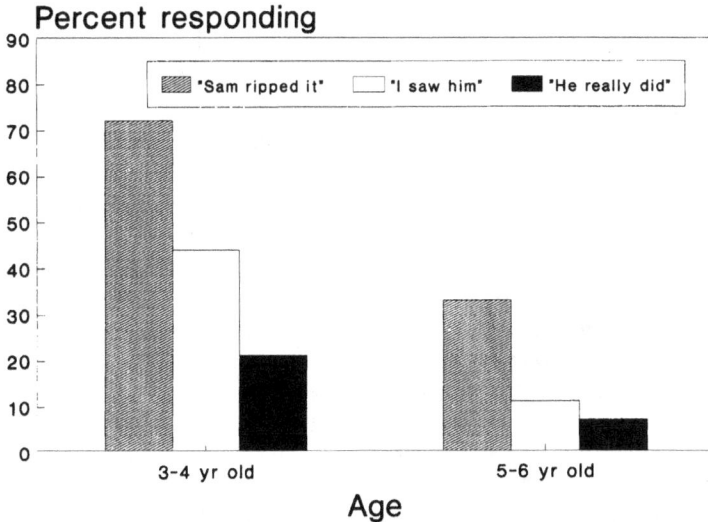

FIG. 2.2. The percentage of children in the condition with both suggestions and stereotype responding to fictitious events. See the text for a description of the various levels of responding.

EXPERIMENT 2: CHILDREN'S REPORTS
OF REAL AND IMAGINED PERSONAL
EXPERIENCES

To learn whether young children would be suggestible about events they had only imagined, Ceci, Crotteau-Huffman, Smith, and Loftus (1994; see also, Ceci, Loftus, Leichtman, & Bruck, 1994) asked preschoolers to think about a number of events repeatedly, creating mental images each time they did so. Events included actual experiences (e.g., an accident that resulted in stitches) and fictitious events that they had not experienced (e.g., getting a finger caught in a mousetrap and having to go to the hospital to have it removed).

Each week for approximately 10 consecutive weeks, preschool children were individually interviewed by a trained adult. They were asked if each of the real and fictitious events had ever happened to them. For example, the interviewer would ask: "Think real hard, and tell me if this ever happened to you. Can you remember going to the hospital with the mousetrap on your finger?" The interviewer asked the children to think "real hard" about all of the events each week, and prompted them to visualize the scenes.

After 10 weeks of thinking about both real and fictitious personal events, 58% of the children in one study produced false narrative accounts to one or more fictitious events, with 25% of the children producing false accounts to the majority of the fictitious events. Thus, the simple act of repeatedly imagining participation in an event caused these preschoolers to falsely report that they had engaged in activities when they had not. In fact, it would seem as though many of the children firmly believed that these fictitious events had actually occurred, with 27% of them initially refusing to accept debriefing. Many insisted, to both the researchers and to their parents, that they remembered the events happening.

An important extension of that study relates to a manipulation of the types of events imagined (Ceci, Loftus, et al., 1994). Under very similar circumstances, children imagined positive, negative, and neutral events in which they were or were not participants. (For ease of exposition, we have collapsed across age groups in Fig. 2.3 because, even though the youngest children made many more errors, the pattern across ages was similar.) In this study, children were shown to have the highest false assent rates to neutral events, such as observing someone board a bus (an increase from 38% to 60% mean assent rate between the first and 11th interviews) and the lowest to negative events (from 13% to 30%), with positive events falling in the middle (these are average values, with younger children assenting more often on each trial and older children less often). These data supply some evidence for the claim that negative events (as in abusive or threatening experiences) are more resistant to false suggestions than neutral ones.

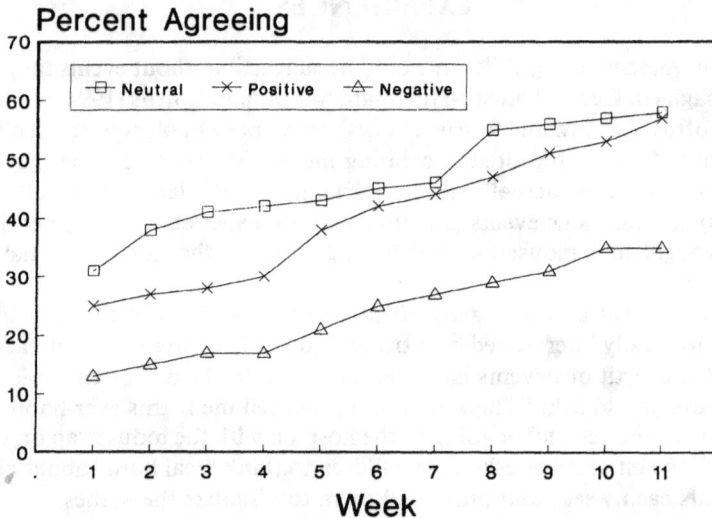

FIG. 2.3. The percentage of children reporting that they had engaged in fictitious events plotted as a function of the number of weeks they had been imagining the events.

However, the findings also imply that "although abusive events may be more resistant to suggestive interviewing methods than other types of events, [they] are by no means immune to the deleterious effects of suggestive interviewing techniques" (Ceci, Loftus, et al., 1994, p. 316).

Experiment 2B: The Persistence of Children's False Beliefs

Given many children's insistence on the truth of the fictitious events they had imagined in the previous study, we decided to follow up on as many of the children as possible, to see whether or not they recalled their prior reports (Huffman, Crossman, & Ceci, 1996). After interviewing 22 of the original children, we found that although the children remembered 91% of the true events, they only assented to 13% of the false events (as opposed to 34% found by Ceci, Crotteau-Huffman, et al., 1994). (This number is still impressive in that these false claims occurred following the original debriefing.) Their high accuracy rate for true events 1 year later makes it unlikely that their "recanting" of false events was due to forgetting. This finding raises additional unanswered questions about the fate and composition of children's false beliefs.

EXPERIMENT 3: CHILDREN'S REPORTS ABOUT A VISIT TO THEIR PEDIATRICIAN

The studies previously discussed detailed ways in which children can seemingly come to believe that they witnessed events that never occurred. However, it could be argued that the acts the children were questioned about were minor, peripheral events that lacked relevance to issues raised by claims of sexual abuse. We feel that it is valid to distinguish between events in which a child is merely a bystander and those that involve actions directly affecting the child and relating to the child's body. Consequently, Bruck, Ceci, Francouer, and Barr (1995) examined children's memories for details about a visit to a pediatrician's office. We looked at the effects of postevent suggestions on children's memories for an inoculation, an event that involves some degree of stress as well as pain and discomfort.

This study was conducted in two phases, both of which involved a group of 5-year-old children who were visiting their pediatrician for an annual checkup. In the first phase, children were given a routine examination by their pediatrician and then led to an "inoculation room" where a research assistant discussed a poster on the wall. Five minutes later, the pediatrician entered the room and administered an oral polio vaccine and a DPT (diptheria, pertussis, tetanus immunization) shot. The research assistant remained present and coded the child's level of distress and how long it took before the child stopped crying and became ready for the next part of the study. The child was then taken to another room by the research assistant and randomly assigned to one of three feedback conditions in which the child was told how he or she had acted while receiving the inoculation.

Children in the pain-denying group were told that the shot did not seem to hurt them at all and that it does not hurt big kids to get a shot (no-hurt condition). Other children were given pain-affirming feedback and told that the shot seemed to have hurt them a lot but that children generally hurt when they get a shot (hurt condition). The final group was simply told that the shot was over and that many children get shots (neutral condition). After giving the child feedback, the research assistant gave the child a treat and read the child a story about a child who gets injured after falling from a tree. The mother in the story gave the fictional child the same feedback that the child participant had received from the research assistant.

One week later, a second research assistant visited the child at home and taught the child how to indicate on rating scales how much the child felt the shot had hurt and how much he or she had cried during the inoculation procedure. We found that the children's reports of how much they cried and hurt during this interview were positively correlated with distress ratings made by the research assistant during the inoculation, but they did not differ on the basis of feedback condition. Hence, in the first interview, the children's reports for a personally relevant, stressful experience were not rendered less accurate by the suggestive feedback given immediately following the event.

In the second phase of the study, children were suggestively interviewed three additional times approximately 1 year later. They were repeatedly given either "no-hurt" feedback (i.e., told that they had been brave and had not cried at the time of the inoculation) or "neutral" feedback (i.e., not told how they acted). For ethical reasons, the pain-affirming "hurt" condition was discontinued to avoid inducing in the children a phobia of doctors. During a fourth interview, the children were again asked to rate how much the short had hurt and how much they cried. This time there were large suggestibility effects, with children in the "no-hurt" condition reporting significantly less hurt and crying than children who were not given feedback.

In the three follow-up interviews, we also provided three groups of children with misleading information about the actions of those present during the medical procedure. Some children were told that the female research assistant had given them the shot and the male pediatrician had shown them the poster. A second group was told that the research assistant had given them the shot, but was given no information about the pediatrician. In the third group, the children were told that the pediatrician had shown them the poster, read them a story, and gave them a treat, but no information was given about the research assistant. Finally, the control group was given no information about the pediatrician or about the research assistant, but was simply told that "someone" had done these things.

During the fourth and final interview, only 1 child out of 32 in the two groups that had not been given misinformation about the research assistant inaccurately reported that she had administered the shot. However, 32% of the children who had been misinformed about the research assistant asserted that she had given them the short. Forty-two percent of the misled children said the research assistant gave them the oral polio vaccine, compared to 16% of the children who were not misled about the research assistant. Interestingly, 38% of the misled children, as opposed to none of the control children, claimed that the research assistant had performed other scripted events that were not accurate, such as checking their ears and nose, although these events had not been suggested. The children who had been misled were, in fact, much more likely to make errors of commission in free recall, with 41 spontaneous false allegations emanating from the misled groups, compared to only one occurring in the group that had not been given false information about either participant. These data are presented in Fig. 2.4.

The results of this study are consistent with those of the Sam Stone study, despite the fact that the events and experiences about which the children were misled were different. In the Sam Stone study, repeated suggestions and stereotypes led to convincing claims of witnessing nonevents. In the inoculation study, misleading information given in repeated interviews after a long delay influenced children's memories of personally experienced, salient, and scripted events that involved pain and discomfort.

EXPERIMENT 4: USING ANATOMICAL DOLLS TO SYMBOLICALLY REPRESENT ACTIONS

In the next study, Bruck, Ceci, Francouer, and Renick (1995) wished to examine whether errors in reporting that had been observed in earlier studies would also occur for events involving genital touching that caused embarrassment rather than pain and discomfort. In order to approach this matter in an ethically acceptable manner, naturally occurring visits by forty 3-year-old children to a professor of pediatrics were studied. The children were assigned to either a genital-examination condition, in which they

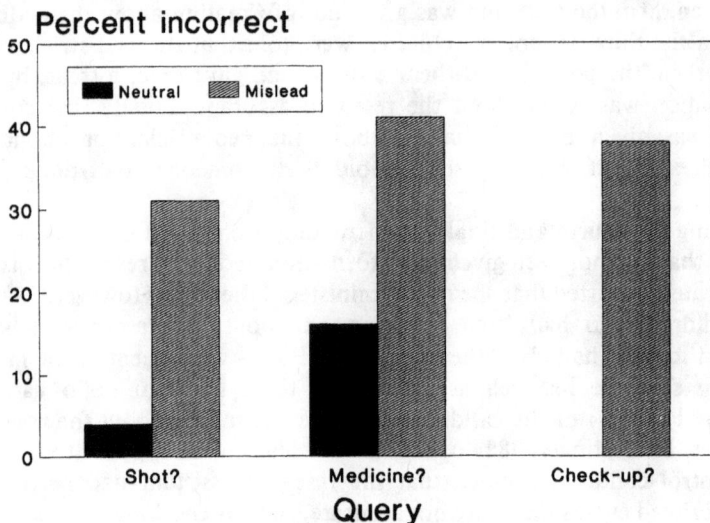

FIG. 2.4. The percentage of children claiming that the research assistant had performed various activities that she had not performed.

received a genital examination before being interviewed, or to a no-genital-examination condition, in which they received a general physical examination before their interview.

Five minutes after the exam, with the children's mothers present, the children were asked to describe in their own words where the doctor touched them. The children were then presented with anatomical dolls and asked to tell and demonstrate where the pediatrician had touched them. The major finding was that 3-year-olds were generally confused by questions about their bodies and about symbolically representing them with anatomical dolls. Approximately 50% of the children who were touched in the genital region did not indicate that they were touched there when questioned either with or without dolls. Thus, they committed errors of omission. Somewhat over half of those who were not touched in the genital region correctly refrained from stating that they were touched there in the doll-assisted questioning condition. Significantly, however, a sizable number of children in both groups made errors of commission when questioned with the dolls. In all, nearly 60% of the total sample indicated genital insertions, used the props in a sexualized manner, or committed other aggressive acts that would otherwise be cause for concern. This is contrary to a commonly held belief that children who have not been sexually touched will not indicate sexual events with dolls. Although research by Goodman and her colleagues did not find that 5-year-olds made errors of commission with the dolls (Saywitz, Goodman, Nicholas, &

Moan, 1991), they also did not find that the dolls were beneficial in eliciting accurate information (Goodman et al., 1990). Hence, on the basis of this research, it would seem best not to use anatomical dolls when interviewing 3-year-olds unless the dolls' incremental validity can be demonstrated, which at this point seems unlikely.

As an example of what can happen when a 3-year-old is presented with an anatomically correct doll, we describe a child from a pilot study who was given a nongenital exam in which her underpants were never removed and the pediatrician never touched her genital or anal areas.

Immediately following the exam, the child was given an anatomically correct doll and committed two errors, interdigitating the doll's vagina and incorrectly using a measuring tape on her head and the doll's ankle. She responded correctly to all other questions about where the doctor touched her and correctly demonstrated the use of other props, such as a stethoscope, light, and reflex hammer, both on herself and on the doll.

Three days later the same child was again shown the anatomically detailed doll. This time the child inserted a stick the pediatrician had used to tickle her foot into the doll's vagina, although on further questioning she denied that this had happened. Most remarkably, when shown the doll for a third time 3 days later, she hammered the stick violently into the doll's vagina with a reflex hammer. She then inserted a toy earscope into the doll's anus. When the interviewer asked: "Did Dr. Emmett really do this to you?" the child adamantly replied that he did. A follow-up question by her father elicited a similar claim. When the father said that her mother did not see Dr. Emmett do this to her, the child replied that he did it when her mother left the room. Thus, repeated exposures to the doll, with a minimum degree of suggestion, resulted in highly sexualized play by this child.

In sum, this study shows that young children have difficulty accurately reporting events that involve their bodies. In addition, the use of anatomically detailed dolls does not appear to facilitate recollections of personally-experienced events that involve bodily touching.

EXPERIMENT 5: THE EFFECT
OF INTERVIEWERS' CONFIRMATORY BIASES
ON CHILDREN'S REPORTS

In the previous sections, we discussed children's suggestibility about autobiographical events that included some type of bodily touching. Although past research has been criticized because of the belief that children will not incorporate false material about events that are personal and/or involve genital touching, we have given contrary examples in which children did accept false material about autobiographical events that included genital touch. In the following experiment, Ceci, Leichtman, and White (in press) decided to more closely simulate a forensic situation by adding an actual interviewer with preexisting hypotheses about the event in question.

Children 3 to 6 years old played a game of "Simon Says" in pairs with an experimenter and then were interviewed 1 month later. The interviewer, a trained social worker, received a one-page sheet containing events that might have occurred during the game. This report contained both factual and erroneous information. For example, if Child A had touched Child B's nose and patted her own head, the interviewer might have been told that Child A had touched Child B's toe (inaccurate) and patted her own head (accurate). We instructed the interviewer to determine what information the child was still able to remember. We asked the interviewer to begin by asking the child for a description of the event, avoiding all forms of suggestions and leading questions. After this free recall period, the interviewer could use any strategies that she felt were necessary to elicit the most factually accurate recall from the child.

When we had supplied the interviewer with accurate information, she elicited the correct information from the children nearly 100% of the time. However, when we misinformed the interviewer, 34% of the 3- to 4-year-olds and 18% of the 5- to 6-year-olds corroborated one or more of the interviewer's false events. In addition, as the interview progressed, children who initially accommodated false information seemed to become more credible in their affect and speech patterns. Thus, we became interested in determining what would happen if we repeated the process a second time with a new interviewer.

One month later, we gave the first interviewer's notes to a second interviewer and asked her to reinterview the children. In the same way that the first interviewer used our information to form biases about the event, the second interviewer's questions built on the biases of the first. Not only did the children's confidence levels about the false information increase, but the number of false events that they accepted as true also increased. Thus, in addition to replicating the finding that children will incorporate false information about autobiographical events involving touch in their memory reports, as was shown in the previous studies, this study also adds interviewer bias as another dimension affecting the suggestibility of children.

EXPERIMENT 6: CRYPTOMNESIA: TWO OPPOSITELY VALENCED DEVELOPMENTAL TRAJECTORIES

Still more evidence underscores the fact that we do not yet fully understand the relationship between age and suggestibility. For the most part, younger children have been found to be more suggestible than older children in many settings. Researchers have attributed these findings to younger children's poorer source attribution and metacognitive abilities. However, the following experiment suggests that, in some instances, older children's superior metacognitive abilities may make them more susceptible to source errors than younger, less cognitively sophisticated children.

In this experiment, we examined children's source misattributions in a group activity that was designed to foster a situation in which children incorrectly anticipated what would be asked of them and were encouraged to engage in advance encoding of answers that would be irrelevant later. The game involved stating or acting out examples of a category and each child was asked to generate a response that had not yet been used by another child. For example, if the category was "colors" and other children had said "blue" and "green," the next child would have to choose a new color such as "red." If the child incorrectly repeated "blue," the researcher would correct the child and then ask him or her to think of a new color. Two weeks after the activity, we asked children to recall as many of their own responses as possible. Then, children were asked to list as many unused responses as they could remember (i.e., those that were not made by any of the children). Finally, we presented the children with a list of responses and asked them to discriminate between the responses they had made and those that were made by others.

Surprisingly, older children (5- to 6-year olds) made more source monitoring errors in which they claimed to have given their peers' responses than younger children (3- to 4-year-olds), with the older children more often claiming that they had made responses that their peers had actually made. In observing the children playing the game, we realized that a potential explanation for this finding was the fact that older children had visibly rehearsed the responses that they were going to make while waiting for their turn. Younger children, on the other hand, waited until their turn and then spontaneously made a response; that is, they did not rehearse their responses in advance. We interpreted this to mean that during the discrimination task, older children were more often deciding whether they had merely thought about the response or verbalized it, whereas younger children, who had not made any attempt at rehearsal prior to their turn, had only been discriminating between their own and other's verbalizations. Possibly, discriminating between two events that involve the same child (e.g., saying vs. thinking) is a more difficult cognitive task than discriminating between two events that involve different children (e.g., self vs. another child saying). At this point, we realized that the advance encoding used by the older children might actually be interfering with their later recall. We sought to test this interpretation by repeating the experiment with one important modification. The experimenter whispered in each child's ear an item or act that he or she should say—provided that no one else said it first. This assured that the younger children would engage in advance encoding just like their older counterparts.

As expected, under these circumstances younger children plagiarized significantly more of their peers' contributions than did older children. Presumably, this occurred because the technique of whispering in their ear was tantamount to making them engage in advance encoding. If correct, this implies that younger children, although deficient in the spontaneous use of advance encoding, exhibit greater memory difficulties than older children when they are encouraged to use this form of encoding. Interestingly, another unexpected piece of evidence from this manipulation added further support for our interpretation of the first experiment: Children's plagiarisms came disproportionately from the children who went immediately before them. Only the children before them could have preempted their advance encoding because of the way the experiment was designed. Thus, children were not making random errors but were specifically failing to recall whether they had been thinking about the response when another child made it or had actually made the response themselves.

In the first portion of this experiment, the older children's metacognitive superiority worked to their disadvantage. Advance encoding of a response led to more errors in the later discrimination task. Younger children actually made fewer errors because they did not plan ahead by rehearsing options before their actual turn. When both groups were encouraged to use advance encoding, the expected age difference resurfaced, with older children making fewer source errors than younger children. In addition to incorporating others' responses as their own, younger children now made the additional implicit memory error of naming the responses of others as ones that were not made at all. Perhaps they had been busy encoding the whispered option while others were responding and this interfered with their later recall.

CONCLUSION

Taken together, the results of these seven experiments demonstrate that suggestibility effects are not confined to any one domain but apply to a wide range of domains and paradigms. Importantly, these findings reveal that suggestibility can be found for virtually all types of events, including bodily touching, painful and embarrassing experiences, and more mundane, stress-free experiences. This is not to say that suggestibility is as prevalent for events such as bodily touching as it is for more everyday, common events, but merely that it is wrong to assume, as some have done, that bodily touching is off limits when it comes to the potential impact of erroneous suggestions. Future research may demonstrate that salient, stressful events are somewhat harder to taint through false suggestions than relatively neutral, superficial events. To date, however, this has not been persuasively demonstrated. Based on what we do know, the safest conclusion is that there is no event domain that is impervious to the deleterious effects of suggestions, especially when they are repeatedly delivered over long retention intervals, as was the case in these seven experiments.

Recently, Eisen, Goodman, and Quin (1995) reported the results of their attempt to inculate false reports in children who had documented histories of abuse and neglect. These investigators made erroneous suggestions about anogenital touching during a 5-day abuse intake assessment. They found that 3- to 5-year-old children responded incorrectly to 21% of misleading questions about anogenital touching, and that sexually abused children were no less suggestible than nonabused children:

> It is also of interest to note that children who have suffered physical and/or sexual abuse, who have been removed from their homes in the midst of an abuse investigation, do not appear to show decrements in memory or increased suggestibility relative to our neglect and non-abused control groups. (p. 18)

Despite these authors' efforts to recast this finding by claiming that it provides no support for the view that sexually abused children are more suggestible than nonabused children, the argument most often made, including by one of the preceding authors in earlier reports, has been that it is harder to make suggestions about bodily touching to sexually abused children, not that it is easier (Goodman et al., 1990).

Although there is some debate over the role of stress (such as that caused by sexual abuse investigations) in susceptibility to suggestions, the most prudent view seems to be that stress can have negative effects on memory and suggestibility or no effect at all, but not positive effects (Ceci & Bruck, 1993).

In summary, recent research has charted the developmental and contextual factors that influence memory and suggestibility and shown that there are no areas of functioning that appear to be impervious to the baleful effects of repeated suggestions made over extended periods of time. Future research thus needs to turn to a new set of issues to explain differences within domains or contexts, namely individual differences. That is, future investigators should begin to concentrate on understanding why it is that some children of the same age are more resistant to false suggestions than others.

REFERENCES

Bruck, M., Ceci, S. J., Francouer, E., & Barr, R. (1995). "I hardly cried when I got my shot!" Influencing children's reports about a visit to their pediatrician. *Child Development, 66,* 193–208.

Bruck, M., Ceci, S. J., Francouer, E., & Renick, A. (1995). Anatomically detailed dolls do not facilitate preschoolers' reports of a pediatric examination involving genital touching. *Journal of Experimental Psychology: Applied, 1,* 95–109.

Ceci, S. J., & Bruck, M. (1993). Suggestibility of the child witness: A historical review and synthesis. *Psychological Bulletin, 113,* 403–439.

Ceci, S. J., Crotteau-Huffman, M., Smith, E., & Loftus, E. W. (1994). Repeatedly thinking about non-events. *Consciousness & Cognition, 3,* 388–407.

Ceci, S. J., Leichtman, M., & White, T. (in press). Interviewing preschoolers: Remembrance of things planted. *Applied Cognitive Psychology.*

Ceci, S. J., Loftus, E. W., Leichtman, M., & Bruck, M. (1994). The role of source misattributions in the creation of false beliefs among preschoolers. *International Journal of Clinical and Experimental Hypnosis, 62,* 304–320.

Eisen, M. L., Goodman, G. S., & Quin, J. (1995, August). *The impact of dissociation, trauma, and stress arousal on memory and suggestibility in the assessment of abused and neglected children.* Paper presented at the 103rd Annual Meeting of the American Psychological Association, New York.

Goodman, G. S., & Clarke-Stewart, A. (1991). Suggestibility in children's testimony: Implications for child sexual abuse investigations. In J. L. Doris (Ed.), *The suggestibility of children's recollections* (pp. 92–105). Washington, DC: American Psychological Association.

Goodman, G. S., Rudy, L., Bottoms, B. L., & Aman, C. (1990). Children's concerns and memory: Issues of ecological validity in the study of children's eyewitness testimony. In R. Fivush & J. Hudson (Eds.), *Knowing and remembering in young children* (pp. 249–284). New York: Cambridge University Press.

Huffman, M. L. C., Crossman, A. M., & Ceci, S. J. (1996, March). *Long term effects of source misattribution error: Are false memories permanent?* Presentation at the biennial meeting of the American Psychology-Law Society, Hilton Head, SC.

Leichtman, M. D., & Ceci, S. J. (1995). The effects of stereotypes and suggestions on preschoolers' reports. *Developmental Psychology, 31,* 568–578.

Myers, J. E. B. (1995). New era of skepticism regarding children's credibility. *Psychology, Public Policy, and Law, 1,* 387–398.

Pope, K., & Brown, L. (1996). *Recovered memories of abuse: Assessment therapy forensics.* Washington, DC: American Psychological Association.

Saywitz, K. J., Goodman, G. S., Nicholas, E., & Moan, S. F. (1991). Children's memories of a physical examination involving genital touch: Implications for reports of child sexual abuse. *Journal of Consulting and Clinical Psychology, 59,* 682–691.

State v. Federico Martinez Macias, No. 41270–168 (168th Judicial Court, El Paso County, TX, 1987).

3

Effects of Stress on Children's Memory for a Natural Disaster

Janat Fraser Parker
Lorraine Bahrick
Brenda Lundy
Florida International University

Robyn Fivush
Emory University

Mary Levitt
Florida International University

In this chapter we explore the effects of stress on children's recall of events surrounding Hurricane Andrew, a Class IV hurricane with 175 miles per hour winds. On August 24, 1992, Hurricane Andrew devastated much of southern Dade County in Florida. It caused over $20 billion in property damage and affected the lives of families and young children for months to come. This event provided a forum for addressing many of the questions and issues raised by current developmental research on children's memory and its relation to stress, in a naturalistic, personally relevant, and highly emotional event context. It thus provided a unique opportunity for us to determine to what extent findings of laboratory and field studies generalize to traumatic naturalistic events.

Research on the effects of natural disasters has primarily focused on determining the stressful nature of disasters on children's psychological and social development. McFarlane (1987) demonstrated that 8 months after exposure to an Australian brush fire, 43% of the children were still talking about the fire and 35% were upset by reminders of the fire. Earls, Smith, Reich, and Jung (1988) noted that 1 year after a severe flood, children were still experiencing nightmares and fears of reoccurrences. Likewise, Lonigan, Shannon, Taylor, Finch, and Sallee (1994) reported on posttraumatic stress disorder (PTSD) symptoms of 5,687 children exposed to Hurricane

31

Hugo. Three months after the hurricane, children completed a self-report PTSD questionnaire (The Reaction Index for Children; Frederick, 1985). Presence of PTSD symptoms was strongly related to children's reported hurricane severity and degree of home damage sustained. Vernberg, La Greca, Silverman, and Prinstein (1996) recently completed an analysis of 568 elementary school children's reactions to Hurricane Andrew. More than 55% of the children reported moderate to very severe levels of PTSD symptoms 3 months after Hurricane Andrew.

Thus, it has been convincingly established that natural disasters are extremely stressful for children. However, very little is known about children's memories for natural disasters and how memory may be related to the level of stress experienced in these events. Recently, Terr (1988) examined a group of children who were under age 5 when they experienced severe trauma, such as their own rape or the murder of a relative. All the children showed some evidence of the trauma in their behavior and those older than 18 to 24 months at the time of the experience were able to verbally recall the trauma. However, there have been no studies of natural disasters that have focused on the amount and type of information recalled about the disaster as a function of stress.

EFFECTS OF STRESS
ON EYEWITNESS TESTIMONY

Research relevant to our understanding of the relation between stress and memory in recall of a disaster can be found in the body of work addressing the effects of stress on eyewitness testimony. The eyewitness studies that are most relevant in the present context are those that are similar to natural disasters in that the children and their emotional reactions are an integral component of the to-be-remembered event. This literature is concerned with establishing the conditions under which children will produce reliable and accurate memories for stressful events such as physical and sexual abuse. This is of obvious practical importance when evaluating the potential for children to give accurate testimony in a court of law.

To circumvent ethical considerations and to avoid exposing children to unnecessary discomfort, researchers have often examined the effects of stress on children's reports of personally experienced naturally occurring events such as visits to the doctor (Baker-Ward, Gordon, Ornstein, Larus, & Clubb, 1993; Goodman, Aman, & Hirschman, 1987; Goodman, Hirschman, Hepps, & Rudy, 1991; Ornstein, Gordon, & Larus, 1992) or visits to the dentist (Peters, 1987, 1991; Vandermaas, Hess, & Baker-Ward, 1993). Other eyewitness studies have used laboratory analogues of stressful eyewitness situations, such as exposure to a fire alarm versus a loud radio (Peters, 1991) or exposure to videotapes of children having routine physical examinations with variations of depicted facial affect by doctor and child (Bugental, Blue, Cortez, Fleck, & Rodriquez, 1992). In both types of research, establishing a control group or basis of comparison for the high-stress groups is important. Two approaches have been used and each approach has distinct advantages and limitations. One approach has been to create a low-stress control group with an event that elicits little stress but is as comparable as possible to the stressful event on other variables. However, the lack of comparability across tasks may introduce confounds. Alternatively, researchers have chosen a stressful event for which there are individual differences in the degree of stress experienced. Participants who experience the least stress are used as controls. The individual difference approach has the limitation that typically a much narrower range of stress is represented. This clearly reduces the likelihood of finding an effect of stress if one is present. Furthermore, those participants who experience the event as very stressful versus those who experience it as only mildly stressful may differ a priori in other important ways that may be related to memory performance. For example, they may have different trait anxiety levels, temperaments, or coping strategies. On the other hand, this approach has the distinct advantage that the memory test itself and the task are identical across stress levels so that no confounds can arise due to type of task.

There is a controversy in both the adult and child memory literature regarding whether stress facilitates or hinders memory of an event. Goodman and colleagues (Goodman et al., 1987; Goodman, Bottoms, Schwartz-Kenney, & Rudy, 1991; Goodman, Hepps, & Reed, 1986; Goodman, Hirschman, et al., 1991) were among the first to explore the effects of stress on children's recall. Taking advantage of the natural variation in the stress experienced by children subjected to inoculations, they observed, in at least one study, that children experiencing the highest stress outperformed children experiencing the lowest stress (Goodman, Hirschman, et al., 1991). However, in most of their studies, 3- to 7-year-old children, who experienced stressful events such as inoculations or venipuncture, performed as well as children who experienced nonstressful events such as washable tattoos. Recently, Eisen, Goodman, and Qin (1995) showed that abused and neglected children's memory for an anogenital examination is unrelated to stress regardless of the stress measure employed (medical staff ratings or physiological indices such as heart rate). Numerous other researchers also have shown no relation between stress and memory. Howe, Courage, and Peterson (1994b, 1995) found that children's stress as rated by parents at the time of a traumatic incident and again during the emergency room procedure was unrelated to recall of either event (Howe et al., 1994b) or to intrusion rates (Howe et al., 1995). Likewise, Baker-Ward et al. (1993)

found that immediate and 6-week recall of children's physical examinations was unrelated to children's stress.

In contrast, Peters (1987) reported a negative impact of stress on 3- to 8-year-old children's abilities to recognize critical individuals from a dentist visit. Peters (1991) found similar negative effects of stress when nursery school children were exposed to a stranger who rubbed them on their heads, or when 3- to 9-year-olds had inoculations administered by a nurse, or when 5- to 10-year-olds saw money being stolen from an experimental room. In these latter studies, Peters included stress measures such as pulse rates, blood pressure, and behavior observations, in addition to the Likert rating scales. Consistent with Peters' findings, Bugental et al. (1992) found that 5- to 6-year-olds showed a significant drop in cognitive processing when exposed to negative affect whereas 9- to 10-year-olds showed a similar although nonsignificant trend. On the other hand, Vandermaas et al. (1993) found that high anxiety as determined from the Behavior Profile Rating Scale (Melamed, Weinstein, Hawes, & Katin-Borland, 1975) had a debilitative effect on the memory of older children but no effect on younger children. Merritt, Ornstein, and Spicker (1994) also found that stress was negatively related to recall of a salient traumatic medical procedure, a voiding cystourethrogram (VCUG). This is considered a very stressful and invasive procedure involving cleansing of the genital areas, passing a catheter into the bladder, and instructing the child to urinate. However, the negative effect on recall was evident only when stress was measured by a behavioral rating but not by a biological salivary cortisol measure.

ATTEMPTS TO EXPLAIN THE STRESS–MEMORY RELATION

The study of the effects of stress on eyewitness memory has a number of difficulties. It has been particularly difficult to calibrate the levels of stress across studies and to determine appropriate nonstress control groups. Furthermore, researchers are beginning to recognize that stress or arousal is a global term that includes many different emotional states from very positive to very negative emotions. On the memory side of the relationship, it has been difficult to compare memory across studies because a variety of measures have been used, ranging from free recall and cued recall to identification of individuals from lineups. Likewise, researchers have focused on different types of information from central to peripheral information and from general knowledge to specific details.

Yerkes and Dodson (1908) were the first to propose a law relating stress and memory. Basically, they claimed that there was an inverted U-shaped relation between stress and memory for tasks of moderate complexity such that the highest level of recall occurred for middle levels of arousal. This function has helped explain some of the divergent findings observed in the eyewitness literature. Deffenbacher (1983) examined the adult memory literature and proposed that studies demonstrating a positive relation between stress and memory were operating on the ascending portion of the inverted U-shaped curve, whereas studies showing a reduction in memory as a function of stress were operating on the descending portion of the curve. Further, Deffenbacher (1991) supported this view by categorizing 15 studies in the adult literature according to the violence level or intensity of personal threat and found that in 13 of the 15 studies, higher arousal resulted in a decrement in recall. More recently, Deffenbacher (1994) argued against a unidimensional concept of arousal and promoted a two-process model where different attentional systems are dominant in tasks involving perceptual intake such as laboratory studies (arousal mode), versus tasks involving cognitive anxiety and physiological activation such as live events (activation mode).

Easterbrook (1959) proposed a hypothesis to explain the empirical relations described by the Yerkes–Dodson curve. He claimed that increases in stress produce greater selectivity of attention such that recall of central information is facilitated whereas recall of peripheral information is debilitated. Studies consistent with greater central recall than peripheral recall with increases in stress are evident in the adult literature (e.g., Christianson, 1984; Christianson & Loftus, 1987, 1991; Kebeck & Lohaus, 1986; Maass & Kohnken, 1989). Exceptions to this pattern have also been noted, however (e.g., Heuer & Reisberg, 1990). There is currently no support for stress impacting peripheral recall more than central recall in the children's literature (e.g., Goodman, Hirschman, et al., 1991; Peters, 1987; Vandermaas et al., 1993). However, the Easterbrook hypothesis may still be relevant for predicting children's memory as a function of stress if methods of measuring memory are carefully examined. Christianson and Loftus (1987) claimed that some memory measurement techniques such as recognition emphasize peripheral information, whereas recall emphasizes central information. Following this line of reasoning, the Easterbrook hypothesis should predict decrements in recognition but not recall as a function of stress (see also Vandermaas et al., 1993). For example, Peters (1987, 1991), who typically measures recognition memory, finds a decrement in memory as a function of stress, whereas Goodman and colleagues, who examine recall memory, find an improvement or no change in memory as a function of stress. In fact, Peters (1991) did not find any effect of stress on recall of the nurse's characteristics in his inoculation study or in free recall of events surrounding the fire alarm. On the other hand, differences in memory measures cannot be the sole explanation because Peters (1991) did observe decrements in responses to objective questions by those participants exposed to a fire alarm versus a loud radio.

It is quite likely that other factors also determine the focus of children's attention and in turn their memory. Notably, Levine and Burgess (1995) suggested that emotions may enhance recall of functionally relevant information and that such information differs for each emotion expressed. They claimed that different emotions produce an increased readiness for certain types of material and a decreased readiness for other types of material. In particular, they showed that emotional arousal enhanced recall for events associated with happiness or anger but not fear or sadness. Their study emphasizes the complexity of analysis that may be required to address the relation between stress and memory.

Ornstein, Merritt, and Baker-Ward (1995) explored the relation between stress and memory by focusing on three different aspects of an event: the level of arousal generated by an event, the prior knowledge and familiarity of an event, and the cohesion or internal structure of an event. They compared three types of medical situations ranging from a well-child checkup (Baker-Ward et al., 1993) to emergency treatment by a plastic surgeon (Baker-Ward, Burgwyn, Ornstein, & Gordon, 1995) to exposure to VCUG (Merritt et al., 1994). They observed the highest recall for the most stressful procedure. However, at the level of individual differences within events, there were no correlations between stress and memory for the least stressful procedure (well-child checkup) but for the more stressful procedures (emergency room and VCUG) there was a negative relation between stress and memory. Basically, the greater the stress the lower the recall, but this was evident only for the behavioral measures. These findings from the same laboratory highlight the problems inherent in comparing across tasks. When different tasks were used for comparison purposes, there was a positive relation between perceived stress and memory, but when individual differences in stress within tasks were explored either there was no relation with memory and stress or a negative relation emerged. As Ornstein et al. (1995) pointed out, these discrepant findings force us to consider how tasks may differ not only in terms of stress engendered but also in terms of prior knowledge and event cohesion.

It is abundantly clear how difficult it is to standardize the levels of arousal generated across studies and events. Furthermore, different measures of stress do not correlate highly. Researchers have used a wide variety of stress measures: self-reports; subjective ratings by parents, researchers, and medical personnel; behavioral indices (e.g., Behavior Profile Rating Scale, Melamed et al., 1975; Preschool Observational Scale of Anxiety, Glennon & Weisz, 1978; Observational Scale of Behavioral Distress, Elliott, Jay, & Woody, 1987); and physiological measures such as blood pressure, pulse rate, and salivary cortisol. Relating stress levels across events especially when measures differ is problematic. Without standardization it is difficult to draw general conclusions regarding the relation between stress and memory and what mediates this relation.

The amount of prior knowledge of a task has an important influence on what and how much children recall (Bjorklund, 1985; Chi & Ceci, 1987). Children may have developed scripts for certain procedures and thus their overall recall may be greater because of the generic commonalities across repeated occurrences (Nelson, 1986). The effects of prior knowledge of the event on memory are currently coming under careful scrutiny by researchers interested in the effects of stress or emotion (e.g., Trabasso, Stein, Rodkin, Munger, & Baughn, in press; Vandermaas et al., 1993). Peters (1997) pointed out that it is imperative that future research incorporate an analysis of the underlying knowledge structure of particular eyewitness events when studying stress and memory. For example, Vandermaas et al. (1993) showed that the negative relation for older children between anxiety and recall of a dental experience was mediated by the familiarity or experience the children had with the dentist office. Clubb, Nida, Merritt, and Ornstein (1993) addressed this issue by reexamining Baker-Ward et al.'s (1993) study of recall of a physical examination in terms of the amount of prior knowledge children had for a physical examination. Event knowledge was related to amount recalled. Recently, Trabasso et al. (in press) recommended online moment-to-moment tracking of children's knowledge of goals and plans, including their emotional responses, to help in the determination of individual differences in memory performance as a function of stress. Thus, when comparing memory for different events as a function of stress, prior knowledge should be controlled.

It is also critical that the number of structural components and natural sequencing involved in an event be taken into account (Ornstein et al., 1995). Children are better able to reconstruct a sequence of actions if the components are causally linked, even when the events are novel (Bauer & Fivush, 1992; Bauer & Mandler, 1989). In addition, Ornstein et al. (1995) and Follmer (1995) suggested that individual differences in behavioral styles such as temperament may determine how children respond to stress, which in turn may influence the attention children give to the characteristics of the event. It is clear that all these aspects of to-be-remembered events must be considered before conclusions regarding the impact of stress can be made.

Attempts to duplicate traumatic events in the laboratory and in the field have been most useful in our understanding of the relation between stress and memory. However, many of these studies do not involve events with stress levels comparable to those experienced in real-life traumas. In actual traumas or disasters the individual's very existence or personal safety is at stake. Laboratory studies typically cannot incorporate the unpredictability of traumatic events and, as Howe, Courage, and Peterson (1994a) pointed out, children are often carefully prepared by parents and professionals (e.g., doctors, dentists, nurses, etc.) for the negative event to be experienced. One advantage of studying recall of information related to an unusual natural disaster is that the children typically have no script for such an event. Furthermore, in natural disasters such as hurricanes, earthquakes, fires, and floods the period of stress ranges from hours to days and weeks rather than minutes. Such an extensive exposure to stress is more analogous to the stress experienced by children who have been physically or sexually abused repeatedly.

AUTOBIOGRAPHICAL MEMORY AND FLASHBULB MEMORY

The recent interest in autobiographical memory in young children is consistent with our emphasis on more naturalistic experiences. Children's recall of personal events has repeatedly demonstrated that young children are able to recall accurately over extended periods of time (see Fivush, 1993, for a review). For example, Hamond and Fivush (1991) interviewed 3- and 4-year-old children about a trip to Disney World that occurred either 6 or 18 months earlier. Children were competent at remembering the event, recalling an average of 40 propositions. Older children provided more elaborate and detailed accounts than younger children but amount recalled did not differ. Other studies have also found accurate long-term recall of single, infrequent events such as the birth of a sibling (Sheingold & Tenney, 1982); going to a zoo, circus, or birthday party (Fivush, Gray, & Fromhoff, 1987; Todd & Perlmutter, 1980); or a trip to an archeological museum (Hudson & Fivush, 1991). However, even though many of these events are emotionally laden in the sense that they are usually positive experiences for the children, autobiographical studies typically have not explored the negative end of the emotional continuum.

On the other hand, recall of traumatic events has been studied for real-life events such as the assassination of President Kennedy (Brown & Kulik, 1977; Winograd & Killinger, 1983), the explosion of the *Challenger* shuttle (Warren & Swartwood, 1992), the shooting of President Reagan (Pillemer, 1984), and the invasion of Iraq in the Gulf War (Weaver, 1993) — the so-called "flashbulb" memory studies. Although most of these studies examined adults' recall, Warren and Swartwood (1992) showed that children from kindergarten through eighth grade were able to recall a great deal about the explosion of the *Challenger* even after long periods of time. Winograd and Killinger (1983) presented questionnaires to college students who were between the ages of 1 and 7 years at the time of the Kennedy assassination and observed that children who were 4½ years and older could remember hearing the news and could remember some of the specific details. However, these events typically are not personal events, but public or national events experienced secondarily through relatives, friends, teachers, or various media. In this respect, they differ markedly from recall of information from a personally experienced disaster.

THE HURRICANE STUDY

The current research had the advantage that "stress" could be objectively defined and manipulated according to the severity of the storm in each child's neighborhood. Storm exposure was rated by the children's mothers via a 7-point questionnaire. On the basis of this questionnaire, the degree of stress or trauma experienced by each family was determined to be low (ratings of 6 or 7), moderate (ratings of 4 or 5), or severe (ratings of 1, 2, or 3). The low-exposure group experienced little or no damage to their homes. The moderate-exposure group suffered damage to their yards, trees, fences, and home exteriors with limited interior damage. The high-exposure group experienced the full force of the hurricane in their homes. The storm penetrated their homes, breaking windows, knocking down walls, and often causing the occupants to move from room to room. Thus, we were able to objectively rate stress for groups within our study but the difficulty of comparing stress levels in our study with those of other studies of course remains.

The study reported here addressed the issue of appropriate control groups by examining low-, moderate-, and high-stress children who all were exposed to a similar event at a different level of intensity. In this manner, we were able to overcome the circularity of Deffenbacher's (1991) placement of particular studies on the ascending versus descending portion of the Yerkes–Dodson curve. With three levels of severity we could make a priori predictions. Presumably, all children had a similar level of knowledge about the event because these young preschoolers had not been exposed to a hurricane before (no hurricanes had been predicted to hit Dade County since the birth of the children). Further, the event itself and tests of memory were similar across different stress levels.

We focused on 3- and 4-year-old children's recall because previous research has been inconsistent in demonstrating age differences in recall of events for 3- and 4-year-olds, with some studies (e.g., Hamond & Fivush, 1991; Pillemer, 1992) observing no differences and others finding a superiority with age (Todd & Perlmutter, 1980). We were also interested in differences in children's spontaneous and prompted recall so interviews began with open-ended questions and followed up with category and specific prompts. Research has suggested that younger children require more structure to support recall than older children and recall is facilitated by cuing (see Pillemer & White, 1989, for a review). It is possible that developmental differences may be evident in open-ended recall that are not present with prompted recall. Furthermore, it is possible that stress may impact spontaneous recall differently from prompted recall.

Memory of events related to the disaster was assessed for three distinct time periods: (a) the prehurricane preparations, (b) the hurricane itself, and (c) the posthurricane recovery period. It should be noted that the prehurricane preparations were very similar from one family to the next and did not differ as a function of the eventual severity of the storm that the family experienced. Thus, in this respect, the low-exposure children are a natural control group because they went through comparable hurricane preparations to the other two groups but only experienced a typical storm. This period was typically characterized by a frenzy of activity including bringing in all unattached objects from patios and yards, purchasing hurricane supplies, and boarding up windows. The second time period involving the hurricane itself differed across severity levels as did the final recovery or aftermath period. The amount of stress experienced by children in the hurricane recovery period covaried with the storm exposure. In the low-exposure group, families typically remained in intact homes and had no more than a few hours of power outage; in the moderate-exposure group, families experienced a disruption of power and basic services for many days and engaged in an extensive clean-up period; in the high-exposure group, families conducted extensive clean-up and often were forced to pack up their remaining belongings and relocate. Thus, for the hurricane itself and the hurricane recovery period, there was likely more potentially recallable information as storm severity increased, whereas this was not true for the hurricane preparation period.

METHOD

Participants

One hundred children (39 three-year-olds and 61 four-year-olds) and their mothers were recruited for participation through local preschools. Only the data from the children and questionnaire information relevant to the children are reported. Children were recruited from three different geographic areas spanning a 15-mile radius to obtain participants from the three storm severity levels and a cross-section of income levels. All children were interviewed at their preschool to provide a uniform and neutral environment with respect to hurricane memory cues. We began interviewing approximately 2 months after the hurricane and completed testing 5 months after the hurricane.

Child Interview: Memory and Subjective Stress Measures

Structured interviews (for details, see Bahrick, Parker, Fivush, & Levitt, in press) began with a warm-up period to establish rapport, followed by an open-ended question asking children to think really hard about the hurricane and tell the interviewer everything they could remember about it. This was followed by nondirective prompts and then open-ended questions about each of the three time periods. The order of open-ended questions focusing on each of the time periods was counterbalanced so that differences in memory from these periods could not be attributed to fatigue or boredom as the interview progressed. After the open-ended question regarding each time period, a standardized series of increasingly more specific questions was presented. Category prompts such as "What did Mommy and Daddy do outside the house?" occurred before a specific prompt such as "Did they do anything with the windows?" Children were always encouraged to talk as much as possible by nondirective prompts such as "tell me more," "what else?" and so forth.

Interviews were tape recorded and transcribed verbatim. We then developed a propositional scoring technique tailored to the hurricane event. A proposition was defined as a clause with a subject and a verb. This scoring technique allowed us to examine the total number of propositions generated by the children for each time period of the hurricane, and whether these propositions were elicited by the initial general question, the open-ended time period questions, category prompts, or specific prompts.

In addition, a detailed breakdown of the content was made differentiating actions, descriptions, and internal states and determining how much of the time the children talked about certain topics such as damage and repair, for example. The degree of elaboration generated by the children was also coded. Although difference in language development is certainly a factor in the amount of material reported by 3- and 4-year-olds, we tried to minimize this factor by our coding system. So, for example, elaborations were coded separately and thus a typical utterance by a 3-year-old, "tree fell," was coded as one proposition just as was a more complete utterance by a 4-year-old, "the big palm tree fell down."

At the completion of the interview the children were given a brief subjective stress rating on a 4-point scale. They were asked to rate how scared and upset or happy and good they felt during each of the three time periods of the storm. To facilitate their understanding of the scale, the children were asked to indicate which of two puppets, a relaxed or frightened one, felt more like they did. They also were asked to make the same ratings for how they thought their mother felt.

Parent Information

All mothers were given a hurricane severity questionnaire designed to objectify the degree of storm exposure. This served as a basis for classifying the participants into high, moderate or low storm severity groups. Forty children were classified in the high-severity group ($N = 13$, age 3; $N = 27$, age 4), 42 in the moderate-severity group ($N = 19$, age 3; $N = 23$, age 4), and 18 in the low-severity group ($N = 7$, age 3; $N = 11$, age 4). The mothers also completed a questionnaire about the extent of damage to their homes and the nature and duration of interruption of basic services, demographic information, and the amount of rehearsal of hurricane events.

The amount of hurricane event rehearsal that the children engaged in may be critical as researchers (e.g., Neisser, 1982) have suggested that flashbulb memories may occur because these stressful events are rehearsed more than less stressful events. To help determine the amount of discussion about the hurricane, rehearsal was assessed by asking mothers to rate the amount of time the family and significant others talked to the children about the hurricane preparations, the hurricane itself, and the hurricane aftermath. Ratings were made on a 3-point scale ranging from 0 (*none*) to 2 (*several times a day*). This rehearsal was assessed for the first week after the hurricane, the weeks just prior to the interview, and the weeks in between. A composite score for rehearsal was calculated for discussion of the hurricane preparations, the hurricane itself, and the hurricane aftermath.

Mothers made subjective ratings of the amount of stress they experienced during each of the three time periods, on a 4-point scale ranging from 1 (*extremely happy and relaxed*) to 4 (*extremely frightened and upset*). They also made similar subjective ratings on a 4-point scale indicating how their child felt. They then were given a questionnaire to complete at home that included two measures of child stress and behavior and six measures of mother stress and behavior. Only the two child measures are discussed here.

Child Frederick Reaction Index Form C (Frederick, 1985). This 20-item questionnaire was designed to assess PTSD symptomatology in children. The scale was modified slightly to fit the hurricane event and to allow children to respond to eight questions that we thought preschoolers could understand and answer (e.g., Do thoughts about the hurricane make you feel afraid and upset?). After the mother asked her child these questions she then completed the 12 remaining items according to her judgment about her child (e.g., feels as good about things he or she likes to do as he or she did before).

Child Well-Being Survey. We developed this 35-item questionnaire to assess changes in ordinary behaviors such as sleeping, eating, attention, and emotionality as a function of the traumatic event. Each item (e.g., wants to sleep with adults, laughs easily, has nightmares) was rated on a scale from 1 (*almost never*) to 5 (*most of the time*) in terms of occurrence prior to the hurricane and again for its occurrence after the hurricane. A difference score was derived between the two sets of scores.

RESULTS AND DISCUSSION

Number of Propositions Recalled

Transcripts of one quarter of the participants were sent to the mothers for review to determine accuracy of recall. Mothers were requested to mark any recall that was not completely accurate and although only nine of the mothers returned these transcripts, the reported errors were minimal. A typical error might involve the mother pointing out that the tiles were orange, blue, and red whereas the child said they were orange, blue, and green. There also was evidence of some time transpositions where the child thought something occurred before the hurricane that actually occurred afterward or vice versa. Other researchers have also noted minimal errors in recall of naturalistic events (Hamond & Fivush, 1991; Sheingold & Tenney, 1982).

The total number of hurricane-relevant propositions generated by the children ranged from 21 to 554, with an overall mean of 154. In general, the children recalled an impressive amount of information about hurricane-related events. This high level of recall is interesting in itself because it appears to be much greater than typically found for less stressful events such as going to Disney World (Hamond & Fivush, 1991) where an average of 40 propositions were remembered.

Because the distribution of propositions was skewed with several children recalling propositions more than three standard deviations above the mean, all analyses on amount recalled were conducted on log transformations as a function of child age and storm severity. There was a main effect of child age, $F(1, 94) = 10.32, p < .01$, with 4-year-olds recalling more propositions about the hurricane ($M = 184$) than 3-year-olds ($M = 124$). This age effect was apparent with this restricted age range and even though developmental differences in the language production of 3- and 4-year-olds were partly minimized by counting propositions independent of elaborations. Most studies of children's event memory have shown higher recall for older children than preschoolers (see Pillemer & White, 1989, for a review) but there are several studies (Hamond & Fivush, 1991; Pillemer, 1992) that have also used this restricted age range in which the age difference did not emerge.

Of even greater interest was the main effect of hurricane severity, $F(2, 94) = 3.14, p < .05$. To assess the nature of the relation between hurricane severity and memory, trend analyses were performed. Figure 3.1 shows a significant quadratic trend across severity levels, $F(1, 94) = 5.84, p < .05$, reflecting an inverted U-shaped relation between number of propositions generated and severity level. The moderate-severity group recalled the most propositions about the hurricane ($M = 177.33$) with the low-severity group ($M = 139.32$) and the high-severity group ($M = 144.21$) recalling less. More detailed analyses were then conducted to examine memory as a function of time period and type of recall. Most but not all propositions could be coded into one of three time periods (hurricane preparations, the hurricane itself, and the recovery period). Propositions were also classified as either

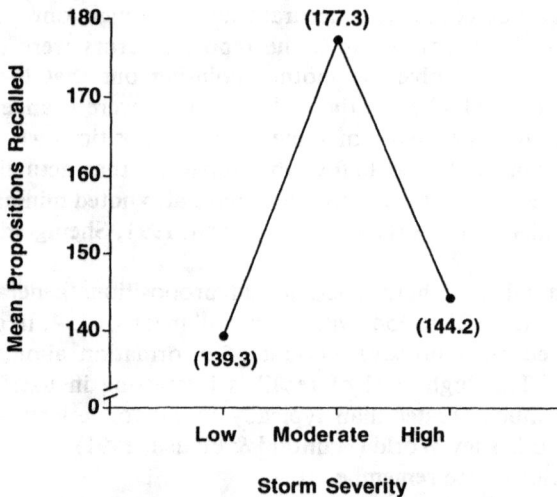

FIG. 3.1. Mean propositions recalled as a function of storm severity.

spontaneous or prompted recall depending on whether they had been elicited by the open-ended questions (the general open-ended question or one of the open-ended questions about the three time periods) or by category or specific prompts.

A four-way analysis of variance (ANOVA) with child age and storm severity as between-subject variables and time period and type of recall as within-subjects variables was then conducted on the log transformations. As before, there were main effects of child age and storm severity. In addition, there were main effects of time period, $F(2, 188) = 139.70, p < .001$, and type of recall, $F(1, 94) = 425.52, p < .001$. There were also several interactions with time period that are discussed later.

We focus first on the main effect of time period. Post hoc Tukey tests revealed that the overall level of recall was much less for hurricane preparations ($M = 22$) than for the hurricane itself ($M = 63$), $p < .05$, or the hurricane aftermath ($M = 58$), $p < .05$. No other means differed from each other. These differences should be viewed in the context of the nature and extent of the three time periods. The preparation period lasted approximately 2 days and was fairly uniform across participants; the hurricane itself was 8 hours; the aftermath ranged anywhere from a few days to several months. Although the hurricane proper was the shortest period, much more was recalled about this period than the preparation period. One could conjecture that this time period is more stressful than the preparation period but it is also possible that some of this differential recall can be attributed to rehearsal, which is discussed later.

These findings must be interpreted in light of the storm severity experienced by the children because the overall analysis revealed an interaction of Time Period × Storm Severity, $F(4, 188) = 3.26, p < .05$. For some children, a typical Florida storm was experienced during Time 2, whereas for other children the hurricane and recovery period were highly unusual, stressful events. To help interpret the interaction between storm severity and time period, results were broken down according to time period and trend analyses were performed. Figure 3.2 shows the effect of storm severity at each of the three time periods separately. Looking first at Time 1, the hurricane preparations, there was a tendency for a quadratic trend with the moderate-severity group recalling the most propositions, although this finding did not reach statistical significance, $F(1, 94) = 2.88, p = .09$. Recall that regardless of storm severity, children all experienced the same kinds of activities during Time 1, the hurricane preparations, because it was not known where the hurricane would make landfall. As stress at the encoding of hurricane preparations presumably was similar across severity groups, any differences that emerge would have to be attributed to retrograde amnesia or interference effects.

For Time 2, the storm itself, the trend analysis revealed no effects of

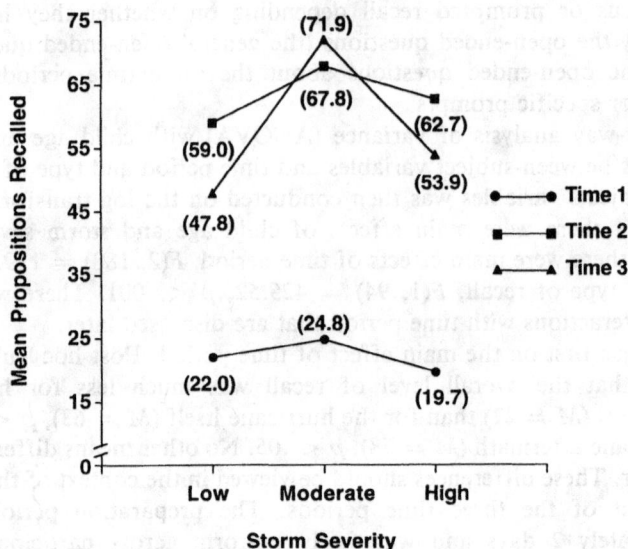

FIG. 3.2. Mean propositions recalled as a function of time period and storm severity.

severity, $F(1, 94) = 1.89, p > .05$. The amount recalled from the 8 hours of the storm itself was comparable for the low-, moderate-, and high-severity groups although the pattern was similar to Time 1. In contrast, a trend analysis of Time 3, the hurricane recovery period, revealed a significant quadratic trend across severity levels, $F(1, 94) = 8.21, p < .01$, with the moderate-severity group recalling the most propositions. It is particularly noteworthy that the high-severity group recalled fewer propositions in the aftermath time period because that group should have had the most content to recall. The stress level of the hurricane and especially its aftermath appears to have a negative impact on their recall. On the other hand, the lower level of recall for the low-severity group may result because of the dearth of material for that group to recall as well as because they experienced a lower level of arousal.

With respect to the significant main effect of type of recall, results revealed significantly less spontaneous recall ($M = 33$) than prompted recall ($M = 110$). This finding of greater prompted or cued recall than free or open-ended recall is consistent with a growing body of child memory research (Fivush et al., 1987; Hamond & Fivush, 1991). We were also interested in whether the age effects that we observed for total number of propositions recalled would be modified as a function of type of recall. As younger children appear to rely more on specific questions, prompts, and structure to facilitate recall (see Pillemer & White, 1989, for a review) it was anticipated that the age difference might disappear with prompted recall.

However, there was no evidence of a Child Age $\times$ Type of Recall interaction, $F < 1$, showing that 4-year-olds are superior to 3-year-olds in the generation of both spontaneous propositions and prompted propositions.

Results also revealed an interaction between type of recall and time period, $F(2, 188) = 14.68$, $p < .001$. Figure 3.3 displays this interaction. Post hoc Tukey tests showed that for open-ended recall, there were more propositions recalled for the hurricane itself ($M = 18.92$) than for the hurricane preparations ($M = 2.99$), $p < .05$, or the hurricane aftermath ($M = 11.37$), $p < .05$. For prompted recall, memory for the hurricane recovery period ($M = 46.50$) was comparable to the hurricane itself ($M = 44.26$) and recall for both these periods was superior to recall for hurricane preparations ($M = 19.21$), $ps < .05$. In other words, the saliency of events surrounding the hurricane itself was particularly evident for the free recall or open-ended measure. However, when the children were aided by prompts they were able to recall comparable amounts of additional information from the hurricane recovery and the hurricane proper periods.

Socioeconomic Class, Retention Interval, and Rehearsal

The main effects observed in this study were reexamined in the context of a number of covariates to determine if they significantly qualified our

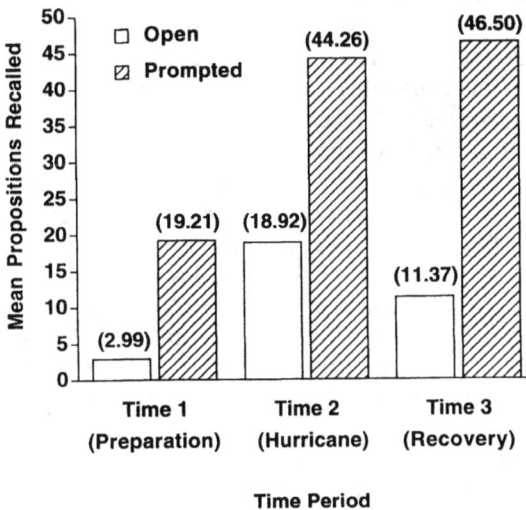

FIG. 3.3. Mean propositions recalled as a function of time period and type of recall.

findings. In order to rule out the role of socioeconomic class we included income, the education of the mother, the education of the father, and the combined education of the mother and father as separate covariates in the preceding analyses. Neither family income nor any measure of parents' education significantly predicted amount recalled, all $ps > .10$. Further, the main effects of children's age and of storm severity as well as the quadratic functions relating storm severity and amount recalled were all significant even when adjusted for the effects of each of these variables, all $ps < .05$.

We also looked at retention interval (length of time from hurricane to memory interview) as a covariate to determine how it impacted the main effects of age and storm severity on amount recalled. We found that it was not a significant predictor of recall, $p > .10$. Further, we included retention interval as a between-subject factor in the major analysis of variance. Children were classified into one of three retention interval conditions by rank ordering them according to retention interval and dividing the participants into three equal groupings. We then compared the children who were tested at the shortest retention interval (60–92 days) with those who were tested at the longest retention interval (109–179 days) in an ANOVA that included the child's age and storm severity as factors. These analyses failed to reveal any main effects or interactions with retention interval, all $ps > .05$, suggesting that children did not show differential recall as a function of retention interval (from 2–5 months). Of course, there may have been some memory loss across the first 2 months following the hurricane that we would not have detected.

It is possible that the lower level of overall recall for hurricane preparations as compared to the hurricane itself or the hurricane aftermath might be because there was less discussion, and less rehearsal of this time period's activities than the other two time periods. Thus, an ANOVA was conducted on the amount of rehearsal reported by the mothers for events that occurred during the three time periods as a function of the child's age and severity of the storm (see Fig. 3.4). This analysis showed that the mean amount of reported rehearsal for the three time periods differed, $F(2,168) = 82.53$, $p < .001$. Post hoc Tukey tests revealed that rehearsal of the hurricane preparations ($M = 1.02$) was lower than rehearsal of the hurricane itself ($M = 1.75$) or the hurricane aftermath ($M = 1.68$), $ps < .05$. It is noteworthy, however, that the amount of talk about hurricane-related events was high for all three time periods. There were discussions at least once a day over this extended retention interval for each of the time periods.

We then evaluated the possibility that the effects of child age, time period, and the quadratic function relating amount recalled with stress might be mediated by differential rehearsal on the part of children. The rehearsal for each of the three time periods was entered in an analysis of

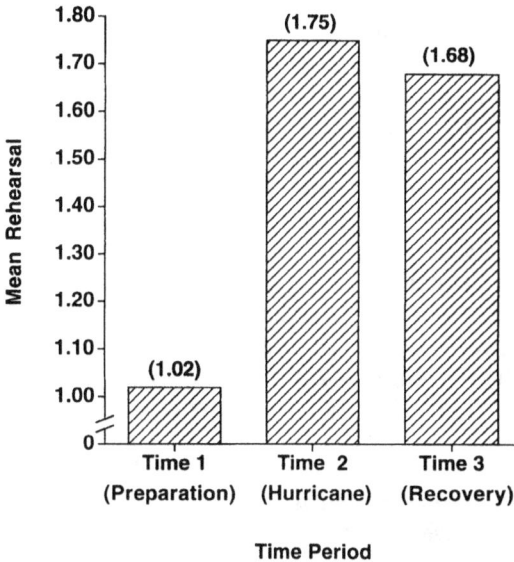

FIG. 3.4. Mean rehearsal as a function of time period.

covariance (ANCOVA) with the child's age and storm severity as between-subjects factors and time as a within-subjects factor. The results indicated that rehearsal was a significant predictor of differential recall for the three time periods, $F(1,167) = 4.36, p < .05$. However, rehearsal summed over the three time periods was not a significant predictor for total number of propositions recalled, $p > .10$. Further, the main effects of child age, time period, and the quadratic effect of storm severity were still present when the means were adjusted for rehearsal. It appears that rehearsal did contribute to differences in the number of propositions generated for the three time periods but it did not qualify any of the main effects.

Stress Measures

In addition to examining recall as a function of hurricane severity we also looked at other measures of stress and their relations with one another. The study contained four distinct measures of child stress in addition to the storm severity measure. These measures included a 4-point subjective stress scale where the child reported on his or her own stress and a 4-point subjective stress scale where the mother reported on the child's stress. The third stress measure required the mothers to administer the Child Frederick PTSD Reaction Index of 20 items. Lonigan et al. (1994) demonstrated evidence of elementary school children's stress after Hurricane Hugo with this instrument. In their study the children, who were 8 years old, filled out their own reaction indices. In the study reported here, the mothers directly asked the children 8 of the questions and filled out the additional 12 questions based on their children's behavior. The final stress measure was the Child Well-Being Survey, which measured changes in habits such as eating, sleeping, and interacting with others.

Of the four measures of child stress, only the PTSD scale was correlated with storm severity, $r = .29$, $p < .01$; the greater the storm severity the greater the amount of PTSD symptomatology. When the individual portions of the Child PTSD were looked at separately, it was the 8 items that were answered directly by the child that were correlated with storm severity, $r = .31$, $p < .01$, whereas the 12 items reported by the mother for the child were not correlated significantly with storm severity. Storm severity was not correlated with any of the other three measures of child stress. This is not surprising as two of these three measures (the children's and the mother's subjective ratings) requested retrospective ratings by the child or mother as opposed to current levels of anxiety or stress. The Child Well-Being Survey, which assessed behavior changes, correlated with total PTSD, $r = .66$, $p < .01$, with the children's 8 responses on the PTSD, $r = .51$, $p < .01$, and the mothers' 12 responses on the PTSD, $r = .61$, $p < .01$.

The relation between stress and memory is indeed complex. It appears that it is dependent on many factors such as the type of event, the type of information (central vs. peripheral), the time of test, and the type of retrieval information. We have looked at hurricane-related recall across different time periods, across varying retention intervals, and as a function of open-ended and prompted questions. Further analyses of our data have explored the type of material recalled such as actions, descriptions, and affect as well as the number of elaborations generated as a function of the severity level of the storm the children experienced (see Bahrick et al., in press).

CONCLUSIONS

Our research shows that 3- and 4-year-old children verbally recall an impressive amount of information about this meaningful real-world event. Further, 4-year-olds remember a substantially greater amount than 3-year-olds, and children of both ages recall more information with prompts than spontaneously. Findings of high levels of memory even in very young children are consistent with recent studies (see Fivush, 1993, for a review). This research provided a solution to a number of problems inherent in conducting naturalistic research on memory and stress. Stress was objectively defined as the degree of hurricane severity and children could be classified into three different stress levels on this basis. Thus, the difficulty of obtaining an appropriate low-stress control group was overcome by identifying individuals who prepared for the hurricane but received only a typical storm. Further, the hurricane offered an objective solution to the typical problem of choosing a viable measure of stress and we therefore did not have to rely on subjective ratings given by young children or by adults about young children. Our results are also not affected by differences in the event or differences in the memory test across stress levels because a single test was given of an event that varied in intensity. Finally, there were no systematic individual differences across stress groups and prior knowledge of the event was minimal and not related to stress level.

In this context, the relation between stress and memory was curvilinear with the greatest recall by children who experienced the moderate level of storm severity. Further, this relation was not qualified by the income of the child's family, the education of either parent, the amount of storm-related rehearsal, or the retention interval. We argue that the range of stress experienced by children in our study exceeds that of most lab and field studies of event memory, given that some children feared for their lives and personal safety whereas others experienced only a normal storm. By classifying children according to three stress levels, we were able to identify a curvilinear relation between memory and stress that cannot be revealed by studies assessing memory for only two stress levels. Thus, the quadratic function presents a broader and more accurate view of the overall relation between memory and stress than prior studies.

ACKNOWLEDGMENTS

This research was supported by a grant from the National Science Foundation (DBS 9300956) to the first two authors.

For a full report of this research see Bahrick, Parker, Fivush, & Levitt (in press).

REFERENCES

Bahrick, L. E., Parker, J. F., Fuvish, R., & Levitt, M. (in press). *Journal of Experimental Psychology: Applied.*

Baker-Ward, L., Burgwyn, E. O., Ornstein. P. A., & Gordon, B. N. (1995, April). Children's reports of a minor medical emergency procedure. In G. Goodman & L. Baker-Ward (Chairs), *Children's memory for emotional and traumatic experiences.* Symposium conducted at the biennial meeting of the Society for Research in Child Development, Indianapolis, IN.

Baker-Ward, L., Gordon, B. N., Ornstein, P. A., Larus, D. M., & Clubb, P. A. (1993). Young children's long-term retention of a pediatric examination. *Child Development, 64,* 1519–1533.

Bauer, P. J., & Fivush, R. (1992). Constructing event representations: Building on a foundation of variation and enabling relations. *Cognitive Development, 7,* 381–401.

Bauer, P. J., & Mandler, J. M. (1989). One thing follows another: Effects of temporal structure on 1-to 2-year-olds' recall of events. *Developmental Psychology, 25,* 197–206.

Bjorklund, D. F. (1985). The role of conceptual knowledge in the development of organization in children's memory. In C. J. Brainerd & M. Pressley (Eds.), *Basic processes in memory development* (pp. 103–142). New York: Springer-Verlag.

Brown, R., & Kulik, J. (1977). Flashbulb memories. *Cognition, 5,* 73–99.

Bugental, D. B., Blue, J., Cortez, V., Fleck, K., & Rodriquez, A. (1992). Influences of witnessed affect on information processing in children. *Child Develo, ment, 63,* 774–786.

Chi, M. T. H., & Ceci, S. J. (1987). Content knowledge: Its role, representation, and restructuring in memory development. In H. W. Reese (Ed.), *Advances in child development and behavior* (Vol. 20, pp. 91–142. Orlando, FL: Academic Press.

Christianson, S.-A. (1984). The relationship between induced emotional arousal and amnesia. *Scandinavian Journal of Psychology, 25,* 147–160.

Christianson, S.-A., & Loftus, E. F. (1987). Memory for traumatic events. *Applied Cognitive Psychology, 1,* 225–239.

Christianson, S.-A., & Loftus, E. F. (1991). Remembering emotional events: The fate of detailed information. *Emotion and Cognition, 5,* 81–108.

Clubb, P. A., Nida, R. E., Merritt, K., & Ornstein, P. A. (1993). Visiting the doctor: Children's knowledge and memory. *Cognitive Development, 8,* 361–372.

Deffenbacher. K. A. (1983). The influence of arousal on reliability of testimony. In S. M. A. Lloyd-Bostock & B. R. Clifford (Eds.), *Evaluating witness evidence* (pp. 235–251). Chichester, UK: Wiley.

Deffenbacher, K. A. (1991). A maturing of research on the behaviour of eyewitnesses. *Applied Cognitive Psychology, 5,* 377–402.

Deffenbacher, K. A. (1994). Effects of arousal on everyday memory. *Human Performance, 7,* 141–161.

Earls, F., Smith, E., Reich, W., & Jung, K. G. (1988). Investigating psychopathological consequences of a disaster in children: A pilot study incorporating a structure diagnostic interview. *Journal of the American Academy of Child and Adolescent Psychiatry, 27,* 90–95.

Easterbrook, J. A. (1959). The effect of emotion on the utilization and organization of behavior. *Psychological Review, 66,* 183–201.

Eisen, M. L., Goodman, G. S., & Qin, J. (1995, July). Eyewitness testimony in victims of child maltreatment: Stress, memory, and suggestibility. In J. F. Parker (Chair), *Effects of stress and arousal upon children's memories.* Symposium conducted at the first biennial meeting of the Society for Applied Research in Memory and Cognition, Vancouver, BC.

Elliott, C. H., Jay, S. M., & Woody, P. (1987). An observation scale for measuring children's distress during medical procedures. *Journal of Pediatric Psychology, 12,* 543–551.

Fivush, R. (1993). Developmental perspectives on autobiographical recall. In G. S. Goodman & B. L. Bottoms (Eds.), *Child victims, child witnesses: Understanding and improving testimony* (pp. 1–24). New York: Guilford.

Fivush, R., Gray, J., & Fromhoff, F. (1987). Two year olds talk about the past. *Cognitive Development, 2,* 393–409.

Follmer, A. (1995, July). The role of behavioral styles in individual and age-related variation in children's memory reports. In B. Knauper (Chair), *Individual differences and developmental effects.* Symposium conducted at the first biennial meeting of the Society for Applied Research in Memory and Cognition, Vancouver, BC.

Frederick, C. J. (1985). Children traumatized by catastrophic situations. In S. Eth & R. S. Pynoos (Eds.), *Posttraumatic stress disorders in children* (pp. 73–99). Washington, DC: American Psychiatric Press.

Glennon, B., & Weisz, J. R. (1978). An observational approach to the assessment of anxiety in young children. *Journal of Counseling and Clinical Psychology, 46,* 1246–1257.

Goodman, G. S., Aman, C., & Hirschman, J. (1987). Child sexual and physical abuse: Children's testimony. In S. J. Ceci, M. P.Toglia, & D. F. Ross (Eds.), *Children's eyewitness memory* (pp. 1–23). New York: Springer-Verlag.

Goodman, G. S., Bottoms, B. L., Schwartz-Kenney, B. M., & Rudy, L. (1991). Children's testimony about a stressful event: Improving children's reports. *Journal of Narrative and Life History, 1,* 69–99.

Goodman, G. S., Hepps, D. H., & Reed, R. S. (1986). The child victim's testimony. In A. Haralambie (Ed.), *New issues for child advocates* (pp. 167–176). Phoenix: Arizona Association of Council for Children.

Goodman, G. S., Hirschman, J. E., Hepps, D., & Rudy, L. (1991). Children's memory for stressful events. *Merrill-Palmer Quarterly, 37,* 109–157.

Hamond, N. R., & Fivush, R. (1991). Memories of Mickey Mouse: Young children recount their trip to Disneyworld. *Cognitive Development, 6,* 433–448.

Heuer, F., & Reisberg, D. (1990). Vivid memories of emotional events: The accuracy of remembered minutiae. *Memory and Cognition, 18,* 496–506.

Howe, M. L., Courage, M. L., & Peterson, C. (1994a, November). *Children's memories of traumatic events.* Paper presented at the annual meeting of the Psychonomic Society, St. Louis, MO.

Howe, M. L., Courage, M. L., & Peterson, C. (1994b). How can I remember when "I" wasn't there: Long-term retention of traumatic experiences and emergence of the cognitive self. *Consciousness and Cognition, 3,* 327–355.

Howe, M. L., Courage, M. L., & Peterson, C. (1995). Intrusions in preschoolers' recall of traumatic childhood events. *Psychonomic Bulletin & Review, 2,* 130–134.

Hudson, J. A., & Fivush, R. (1991). As time goes by: Sixth graders remember a kindergarten experience. *Applied Cognitive Psychology, 5,* 346–360.

Kebeck, G., & Lohaus, A. (1986). Effect of emotional arousal on free recall of complex material. *Perceptual and Motor Skills, 63,* 461–462.

Levine, J. L., & Burgess, S. L. (1995, July). Beyond "arousal": Effects of specific emotions on memory. In L. Levine (Chair), *Event memory.* Symposium conducted at the first biennial meeting of the Society for Applied Research in Memory and Cognition, Vancouver, BC.

Lonigan, C. J., Shannon, M. P., Taylor, C. M., Finch, A. J., Jr., & Sallee, F. R. (1994). Children exposed to disaster: II. Risk factors for the development of post-traumatic symptomatology. *Journal of the American Academy of Child and Adolescent Psychiatry, 33,* 94–105.

Maass, A., & Kohnken, G. (1989). Eyewitness identification: Simulating the "weapon effect." *Law and Human Behavior, 13,* 397–408.

McFarlane, A. C. (1987). Posttraumatic phenomena in a longitudinal study of children following a natural disaster. *Journal of the American Academy of Child and Adolescent Psychiatry, 26,* 764–769.

Melamed, B. G., Weinstein, D., Hawes, R., & Katin-Borland, M. (1975). Reduction of fear-related problems with use of film modelling. *Journal of the American Dental Association, 90,* 822–826.

Merritt, K., Ornstein, P. A., & Spicker, B. (1994). Children's memory for a salient medical procedure: Implications for testimony. *Pediatrics, 94,* 17–23.

Neisser, U. (1982). Snapshots or benchmarks? In U. Neisser (Ed.), *Memory observed: Remembering in natural contexts* (pp. 43–48). New York: Freeman.

Nelson, K. (1986). *Event knowledge: Structure and function in development.* Hillsdale, NJ:

Lawrence Erlbaum Associates.

Ornstein, P. A., Gordon, B. N., & Larus, D. (1992). Children's memory for a personally experienced event: Implications for testimony. *Applied Cognitive Psychology, 6,* 49–60.

Ornstein, P. A., Merritt, K., & Baker-Ward, L. (1995, July). Children's recollections of medical experiences: Exploring the linkage between stress and memory. In J. F. Parker (Chair), *Effects of stress and arousal upon children's memories.* Symposium conducted at the first biennial meeting of the Society for Applied Research in Memory and Cognition, Vancouver, BC.

Peters, D. P. (1987). The impact of naturally occurring stress on children's memory. In S. J. Ceci, M. P. Toglia, & D. F. Ross (Eds.), *Children's eyewitness memory* (pp. 122–141). New York: Springer-Verlag.

Peters, D. P. (1991). The influence of stress and arousal on the child witness. In J. L. Doris (Ed.), *The suggestibility of children's recollections* (pp. 60–76). Washington, DC: American Psychological Association.

Peters, D. P. (1997). Stress, arousal, and children's eyewitness memory. In N. L. Stein, P. A. Ornstein, B. Tversky, & C. J. Brainerd (Eds.), *Memory for everyday and emotional events* (pp. 351–370). Mahwah, NJ: Lawrence Erlbaum Associates.

Pillemer, D. B. (1984). Flashbulb memories of the assassination attempt of President Reagan. *Cognition, 16,* 63–80.

Pillemer, D. B. (1992). Preschool children's memories of personal circumstances: The fire alarm study. In E. Winograd & U. Neisser (Eds.), *Affect and accuracy in recall: Studies of "flashbulb" memories* (pp. 121–137). New York: Cambridge University Press.

Pillemer, D. B., & White, S. H. (1989). Childhood events recalled by children and adults. In H. W. Reese (Ed.), *Advances in child development and behavior* (Vol. 21, pp. 297–340). Orlando, FL: Academic Press.

Sheingold, K., & Tenney, Y. J. (1982). Memory for a salient childhood event. In U. Neisser (Ed.), *Memory observed* (pp. 201–212). San Francisco: Freeman.

Terr, L. C. (1988). What happens to early memories of trauma? A study of twenty children under age five at the time of documented traumatic events. *Journal of the American Academy of Child and Adolescent Psychiatry, 27,* 96–104.

Todd, C., & Perlmutter, M. (1980). Reality recalled by preschool children. In M. Perlmutter (Ed.), *Children's memory: Vol. 10. New directions for child development* (pp. 69–85). San Francisco: Jossey-Bass.

Trabasso, T., Stein, N. L., Rodkin, P. C., Munger, M. P., & Baughn, C. R. (in press). Knowledge of goals and plans in the on-line narration of events. *Cognitive Development.*

Vandermaas, M. O., Hess, T. M., & Baker-Ward, L. (1993). Does anxiety affect children's reports of memory for a stressful event? *Applied Cognitive Psychology, 7,* 109–127.

Vernberg, E. M., La Greca, A. M., Silverman, W. K., & Prinstein, M. J. (1996). Prediction of posttraumatic stress symptoms in children after Hurricane Andrew. *Journal of Abnormal Psychology, 105,* 237–248.

Warren, A. R., & Swartwood, J. N. (1992). Developmental issues in flashbulb memory research: Children recall the *Challenger* event. In E. Winograd & U. Neisser (Eds.), *Affect and accuracy in recall: Studies of "flashbulb" memories* (pp. 95–120). New York: Cambridge University Press.

Weaver, C. A., III. (1993). Do you need a "flash" to form a flashbulb memory? *Journal of Experimental Psychology: General, 122,* 39–46.

Winograd, E., & Killinger, W. A. (1983). Relating age at encoding in early childhood to adult recall: Development of flashbulb memories. *Journal of Experimental Psychology: General, 112,* 412–422.

Yerkes, R. M., & Dodson, J. D. (1908). The relation of strength of stimulus to rapidity of habit formation. *Journal of Comparative Neurology and Psychology, 18,* 459–482.

4

Interviewing Child Victim-Witnesses: How You Ask Is What You Get

Nancy E. Walker
Jennifer S. Hunt
Creighton University

Persons who do not have the use of reason, such as idiots, lunatics during lunacy, and children who do not understand the nature of an oath, shall be incompetent witnesses.

—Code of Georgia § 38–1607 (1994)

This excerpt from the Georgia Code of Statutes illustrates a serious fallacy in the construction of our judicial system. The western legal system is structured by and for fully functioning adults who often do not take the perspectives and limitations of others into account. A prime example is the child victim-witness. Children who enter into the legal system are accosted by strangers who use language they cannot understand (Brennan & Brennan, 1988; Perry et al., 1995; Saywitz, Jaenicke, & Camparo, 1990) to demand information they may be reluctant to give. Should they be unable to relate their accounts in the format adults expect, children may be considered unreliable and therefore may be excluded from further legal proceedings.

The belief that children cannot be competent witnesses, however, is a misperception. The controlling party in an interview of a child is in fact the adult interviewer, whose use of language and questioning techniques directly affects the quality and quantity of children's responses. The skill of the interviewer influences whether a child describes a true memory, relates a false belief, affirms details suggested by others, embellishes fantasies, or provides no information at all. The nature of the interview process itself likely contributes as much to the perceived competency of the witness as does the maturity of the child.

In recent years, psychologists have brought this perspective into the legal system, influencing judges and legislators as never before. In addition to serving as expert witnesses for various cases involving alleged child abuse, psychologists have influenced the courts through the use of amicus briefs (e.g., *Maryland v. Craig*, 1990; *State v. Michaels*, 1994). For example, in *State v. Michaels* (1994), an amicus brief signed by more than 40 researchers demonstrated the causative link between the use of highly suggestive interviewing techniques and children's skewed memories. The brief's application of scientific research to the interviews of the children who purported to have been molested by WeeCare day-care teacher Kelly Michaels raised the issue of whether the

> interview techniques used by the State in this case were so coercive or suggestive that they had a capacity to distort substantially the children's recollections of actual events and thus compromise the reliability of the children's statements and testimony based on their recollections. (*State v. Michaels*, 1994, p. 1377)

Clearly, the data presented in the brief influenced the appellate court's decision to reverse Michaels' conviction.

Psychological research on communicating with child victim-witnesses has had two major foci: (a) an assessment of the extent to which children are suggestible, and (b) the development of interviewing techniques (both questions and protocols) that elicit complete, unbiased reports from children. The amicus brief in the *Michaels* case primarily examined the first issue. However, in light of the influence those data had on the *Michaels* case, we believe it is important to summarize the research involving interview design. Without appropriate interviewing, truth finding may be seriously compromised, if not completely obscured. A summary of the research on interview design can be used not only to improve the training of interviewers and to guide future research, but also to guide statutory reform aimed at helping child victim-witnesses to provide accurate reports.

Our purposes for this chapter, therefore, are threefold. First, we review recommendations for proper interviewing techniques for child witnesses that are based on professional experience and empirical research. Second, we examine in what ways — or even whether — United States statutes address the issue of interviewing child victim-witnesses. Finally, we use those recommendations and statutes as a backdrop for analyses of 42 Child Protective Services interviews of children who allegedly had been sexually abused. We examine both the structure of the interviews and particular questioning techniques in order to determine whether they conformed to the recommendations described. We also assess the impact of age on children's ability to respond to various questioning techniques.

GUIDELINES FOR INTERVIEWING: PROFESSIONALS' RECOMMENDATIONS AND CURRENT STATUTES

We reviewed recommendations offered by several researchers and policy groups familiar with the special interview needs of child victim-witnesses.[1] Our sources included one professional organization (the American Professional Society on the Abuse of Children; APSAC, 1990), three empirically based protocols for interviewing (The Cognitive Interview [Fisher & Geiselman, 1992], The Structured Interview [Koehnken, 1995], and The Stepwise Interview [Yuille, Hunter, Joffe, & Zaparnuik, 1993], two books on child witnesses (Jones, 1992; Perry & Wrightsman, 1991), one report commissioned by the National Center on Child Abuse and Neglect (NC-CAN; Saywitz, Nathanson, Snyder, & Lamphear, 1993), one British policy statement on interviewing child witnesses (Home Office, 1992), and one article offering recommendations for practice (McGough & Warren, 1994).

Although this sample from North America and Europe represents various perspectives and interests, the recommendations for sound interviewing practices are quite consistent (see Table 4.1). For example, every professional recommended building rapport with children before incident-related questioning begins. Each one also recommended requesting a free narrative report before engaging in direct questioning and asking direct questions only if free narrative reports are inadequate. Nearly all of the professionals specifically recommended obtaining official information and discussing the "ground rules" for the interview, and several suggested asking developmentally appropriate questions, formally closing the interview when questioning has been completed, and using demonstrative aids only if necessary. Some recommended explaining the interview purpose and conducting a practice interview before forensically relevant questioning begins. No one in our sample recommended asking children to differentiate between "good" and "bad" touches.

Because United States statutes provide another source of guidelines for interviewing child victim-witnesses, we also reviewed statutes on communi-

---

[1]Throughout this chapter, we use the term *professionals* to refer collectively to the researchers and policy groups whose recommendations we reviewed.

TABLE 4.1

Professionals' Recommendations for Interviewing Child Witnesses

Author	APSAC	Fisher & Geiselman	Koehnken et al.	Yuille et al.	Home Office (United Kingdom)	Jones	Perry & Wrightsman	McGough & Warren	Saywitz et al.	Number of Professionals Explicitly Endorsing Each Recommendation	Percentage of Professionals Explicitly Endorsing Each Recommendation
Source	Guidelines for Psychosocial Evaluation . . .	Cognitive Interview	Structured Interview	Stepwise Interview	Memorandum of Good Practice	Interviewing the Sexually Abused Child	The Child Witness	Article for Practitioners	NCCAN Report		
Recommendations											
Build rapport	X	X	X	X	X	X	X	X	X	9 of 9	100%
Explain interview purpose		X	X	X	X		X			5 of 9	55.6%
Discuss ground rules	X	X	X	X	X	X	X	X		8 of 9	88.9%
Obtain official information	X	X	X	X	X	X	X	X		8 of 9	88.9%
Conduct practice interview		X	X	X				X		4 of 9	44.4%
Request free narrative	X	X	X	X	X	X	X	X	X	9 of 9	100%
Ask direct questions	X	X	**	**	**	X	**	**	**	3–9 of 9	33.3–100%**
Ask developmentally appropriate questions	X		X		X		X	X	X	7 of 9	77.8%
Use demonstrative aids	X			**	**	**	**	**		1–6 of 9	11.1–66.7%**
Differentiate good/bad touch										0 of 9	0%
Formally close interview	X	X	X	X	X	X	X		X	7 of 9	77.8%

Note. X = Recommended practice. ** = Use only if necessary.

cating with child victim-witnesses from all 50 states. In the following sections, we summarize those statutes addressing interviewer training, interview climate, and the number of interviews, comparing them with the recommendations for interviewing children offered by our sample of professionals.

Interviewer Training

If an interviewer plans to question a person from another culture, it helps for the interviewer to be knowledgeable about that individual's language and customs. Therefore, as most of the professionals in our sample either implied or explicitly stated, it stands to reason that interviewers who question youth should have a solid grounding in child development. For example, the *Memorandum of Good Practice* published by the United Kingdom's Home Office (1992) cautioned that "all interviews should be undertaken only by those with training, experience and an aptitude for talking to children" (p. 3).

The following excerpts from a Child Protective Services worker's interview of a 3-year-old child demonstrate how ignorance of child development can jeopardize interview integrity:

> Hmm, you know what? I didn't—you know, I've just never interviewed anybody three years of age before and it's just got me all shook up . . .

> Okay. We don't really know the difference between the truth and a lie. We don't really know the difference between a good touch and a bad touch . . .

> Uhhhh [pause] let's see. What to do. [Pause] Try the direct approach . . .

> Okay. Let me just ask you this, D. Have you ever said, "Mommy sucks my tanner?" (Perry, 1995)

Although it is crucial that interviewers understand child development, only four U.S. states (Illinois, New Mexico, Utah, and Washington) specifically require special training for individuals who interview child witnesses. The New Mexico law is illustrative:

> A person who serves as a judge, prosecutor, guardian ad litem, treatment guardian, court appointed attorney, court appointed special advocate, foster parent, mental health commissioner or mental health treatment service provider for a child subject to an abuse or neglect petition, a family in need of services petition or a mental health placement shall receive periodic training, to the extent of available resources, to develop his knowledge about

children, the physical and psychological formation of children and the impact of ethnicity on a child's needs. (New Mexico Statutes § 32A-18-1.A [1993])

In our opinion, all jurisdictions should encourage professionals who interview children to be trained in child development, particularly in the area of language development and comprehension.

Interview Climate

The climate of the interview is an especially important consideration. An atmosphere that is overly friendly and reassuring may lead to fabrication of details (Leichtman & Ceci, 1995), whereas a hostile or accusatory context may lead to increased errors in children's reports (Lepore & Sesco, 1994; Tobey & Goodman, 1992). An environment that is neutral—warm but not effusive, and professional but not intimidating—is most likely to produce accurate reports (Warren & Lane, 1995).

Although several states have statutory language expressing the importance of interview context, the differences among jurisdictions are striking. For example, some states (e.g., Connecticut and Massachusetts) require that children be protected from harassment, whereas other states (e.g., Delaware and Washington) mandate that legal procedures be explained to child witnesses; still other states (e.g., Alaska and Iowa) recommend limiting the duration of a child's in-court testimony.

Prohibition Against Harassment. Connecticut law specifically prohibits harassment of child witnesses:

> The attorneys for the defendant and for the state shall question the child while seated at a table positioned in front of the child, shall remain seated while posing objections and shall ask questions and pose objections in a manner which is not intimidating to the child. (Connecticut General Statutes § 54-86g (b)(4) [1958])

Similarly, California, Idaho, Massachusetts, Nevada, Oregon, and Utah all require that children be protected from justice system abuse. The Utah statute is representative: "Children have the right to protection from physical and emotional abuse during their involvement with the criminal justice process" (Utah Code § 77-37-4(1) [1993]). The Utah statute adds a unique further specification:

> Children are not responsible for inappropriate behavior adults commit against them and have the right not to be questioned, in any manner, nor to have

allegations made, implying this responsibility. Those who interview children have the responsibility to consider the interests of the child in this regard. (Utah Code § 77-37-4(2) [1993])

Alaska also adds an interesting statutory twist, noting that "The court may allow the child to testify while sitting on the floor" (Alaska Statutes Code of Criminal Procedure, § 12.45.046(c) [1990]). Most states, of course, are not as specific as Alaska; in fact, the vast majority are silent on the general topic of interview climate, an omission we find troublesome.

Procedural Explanations. The majority of the professionals in our sample recommended explaining the interview's purpose to the child and using developmentally appropriate language (see Table 4.1). For example, the Home Office's (1992) *Memorandum of Good Practice* suggested: "At some early point during the rapport phase the reason for the interview should be briefly explained in a way that takes account of the child's needs, and which does not refer to the alleged offence" (p. 16).

However, only seven U.S. states (Delaware, Florida, North Dakota, Pennsylvania, Rhode Island, Washington, and Wisconsin) have laws requiring that proceedings be explained to children in age-appropriate language. The Washington statute provides one example: A child has the right "to have explained in language easily understood by the child, all legal proceedings and/or police investigations in which the child may be involved" (Code of Washington § 7.69A.030(1) [1995]). To us, this requirement seems to be fundamental, yet only 14% of U.S. states specifically address the issue.

Limited Interview Duration. Most individuals, whether they are developmental psychologists or not, would recognize the wisdom of the Home Office's (1992) recommendation that "at appropriate intervals during the interview the child may need to be offered a break" (p. 12). Similarly, Jones and McQuiston (1988) asserted that "the interview should proceed at the child's tempo and not that dictated by the pressures of the system" (pp. 16–17). However, only Alaska and Iowa have enacted statutes that recommend limiting the amount of time that a child spends on the witness stand. Iowa's law reads:

A court may, upon its own motion or upon the motion of a party, order the court testimony of a child to be limited in duration in accordance with the developmental maturity of the child. The court may consider or hear expert testimony in order to determine the appropriate limitation on the duration of a child's testimony. However, the court shall, upon motion, limit the duration of a child's uninterrupted testimony to one hour, at which time the court shall allow the child to rest before continuing to testify. (Iowa Code § 910A.14.4 [1994])

We believe that all jurisdictions should adopt similar guidelines.

Number of Interviews

Some of the published recommendations we reviewed suggest limiting the number of interviews to which child witnesses are subjected (Home Office, 1992; Perry & Wrightsman, 1991; Walker, 1994). Utah's statutes reflect this sentiment: "Child victims and witnesses have the right to have interviews relating to a criminal prosecution kept to a minimum" (Utah Code § 77-37-4(3) [1993]). The statutes of Alabama, Florida, and New York concur.

Recently, however, some psychologists (Poole, 1995; Poole & Warren, 1995) have been reevaluating their positions on repeated interviews. Research by Fivush and her colleagues (Fivush & Hamond, 1990; Fivush & Shukat, 1995) has revealed that children provide different, although consistently accurate, pieces of information at different times. As a result, repeated, nonsuggestive questioning can make children's memory reports more complete.

Additional interviews therefore may be necessary to reveal new forensically relevant information. We offer, however, two caveats. First, interviewers must pay special attention to the questions they ask. Questions that are suggestive or that pressure children to provide answers tend to maintain errors across repetitions (e.g., Warren & Lane, 1995), whereas repeated specific or yes–no questions often lead to changes in children's responses (Poole & White, 1995). Second, we are by no means advocating unlimited interviews of already victimized children; good judgment and moderation must be exercised. Poole (1995) summarized the situation as follows:

> The fact-finding process would often be served better by a two-interview process, an initial interview to get preliminary information about the case, and a follow-up interview to clarify questions and explore other issues. There is no evidence that this process would reduce accuracy, provided interviews are conducted in a nonsuggestive way. (p. 4)

INTERVIEW STRUCTURE

However refined professionals' recommendations and/or statutes regarding interviewing children become, they mean very little if interviewers do not follow them. We concur with the sentiments of Yuille and his colleagues (1993), who commented:

> Our goal should not be to hide poor interviews, for it is important that the adequacy of the methods used to obtain children's evidence be assessed. A more appropriate goal would be to educate interviewers in order to enable them to conduct interviews that can withstand public scrutiny. (p. 101)

In the study reported in the following, we begin this process of scrutinizing actual investigative interviews of children. We analyzed the linguistic features of 42 transcripts of Child Protective Services (CPS) interviews of children from one mid-South state. The interviews involved 30 girls and 12 boys between 2 and 13 years old who were alleged to have been sexually abused. The sample consisted of 16 interviews of children 2 to 4 years old, 11 of children 5 to 7 years old, 9 of children 8 to 10 years old, and 3 of adolescents 11 to 13 years old. In three transcripts, the age of the child was not specified.

All of the interviews were conducted by Department of Human Services workers. In addition, a police officer participated in three interviews, and a worker from the sheriff's department participated in one interview. Overall, 43 interviewers were included in our sample. Although most of those interviewers did not specify their background or training, seven interviewers explicitly referred to themselves as social counselors.

Most interviewers ($n = 38$) were involved in only one of the interviews in the sample; however, five interviewers were involved in multiple interviews (two in two interviews, two in three interviews, and one in four interviews). In most interviews ($n = 31$), a single interviewer was present, but there were 10 interviews with two interviewers, and 1 interview with three interviewers. Camera operators or silent observers who were not related to the child were present in three interviews.

We divided each interview into its structural components: rapport-building, statement of interview purpose, establishment of ground rules, competency evaluation, discussion of "good" and "bad" touches, gathering of official information, discussion of the alleged abuse, use of demonstrative aids, and closing remarks. We determined the percentage of interviews containing each structural component (see Fig. 4.1). We also counted the number of words spoken by both interviewer and child in each interview section in order to determine how interview time was allocated (see Fig. 4.2). In addition, we conducted both quantitative and qualitative analyses of question form and content, examining the effects of several question forms on children's responses. Using two raters, interrater reliability for all analyses ranged from .63 to 1.00, with nearly all coefficients greater than .80.

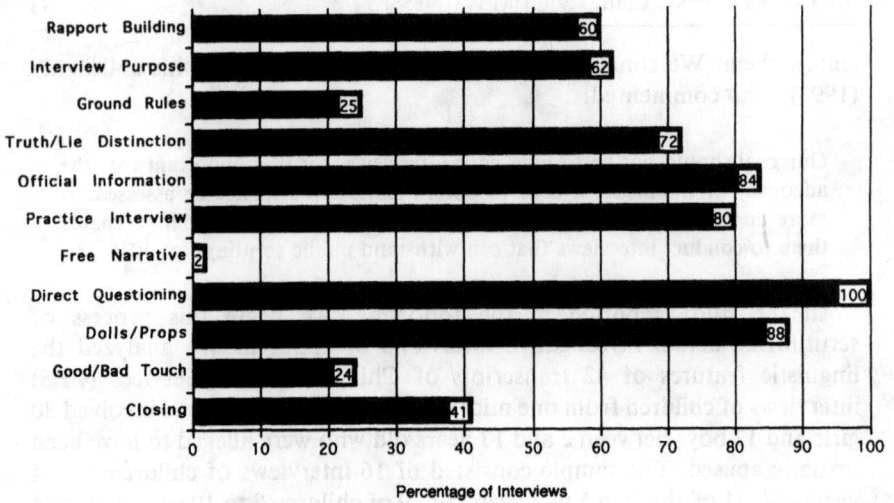

Percentage of Interviews

FIG. 4.1. Percentage of interviews including recommended interview segments.

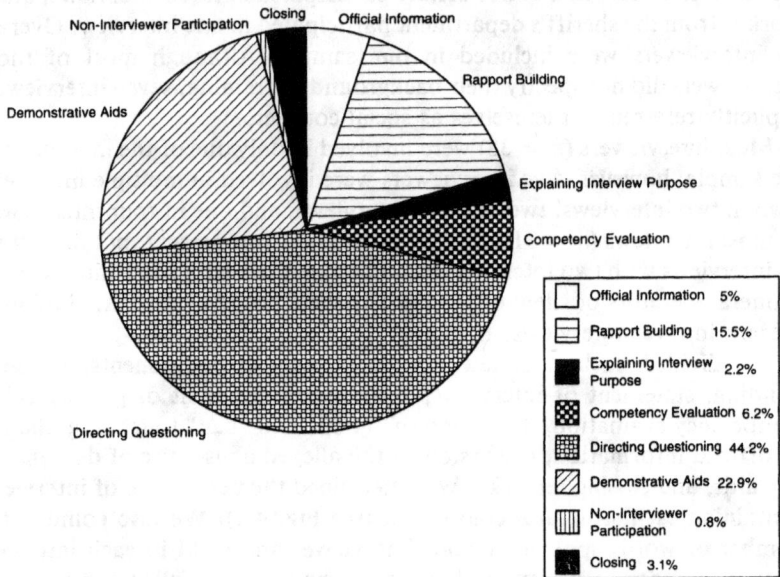

☐	Official Information 5%
☰	Rapport Building 15.5%
■	Explaining Interview Purpose 2.2%
▨	Competency Evaluation 6.2%
▦	Directing Questioning 44.2%
▨	Demonstrative Aids 22.9%
▥	Non-Interviewer Participation 0.8%
■	Closing 3.1%

FIG. 4.2. Percentage of time spent in each interview segment.

64

Rapport Phase

All of the professionals in our previously described sample specifically emphasized the importance of the rapport-building phase of the interview (see Table 4.1). For example, the United Kingdom's Home Office (1992) noted:

> The main aim of the first phase of the interview is to build up a rapport between the interviewer and the child in which the child is helped to relax and feel as comfortable as possible in the interview situation. However, this phase serves a number of important additional functions. If used correctly, it should supplement the interviewer's knowledge about the child's social, emotional and cognitive development, and particularly about his or her communication skills and degree of understanding . . . . *A rapport phase, however brief, should not be omitted even if the child has had significant previous contact with the interviewer.* (pp. 15-16)

Similarly, Koehnken (1993) advised:

> Before you begin to ask the child about the event it is very important to create a relaxing atmosphere and to make the child feel secure and confident. A good way to achieve this is to ask some questions which can be answered positively and therefore create a positive mood. You could, for example, ask what the child's favourite subjects are, if he or she has a pet, or you could talk about friends, hobbies, favourite games, toys, etc. . . . Building rapport here requires that you interact meaningfully with the child, contributing as an interested party, not simply asking a series of census-like questions. (p. 8)

Yuille et al. (1993) asserted that effective rapport building increases the quantity of children's free narrative. Recent work by Lamb and associates in Israel (Lamb et al., 1996) confirmed the assertions made by Yuille and colleagues. When interviewers spent adequate time on rapport-building activities, the first substantive open-ended question regarding abuse produced four times as much information as when inadequate time was spent on rapport building.

However, in 17 (40%) of the 42 interviews in our CPS sample, interviewers did not make any attempts to establish rapport with the child being questioned (see Fig. 4.1). In the 60% of the interviews in which interviewers did try to build rapport, they primarily used specific questions (e.g., "What is your dog's name?") rather than open-ended questions (e.g., "What do you like to do after school?"). As a result, interviewers talked three times more than children during the so-called rapport-building phase (Wilcoxon $T = -4.979, p < .0001$), a pattern that was consistent across all age groups.

These data suggest that a significant proportion of the interviewers in our sample never attempted to establish rapport, and that those who tried to do so in fact dominated the activities rather than facilitating verbalization from children. We therefore conclude that proper rapport building was woefully absent from our sample of CPS interviews.

Statement of Interview Purpose

Several of the professionals we sampled also endorsed the importance of stating the interview's purpose. Koehnken (1993) offered the following perspective:

> The child may not exactly know why he or she is being interviewed. However, unless it is clear what the purpose of the interview is it will be difficult to get the required information . . . . You should not assume that the child will volunteer relevant information without being told to do so. (p. 9)

Despite the importance of stating the interview's purpose, however, in only 62% of the interviews in our sample did the CPS workers inform the child why the interview was being conducted (see Fig. 4.1). Again, we conclude that a sizable proportion of the interviewers in our sample failed to follow recommended practice.

Establishment of Ground Rules

Eight of the nine professionals in our sample recommended establishing the ground rules for the interview before formal questioning begins. For example, one might say:

> I'm going to ask you some questions, and I want you to tell me what really, really happened. I don't want you to guess or to make anything up. If you don't know the answer to my question, that's okay; just say "I don't know." If you don't understand my question, that's okay, too; just say "I don't understand that question."

This phase is important because it conveys to the child the need to speak the truth and the acceptability of revealing lack of knowledge or comprehension (Home Office, 1992). Laboratory studies by Saywitz, Moan, and Lamphear (1991) and Hardie (1991) found that children prepared in this manner resisted significantly more misleading questions than did children who had not received such instruction. Similarly, Memon, Holley, Wark, Bull, and Koehnken (1995) found that children who frequently used "don't know" responses gave more accurate interviews overall.

In fewer than 25% of our sample of CPS cases, however, was there a discussion about the ground rules for the interview (see Fig. 4.1). More than three fourths of the interviews proceeded without an explanation to the child of how the interview would be conducted. Once again, the CPS interviewers in our sample failed to follow professionals' recommendations.

Competency Evaluation

In criminal proceedings a witness may give evidence only if he or she is competent. A witness is considered competent if he or she observed the events in question, stored a memory of those events, can communicate what happened, and is capable of telling the truth. All 50 U.S. states consider children competent to testify in sexual abuse cases unless explicitly demonstrated to be incompetent (Perry & Wrightsman, 1991). However, most statutes provide no direct guidance regarding how competence must be evaluated.

Conventional wisdom suggests that assessment of a child's competence should involve asking a series of questions whose answers imply that the child understands the obligation to be truthful. For example, an interviewer might ask the child to explain the difference between the truth and a lie, to determine whether a hypothetical question connotes truth (e.g., "If I say my shirt is red, am I telling the truth?"), and/or to explain what happens when the child tells a lie (e.g., that some punishment ensues).

A recent study by Walker and McKinley-Pace (1995), however, suggests that such approaches may be counterproductive. The researchers analyzed 71 forensic interviews of children 2 to 13 years old who testified in various civil and criminal proceedings. They found that as the time spent in truth–lie questioning increased, the children in their sample became more likely to provide misleading or irrelevant responses to those questions.

Walker and McKinley-Pace (1995) also found that, in their sample, 50% of the truth–lie queries were made during the first 2 minutes of the interview (i.e., before rapport had been established). In addition, the majority (61%) of the truth–lie questions requested yes–no responses (e.g., "Do you know the difference between the truth and a lie?"). The researchers concluded that, although more study of the assessment of children's understanding of the truth is warranted, the current methods of appraisal appear to be "inefficient and uninformative at best. At worst, [they are] prejudicial to the perception of children's testimonial competence."

In 72% of our sample of CPS interviews, the interviewers asked children questions to assess their understanding of the truth. In this regard, we give the interviewers good marks for effort, if not necessarily, as Walker and McKinley-Pace (1995) suggested, for appropriate questioning.

Discussion of "Good" and "Bad" Touches

Closely related to the assessment of a child's understanding of the difference between the truth and a lie is the assessment of a child's understanding of the difference between "good" and "bad" touches. This method of competency evaluation has been given little attention by professionals on interviewing children. Although none of the professionals in our sample recommended including such an assessment, none specifically condemned the practice either (see Table 4.1).

We would argue that discussions of the difference between "good" and "bad" touches do not elicit useful information and, in fact, may diminish perceptions of a child's competency. Children under the age of 12 do not possess the reasoning abilities required to process abstractions, particularly in the legal context (Perry & Teply, 1984–1985). However, discussions about "good" and "bad" touches incorporate two abstract concepts: (a) touch, and (b) good versus bad. The word *touch*, as used by adults, encompasses a variety of actions (e.g., fondling, probing, patting). A child, however, may use a restricted definition of touch that precludes, for example, penetration with a finger (Walker, 1994). Even if a child broadly defines touch, he or she still may experience difficulties with the abstract concepts of good and bad. As a result, children may answer "good touch"–"bad touch" questions in a way that underestimates their true understanding of what constitutes an inappropriate action.

Twenty-four percent of the interviews in our sample included discussions about the differences between "good" and "bad" touches. For the reasons already stated, we believe such practice should be discouraged. However, we advocate further empirical investigation into children's understanding of the concepts of "good" and "bad" touches, as well as the effects of "good touch"–"bad touch" assessments.

Gathering of Official Information

Intuitively, it seems obvious that interviewers should gather basic information regarding the identity and status of the child being questioned. For example, an interviewer might ask the child's name, address, and/or year in school, as well as inquiring about with whom the child lives. Eight of the nine professionals in our sample specifically recommended such practice (see Table 4.1). Some professionals, however, cautioned against opening an interview with such questions. Fisher and Geiselman (1992) suggested that it is better to ask for such information at the end of the interview, because gathering official information (for which there is only one right answer) tends to suppress rapport building.

In 84% of the interviews in our CPS sample, interviewers collected information regarding the child's identity and status; in 16% of the interviews they did not gather even this basic information (see Fig. 4.1).

Those interviewers who did ask for the information tended to do so at the beginning of the interview.

Discussion of the Alleged Abuse

Use of Free Narrative.   All of the professionals in our sample strongly recommended requesting a free narrative from the child before proceeding to direct questioning regarding the alleged incidents of forensic concern (see Table 4.1). Children's spontaneous, free recall reports, although typically less detailed than those elicited by specific questioning, tend to be more accurate than reports obtained through direct questioning (Dent, 1991).

The United Kingdom's Home Office (1992) *Memorandum of Good Practice* offered advice that the child should be encouraged to:

> provide *in his or her own words* and at his or her own pace an account of the relevant event(s). This is the heart of the interview and the interviewer's role is to act as a facilitator, not an interrogator. Only the most general, open-ended questions should be asked in this phase, for example: "Why do you think we are here today?"; "Is there anything that you would like to tell me?" If the child responds in a positive way to such questions then the interviewer can encourage the child to give a free narrative account of events. Every effort must be made to obtain information from the child which is spontaneous and free from the interviewer's influence. (p. 17)

Similarly, Koehnken (1993) recommended:

> ask the child to describe in narrative style his or her general recollections of the event. You might say, "Tell me everything you can, even the little things you think aren't important." *It is essential not to interrupt the child during his or her narration or to ask specific questions!* The single most important skill an interviewer can learn is not to interrupt the child in the middle of a narrative response! (p. 11)

Clearly, professionals are unequivocal about the importance of the uninterrupted, free narrative portion of the interview. In our CPS sample, however, only 2% of the interviews began the incident-relevant portion of the conversation with open-ended questions (see Fig. 4.1). In fully 98% of the CPS interviews, this step considered critical by every one of the professionals whose recommendations we reviewed was omitted! Unfortunately, failure to include open-ended questions does not seem to be limited to our sample of interviewers. Lamb et al. (1996) obtained strikingly similar results (2.2%) when they analyzed interviews conducted by specially trained Israeli "youth investigators."

Use of Direct Questions.   All of our professionals acknowledged that it may be appropriate, and even necessary, to ask direct questions following the free narrative portion of the interview (see Table 4.1). Warren and McGough (1995) elucidated the dilemma inherent in this approach: "The major issue confronted by interviewers is likely to be the paradox that young children need help recalling experiences, but that direct, specific questions and other recall prompts may produce distortions and suggestibility" (p. 21). We therefore concur with the six professionals in our sample who urged practitioners to ask direct questions only if necessary, that is, if the free narrative does not provide sufficient information.

Although the vast majority of the CPS interviewers in our sample failed to elicit a free narrative recollection of the allegedly abusive events, 100% asked direct questions regarding the forensically relevant incidents (see Fig. 4.1). Moreover, in an additional analysis of the CPS interviews, Warren et al. (1995) found that 64% of those direct questions required only a yes or no response. Fully 90% of the overall questions asked by the sample of interviewers were specific as opposed to general. Those proportions were similar in both abuse and nonabuse questioning phases of the interviews. Clearly, the interviewers in our sample relied excessively on direct and specific questioning.

Use of Demonstrative Aids

Several states permit the use of anatomically detailed dolls when children provide evidence in cases of alleged sexual abuse. The New York statute is illustrative: "A child witness should be permitted in the discretion of the court to use anatomically correct dolls and drawings during his testimony" (Laws of New York § 642-a [1996]). However, widespread concern about the potential suggestiveness of anatomical dolls (Wolfner, Faust, & Dawes, 1993) has influenced some jurisdictions to ban their use (Bruck, Ceci, Francoeur, & Renick, 1995).

Despite the fact that statutes often permit the use of demonstrative aids in child sexual abuse cases, expert opinion is divided on the advisability of using such aids as anatomically detailed dolls (see Table 4.1). Most researchers suggest using such props only as a last resort (e.g., McGough & Warren, 1994; Perry & Wrightsman, 1991; Yuille et al., 1993). Indeed, in our sample of professionals, only the American Professional Society on the Abuse of Children (1990) fully endorsed the use of demonstrative aids.

Despite the caution recommended by most of the professionals in our sample, in 88% of our sample of CPS transcripts, interviewers encouraged children to use anatomically detailed dolls (see Fig. 4.1). On average, nearly 23% of interview time involved the use of demonstrative aids (see Fig. 4.2). However, although interviewers in general may have relied too much on the use of such aids, they did consider the age of the child. Nearly 36% of the interview time for 2- to 4-year-olds was devoted to demonstrative aids, compared with only 10% of the interview time for adolescents. Whether the age disparity in the use of anatomical dolls in our sample of interviews reflects recommended interview practice is debatable. Although Jones (1992) asserted that anatomical dolls are most appropriate for preverbal and barely verbal children, recent empirical evidence suggests otherwise. DeLoache (1995) found that preschool-age children typically are unable to use dolls to represent themselves or others, and Salmon, Bidrose, and Pipe (1995) found that props did not, in fact, enhance event recall for the very young children in their sample.

Use of Closing Remarks

Seven of the nine professionals in our sample noted that the interview's closing phase is critical. The Home Office (1992) offered several specific suggestions for closing the interview:

> The interviewer should be careful to ensure that all interviews end appropriately. Every effort should be made to ensure that the child is not distressed but is in a positive frame of mind.
>
> During this phase the interviewer may need to check with the child that he or she (the interviewer) has correctly understood the important parts, if any, of the child's account. If this is considered necessary, care should be taken not to convey disbelief. Any recapping should use the child's own language, *not* a summary provided by the interviewer in adult language (which could contain errors but with which the child may nevertheless agree).
>
> It may then be appropriate to revert to some of the "neutral" topics mentioned in the rapport phase . . . . The child should be thanked for his or her time and effort and asked if there is anything more he or she wishes to say. An explanation should be given to the child of what may happen next, but, again, promises which cannot be kept should not be made. The child should always be asked if he or she has any questions and these answered as appropriately as possible.
>
> It is good practice to give to the child (or, if more appropriate, the accompanying adult) a contact name and telephone number in case the child later decides that he or she wishes to discuss further matters with the interviewer. (p. 21)

In 59% of the interviews in our CPS sample, interviewers abruptly ended the session and dismissed the child (see Fig. 4.1). Only 41% of the interviews ended with a formal closing such as those recommended by the Home Office (1992). Interviewers in our sample spent significantly more time closing the interview with children 8 to 13 years old ($n = 12$) than with children 2 to 7 years old ($n = 27$), $F(1, 37) = 6.059, p < .05$. We believe it is important for interviews with children of all ages to be closed gracefully.

Interview Protocols

Psychologists have used the research on interview structures and individual questioning techniques to design protocols for the entire interview. Although none of the interviewers in our sample appeared to follow a specific protocol, we outline three interview protocols in order to illustrate how the research we previously reviewed may be synthesized.

The Stepwise Interview.   The Stepwise Interview (Yuille et al., 1993) divides the interview into nine stages. 'As interviewers progress through these stages, they move from open, nonleading questions to more specific questioning techniques. The Stepwise Interview begins with rapport building. An important component of the rapport building involves asking the child to relate two events that are unrelated to the issue(s) of forensic concern (e.g., birthday parties, after-school activities). Besides providing the interviewer with information about the child's capacity for recall, these narratives serve as a practice interview for the child.

After the two narratives, the interviewer discusses the need to tell the truth. The interviewer then moves to a discussion about the matter(s) of forensic concern by using open-ended questions. Once the child introduces the topic, the interviewer asks him or her to provide a narrative. The child's account is clarified with general questions (e.g., "Can you tell me more about that?"); specific questions and/or anatomical dolls are used only if necessary. Finally, the interviewer closes the interview by thanking the child and explaining the next phase of the investigative procedure (Yuille et al., 1993).

The Structured Interview.   The Structured Interview (SI; Koehnken, 1995) consists of five stages: rapport building, free recall, questioning, review, and closing. During the rapport-building phase, the interviewer engages in casual conversation by asking open-ended questions unrelated to the forensically relevant event(s). The interviewer also informs the witness that the interviewer does not have any knowledge of the event(s) in question and that the witness should set the pace for the interview. In the free-recall phase, the interviewer requests a free narrative account from the witness. In the questioning phase, the interviewer asks questions based solely on the information provided by the witness during the free-recall phase. The interviewer begins with open-ended questions, following them with closed questions if necessary. The interviewer specifically is instructed to avoid the use of leading, misleading, and forced-choice questions. During this phase, the interviewer also cautions the witness not to fabricate responses. Finally, the interviewer reviews the information obtained during the free-recall and questioning phases, then closes the interview.

The Cognitive Interview. The Cognitive Interview (CI; Fisher & Geiselman, 1992) rests on the assumption that different information can be retrieved with different memory searches. The CI consists of the same five stages used in the SI (rapport building, free recall, questioning, review, and closing; Fisher & McCauley, 1995). However, persons questioned with a CI also are taught several mnemonic approaches designed to maximize information retrieval. These techniques include reinstating the context of the original event, relating the event from different perspectives (e.g., describing what another person present at the event would have seen), and recounting the event in different orders (e.g., reverse chronological order). Interviewers using CI techniques also promote complete memory searches by encouraging witnesses to relate every detail they can remember, no matter how seemingly trivial (Fisher & McCauley, 1995; Geiselman, Saywitz, & Bornstein, 1993). Research indicates that CI techniques are helpful for both adults and children (see Fisher & McCauley, 1995, for a review), although there is evidence that older children benefit more than younger children from CI training (Geiselman et al., 1993).

Memon et al. (1995) compared the CI with the SI. The researchers showed 97 eight- and nine-year-old children a video of a magic show. Ten to 12 days later, the children completed an interview sequence consisting of a misleading initial questionnaire, a CI or SI, and then a follow-up questionnaire. Memon and her colleagues found that the use of CI or SI did not induce a significant difference in the amount of information provided by children. However, the use of cognitive techniques seemed to buffer children against misleading suggestions. Children in the CI condition included less misleading information from the initial questionnaire on the follow-up questionnaire, and their overall levels of accuracy were higher. Memon et al. concluded that, after a long delay, CI techniques may not elicit more information than SI techniques, but the information gained from CI is likely to be more reliable.

FAULTY AND NONPRODUCTIVE
QUESTIONING TECHNIQUES

In an interdisciplinary statement regarding investigation of child sexual abuse, Lamb (1994) noted that "few systematic attempts have been made to evaluate the amount of detail and the accuracy of information yielded by children in response to different types of questions" (p. 155). The second part of our analysis of the CPS interviews was an attempt to fill that gap by evaluating the impact of question forms not endorsed by professionals. We found that when interviewers do not follow professionals' recommendations in their direct questioning, they seem to fall into one of two traps: faulty questioning or nonproductive questioning. In this section, we define and provide examples of each of those traps, demonstrating how their use jeopardizes interview integrity.

Faulty Questioning Techniques

Faulty questions lead to responses as opposed to answers. Walker (1994) explained that children follow the conversational rule that every question requires an answer. Therefore, even when interviewers ask questions that children cannot understand, they tend to get responses; those responses, however, do not necessarily provide the requested information. Some examples of faulty techniques include instances in which an interviewer alters a child's statement (what we refer to as *modification*), forced-choice questions, and multipart questions.

Modification.   We defined a modification as an instance in which an interviewer reworded a child's statement in a way that changed its meaning or claimed that the child made a statement that he or she had not made. Although modification presumably can be accidental, it sometimes occurs when interviewers want children's statements to match information from other sources (Geiselman et al., 1993) or the interviewers' own biases or preconceptions. It also can be used to speed up a slow interview. However, interviewers who attempt this practice not only risk discrediting their interviews, they also run the risk of introducing misinformation into children's memories.

Modifications occurred in 74% ($n = 31$) of our sample of interviews. Interviewers made a total of 80 modifications ($M = 2.58$, SD $= 1.52$) across those interviews.[2] Interviewers' use of modification did not vary by the age of the child, $F(3, 35) = .80$, ns (see Table 4.2).

---

[2]As we noted earlier, in five instances, an interviewer conducted more than one interview.

TABLE 4.2
Children's Response Patterns to Interviewers' Modifications

	Age 2-4	Age 5-7	Age 8-10	Age 11-13	All Ages
Number of interviews	16	11	9	3	39
Number of interviews with modifications	11	8	7	2	31
Mean percentage of agreement responses	50	46	39	25	46
Mean percentage of disagreement responses	21	21	35	50	26
Mean percentage of responses ignored	29	33	25	25	28

In the first analysis, we investigated children's reactions to interviewers' modifications. We divided children's responses into three categories. *Agreement* occurred when the child explicitly agreed with the interviewer's modification. For example:

Interviewer: Can you tell me what grandpa did to Sean?
Child: He sucked her.
Interviewer: He sucked her. Okay. What did he do to Jean?
Child: (no response)
Interviewer: Do you know?
Child: (no response)
Interviewer: So he sucked them. Who did he suck?
Child: Both of them. (Hunt, Komori, Kellen, Galas, & Gleason, 1995)

Disagreement occurred when the child explicitly corrected the interviewer:

Child: . . . one day after school when I was going to Howard Elementary.
Interviewer: When you were going to Highland Elementary.
Child: Howard. (Hunt et al., 1995)

Ignoring occurred when the child did not comment on the interviewer's modification:

Interviewer: Do you know how old they are?
Child: (nods)
Interviewer: How old?
Child: Three months old.

However, the interviewers who participated in multiple interviews did not ask disproportionate numbers of any question form included in our analyses.

Interviewer: Three years old . . . okay. What we're gonna do today
                  is get our doll . . . and I'm gonna let you tell me what
                  you call all her body parts, okay? What is this?
Child: Haaair. (Hunt et al., 1995)

We entered into a chi-square analysis each child's overall response
pattern (e.g., a child might agree 50% of the time, disagree 15% of the time,
and ignore modifications 35% of the time).[3] The analysis revealed a
significant difference in children's responses to modifications. Children
were most likely (46%) to agree with modifications, $\chi^2(2, n = 31) = 7.29$,
$p < .05$. Less frequently, they disagreed with the modification (26%) or
ignored interviewers' modifications and continued on with the interview as
if nothing had happened (28%).

We also examined the impact of a child's age on his or her tendency to
agree or disagree with a modification. We found an interesting age trend
that did not reach significance in our sample, but that we believe merits
further investigation. In our sample, the tendency to ignore modifications
was not correlated with the age of the child, $r = -.03$. However, the child's
age had a weak negative correlation with agreeing with a modification ($r =
-.15$) and a weak positive correlation with disagreeing with a modification
($r = .19$). In other words, younger children were somewhat more likely to
agree with modifications than were older children, whereas older children
were somewhat more likely to disagree with modifications than were
younger children. Table 4.2 provides a breakdown of response patterns by
age group. These numbers suggest that a child's willingness and/or ability to
openly disagree with an interviewer may be developmental in nature. It
appears that children, especially young children, often are either unable or
unwilling to contradict interviewers, even when interviewers twist their
words to mean something else.

We next investigated the effect of a child's agreement with a modification
on the interviewer by counting how many times interviewers repeated
modified statements throughout the interviews. We believe that repeating
modifications is a dangerous practice because it reinforces potentially faulty
information, possibly embedding misinformation within children's memories. In 29% ($n = 9$) of the interviews that contained modifications, the
interviewer continued to repeat the modified information. In six of those

---

[3]In all of our analyses, we used each child rather than each question as the unit of analysis
in order to maintain independent observations. In order to investigate whether the peculiarities
(e.g., level of persuasiveness) of those particular interviewers who participated in more than
one interview moderated our results, we examined the patterns of responses elicited by those
interviewers. For no analysis did we find any interactions with individual interviewers; hence,
we collapsed across interviewers for all analyses.

interviews, the child had explicitly agreed with the modification. The child had ignored the modification in two interviews. In only one instance had the child disagreed openly with the modification. Although no definite conclusions can be drawn from this small number of cases, the pattern seems to suggest that interviewers are more likely to repeat modifications with which children agree rather than disagree; in fact, interviewers rarely continued to refer to modified statements when children overtly disagreed with them. It appears, then, that in order to prevent interviewers from repeating modifications, children might have to explicitly correct interviewers, a task that, unfortunately, younger children do not seem to be willing and/or able to do.

Forced-Choice Questions. Forced-choice questions occur when interviewers phrase questions in a way that presents a limited number of response options:

Interviewer: Did he do it real real hard or real real fast?
Child: Fast. (Hunt et al., 1995)

Forced-choice questions can be considered leading because they suggest to children that there is a limited number of correct responses to a question, thereby inhibiting children's ability to provide their own answers (Jones, 1992). Yuille et al. (1993) recommended that interviewers should avoid forced-choice questions, especially if they contain only two response choices.

In our sample, forced-choice questions occurred in 88% ($n = 37$) of the interviews; interviewers asked 170 forced-choice questions ($M = 5.21$, SD $= 4.00$) in those interviews. Interviewers' use of forced-choice questions did not vary by age of child, $F(3, 35) = .48$, ns (see Table 4.3).

Although in our sample forced-choice questions amounted to only 1% of the total questions asked by interviewers, we believe they are important because they often were used to obtain critical information, such as details

TABLE 4.3
Children's Response Patterns to Forced-Choice Questions

	Age 2-4	Age 5-7	Age 8-10	Age 11-13	All Ages
Number of interviews	16	11	9	3	39
Number of interviews with forced-choice questions	13	10	9	3	37
Mean percentage selecting first option	44	41	22	17	34
Mean percentage selecting second option	26	37	35	11	31
Mean percentage providing meaningful alternative answers	17	14	19	72	21
Mean percentage providing nonanswer responses	13	8	24	0	14

about the alleged abuse or perpetrator. It is particularly striking, therefore, that the children in our sample chose one of the answers suggested by the interviewer 65% of the time. Only 21% of the time did they provide a meaningful alternative answer. The low proportion of meaningful alternative responses in part may reflect the accuracy of the interviewers' response options (especially if the interviewer had background information, e.g., from a previous interview). Nevertheless, we believe that the strong adherence of the children in our sample to the response options provided by the interviewers supports the assertion that forced-choice questions are leading in nature (Jones, 1992; Lunning & Eilts, 1996; Warren & McGough, 1995).

We also examined the impact of age on responses to forced-choice questions (see Table 4.3 for a breakdown of responses by age group). Again we found an interesting nonsignificant pattern that merits further investigation with a larger sample. We found that selecting the first response was negatively correlated with age ($r = -.23$), whereas supplying a meaningful alternative answer was positively correlated with age ($r = .23$). In other words, younger children were more likely than older children to demonstrate a primacy effect, simply responding with the first option presented to them by the interviewer. Older children, on the other hand, were more likely than younger children to respond with their own unique (and presumably correct) answer. The latter correlation, however, largely reflects an increase in meaningful alternative answers in the 11- to 13-year-old age group. This pattern is consistent with Piagetian theory, which asserts that adolescents tend to operate at a more advanced cognitive level. It seems, therefore, that older children either are better able and/or more willing to look beyond the options presented by an interviewer and answer forced-choice questions like any other type of question.

Multipart Questions. Multipart questions occur when two or more inquiries with potentially different responses are contained within the same question:

Interviewer: Would it be a special time when you would go up there with [him], or would there be anybody there at his house?
Child: Yes. (Hunt et al., 1995)

Because children have difficulty attending to multiple ideas at one time, they have difficulty understanding and answering multipart questions (Walker, 1994). In fact, Perry and her colleagues (Perry et al., 1995) demonstrated that multipart questions are difficult for all interviewees, adults as well as children.

In our sample, multipart questions were asked in 86% (*n* = 36) of the interviews. In those interviews, interviewers asked 161 multipart questions (*M* = 4.47, SD = 3.69). The age of the child did not impact the number of multipart questions asked by interviewers, $F(3, 35) = 1.14$, *ns* (see Table 4.4).

Overall, we found that 61% of children's responses to multipart questions did not appear to answer any of the questions asked by the interviewer. Children responded to all parts of the question only 5% of the time. A nonsignificant age trend suggests that age is positively correlated with answering all inquiries embedded in a multipart question ($r = .25$). Again, this correlation largely reflects an increase in complete answers in the 11- to 13-year-old age group, as would be predicted by Piagetian theory. (See Table 4.4 for a breakdown of responses by age group.) Thus, older children may be better able to recognize when multiple questions have been asked and to know that each question part requires a response.

Nonproductive Questioning Techniques

Nonproductive questions do not generate interpretable responses from children. Children respond to such questions with confusing nonverbal responses or verbal responses that are completely unrelated to the question. Although nonproductive questions do not run the risk of gathering misinformation as faulty questions do, they do not help the interview. Instead they serve only to prolong the interview, tiring and most likely confusing the child. Some examples of nonproductive techniques include questions that generate nonverbal responses and "Can you . . . ?" questions, such as "Can you tell me where you go to school?"

Questions Eliciting Nonverbal Responses. The first nonproductive technique we examined was the use of questions that elicit nonverbal

TABLE 4.4
Children's Patterns of Responses to Multipart Questions

	Age 2–4	Age 5–7	Age 8–10	Age 11–13	All Ages
Number of interviews	16	11	9	3	39
Number of interviews with multipart questions	13	9	9	3	36
Mean percentage of responses to first inquiry	1	2	6	0	3
Mean percentage of responses to second inquiry	14	36	9	0	18
Mean percentage of responses to all inquiries	3	5	4	17	5
Mean percentage of unclear, question-related responses	11	12	14	17	13
Mean percentage of nonanswer responses	72	45	68	67	61

responses. Some may argue that nonverbal responses are useful because the child in fact responds to the question. We found, however, that of the 31 different types of nonverbal responses given by children in our sample, only two of them (i.e., head nod "yes" and head shake "no") had an unambiguous meaning. The other 29 (e.g., shrugging or looking away) had unclear interpretations. We therefore believe that interviewers should strive to obtain verbal as opposed to nonverbal responses.

The children in our sample gave a total of 1,752 nonverbal responses. One hundred eighty-eight (10.7%) of those nonverbal responses were elicited by various statements and were not analyzed further.[4] Every child gave at least one nonverbal response during his or her interview; the number of nonverbal responses given by each child ($M = 37.24$, SD $= 28.12$) did not differ significantly by age, $F(3, 35) = 1.81$, $p > .15$ (see Table 4.5).

We found that almost any kind of question can lead to a nonverbal response. However, because we knew that the overall composition of questions in the interviews was 90% specific questions (i.e., questions that elicit brief, specific answers) and 10% open questions (i.e., questions that encourage narrative responses; Warren et al., 1995), we collapsed the various questions that elicited nonverbal responses into those two categories.[5] We found that specific questions resulted in a disproportionate amount of nonverbal responses, $\chi^2 (1, n = 42) = 7.11$, $p < .01$. Specific questions led to 98% of the overall nonverbal responses, whereas open questions resulted in only 2% of those responses. Although weak correlations suggest that younger children may give more nonverbals in response to specific questions than do older children ($r = -.15$), the actual differences between the age groups are extremely small (see Table 4.5). It appears the disparity in nonverbal responses between specific and open questions is roughly the same for children of all ages.

Our results confirm the suspicions of a number of professionals (e.g., Home Office, 1992; Jones, 1992; Koehnken, 1995; McGough & Warren, 1994; Myers, 1992; Perry & Wrightsman, 1991; Yuille et al., 1993) that open-ended questions are a better means of obtaining forensically relevant information from children than are specific questions. We find it troubling

---

[4]The focus of our analyses was questions, not statements. Moreover, many of the statements made by interviewers were not designed to elicit information from children (e.g., statements explaining the role of the interviewer); therefore, it was inappropriate to include them in our analyses.

[5]The collapsed Specific category consisted of general specific questions as well as leading questions (i.e., questions that suggest a particular answer), tag questions (i.e., questions that end by asking for confirmation of a statement), multiple questions (i.e., several simultaneous inquiries), "Can you . . . ?" questions (i.e., questions that begin with "Can you"), "Will you . . . ?" questions (i.e., questions that begin with "Will you"), and " . . . or anything?" questions (i.e., questions that end with "or anything").

TABLE 4.5
Children's Nonverbal Responses by Question Type

	Age 2–4	Age 5–7	Age 8–10	Age 11–13	All Ages
Number of interviews	16	11	9	3	39
Mean number of nonverbal responses	30	36	55	24	37
Mean percentage of nonverbal responses to specific questions	98	99	97	95	98
Mean percentage of nonverbal responses to open questions	2	1	3	5	2

that the interviewers in our sample overwhelmingly favored the question form that was most likely to elicit unclear responses.

"Can you . . . ?" Questions. Finally, we examined children's responses to "Can you . . . ?" questions. In these instances, interviewers either asked children "Can you tell me *X*?" or "Can you show me *X*?"

Interviewer: Can you tell me what you call that?
Child: (nods affirmatively)
Interviewer: What do you call that?
Child: Blue stuff. (Hunt et al., 1995)

"Can you . . . ?" questions are problematic because of their complexity. Walker (1993, 1994) found that even older children have difficulty following, remembering, and breaking down questions with several component phrases. In addition, "Can you . . . ?" questions are nonproductive because they do not actually ask for the information the interviewer is seeking. Although presumably an interviewer who asks "Can you tell me where he hit you?" is seeking a qualitative answer such as the name of a body part, in reality he or she is making a metacognitive inquiry, as the following example illustrates:

Question: Can you tell me where he hit you?
Answer: Yes, I can.

"Can you . . . ?" questions appeared in 88% ($n = 37$) of the transcripts in our sample. In those interviews, CPS workers asked 246 "Can you . . . ?" questions ($M = 6.65$, SD = 5.48). Interviewers asked marginally more "Can you tell . . . ?" questions ($n = 148$) than "Can you show . . . ?" questions ($n = 98$), $t(41) = 1.95$, $p < .06$. However, there were no significant differences in responses to those two question forms, so we collapsed them in the analysis. The age of the child did not influence the frequency with which interviewers asked "Can you . . . ?" questions F(3, 35) = .35, ns (see Table 4.6).

TABLE 4.6
Children's Patterns of Responses to "Can You . . . ?" Questions

	Age 2-4	Age 5-7	Age 8-10	Age 11-13	All Ages
Number of interviews	16	11	9	3	39
Number of interviews with "Can you . . . ?" questions	13	11	8	2	37
Mean percentage of qualitative responses	39	67	64	79	53
Mean percentage of yes/no responses	35	28	10	13	28
Mean percentage of nonanswers	26	6	26	8	19

Overall, children were more likely to respond to "Can you . . . ?" questions with qualitative responses (53%) than with yes–no responses (28%) or with nonanswers, such as unclear responses or nonverbals (19%). However, both of the latter categories constitute uninformative responses. As a result, a total of 47% of children's responses to "Can you . . . ?" questions did not provide interviewers with any useful information.

We found significant age trends in children's abilities to answer "Can you . . . ?" questions. (See Table 4.6 for a breakdown of responses by age.) Age was significantly correlated with giving qualitative responses to "Can you . . . ?" questions, $r = .38$. That trend largely reflects the low number of qualitative responses given by children 2 to 4 years old. Conversely, age had a marginally significant negative correlation with providing yes–no responses, $r = -.29$. A substantial difference in the number of yes–no responses seemed to occur between children 7 or younger and children 8 or older. Overall, it appears that children 8 and older frequently are able to give qualitative responses (i.e., answers to the intended questions) to "Can you . . . ?" questions; children 7 and younger, however, often give "Yes" or "No" responses (i.e., literal answers to the metacognitive inquiries), a finding that fits well with predictions grounded in Piagetian theory.

As a whole, "Can you . . . ?" questions often seem to be less productive for interviewers who want to obtain informative responses, especially from younger children. We suggest, therefore, that interviewers use direct, open-ended requests when they ask for information. For example, "Tell me where he hit you" may be a better request than "Can you tell me where he hit you?"

CONCLUSIONS AND RECOMMENDATIONS

Although the results of our analyses of CPS interviews provided useful information, we are aware that our study had limitations. In particular, the sample of interviews used in our study was limited both in quantity and in geographical diversity.

Despite these limitations, however, our study, as well as the other research described in this chapter, demonstrate that interviewers' questioning techniques clearly affect the quality and quantity of children's responses. However, both the courts and many front-line interviewers appear to have paid little attention to the question of interview quality. If we are to obtain reliable testimony from children, both groups need to become familiar with and heed empirical findings bearing on the issue of questioning child witnesses. In the following, we discuss the implications of our findings for legislators, practitioners, and researchers.

Implications for Legislators

We believe that it is premature, and most likely counterproductive, to enact statutes endorsing particular questioning techniques. However, it seems prudent to enact statutes requiring that questioning of children be developmentally appropriate. Portions of three existing U.S. statutes provide helpful guidance in this regard.

Minnesota permits children to use children's language: "A child describing any act or event may use language appropriate for a child of that age" (Minnesota Statutes § 592.02(m) [1993]). That requirement seems fundamental to judicial fairness.

Wisconsin, Pennsylvania, and Washington statutes take an additional step by encouraging officials to inform the court of the child's comprehension of proceedings:

> Counties are encouraged to provide the following additional services on behalf of children who are involved in criminal or delinquency proceedings as victims or witnesses: . . . Advice to the judge, when appropriate and as a friend of the court, regarding the child's ability to understand proceedings and questions. (Wisconsin Statutes § 950.055(2)(b) [1995])

Once again, we endorse that approach.

California's statute is the most comprehensive of all, specifically requiring that questions posed to child witnesses be developmentally appropriate:

> With a witness under the age of 14, the court shall take special care to protect him or her from undue harassment or embarassment, and to restrict the unnecessary repetition of questions. The court shall also take special care to insure that questions are stated in a form which is appropriate to the age of the witness. The court may in the interests of justice, on objection by a party, forbid the asking of a question which is in a form that is not reasonably likely

to be understood by a person of the age of the witness. (California Codes §
765(b) [1993])

We believe that California's statute should serve as a model for other states.

Implications for Practitioners

If interviewers are to conduct informative, nonbiasing interviews, they must
be taught appropriate interviewing techniques, as well as the potential
dangers of using inappropriate techniques. Professional trainers need to
translate robust empirical findings into easily accessible, affordable training
for judges, attorneys, law enforcement personnel, CPS workers, and other
professionals who interview children in forensic contexts.

Implications for Researchers

Interview analysis provides an honest appraisal of what actually is happening in child interviews. The information gathered from such analyses
provides valuable direction for both laboratory research and the development of training programs. Therefore, we advocate using interview analysis
to achieve the following goals. First, we believe that researchers should
continue investigating the effects of particular question forms on children's
responses. We also hope that researchers will replicate our study using
larger samples from a variety of areas. In addition, interviews conducted by
agencies other than CPS (e.g., police departments, prosecutors' offices)
should be analyzed to see if differences in interviewing techniques exist
among the various groups. Finally, researchers should assess whether
trained interviewers in fact do conduct better interviews of child victim-
witnesses.

ACKNOWLEDGMENTS

We wish to thank Carolyn Boyd, Charles Wilson, Barbara Boat, and Mark
Everson for providing transcripts of interviews. We also acknowledge Lori
Komori, Lisa Kellen, Julie Galas, Traci Gleason, David Van Dyke, Debora
Hulse Nelson, Cara Porter Woodall, Kirstin Elliott, Matthew Nguyen, Paul
Bock, and Kurt Sturm for their research assistance. Finally, we are grateful
for the insightful feedback provided by Amye Warren, J. Don Read,
Michael Toglia, Maggie Bruck, and Alex Rothman.

The writing of this chapter was supported in part by a National Science Foundation Graduate Research Fellowship to Jennifer S. Hunt, who now is at the University of Minnesota.

Some of the data included in this chapter were reported at the annual meeting of the Midwestern Psychological Association, Chicago, IL, May 1995, and at the annual meeting of the American Professional Society on the Abuse of Children, Tucson, AZ, June 1995.

REFERENCES

Alaska Statutes Code of Criminal Procedure, § 12.45.046(c) (1990).

American Professional Society on the Abuse of Children (APSAC). (1990). *Guidelines for psychosocial evaluation of suspected sexual abuse in young children.* Chicago: Author.

Brennan, M., & Brennan, R. (1988). *Strange language: Child victims under cross examination.* Wagga Wagga, Australia: Charles Sturt University-Riverina.

Bruck, M., Ceci, S. J., Francoeur, E., & Renick, A. (1995). Anatomically detailed dolls do not facilitate preschoolers' reports of a pediatric examination involving genital touching. *Journal of Experimental Psychology: Applied, 1,* 95–109.

California Codes, § 765(b) (1993).

Code of Georgia, § 38-1607 (1994).

Code of Washington, § 7.69A.030(1) (1995).

Connecticut General Statutes § 54-86g(b)(4) (1958).

DeLoache, J. (1995). The use of dolls in interviewing young children. In M. S. Zaragoza, J. R. Graham, G. C. N. Hall, R. Hirschman, & Y. S. Ben-Porath (Eds.), *Memory and testimony in the child witness* (pp. 160–178). Thousand Oaks, CA: Sage.

Dent, H. R. (1991). Experimental studies of interviewing child witnesses. In M. Gruneberg, P. Morris, & R. Sykes (Eds.), *Practical aspects of memory* (pp. 236–243). London: Academic.

Fisher, R. P., & Geiselman, R. E. (1992). *Memory-enhancing techniques for investigative interviewing: The cognitive interview.* Springfield, IL: Thomas.

Fisher, R. P., & McCauley, M. R. (1995). Improving eyewitness testimony with the cognitive interview. In M. S. Zaragoza, J. R. Graham, G. C. N. Hall, R. Hirschman, & Y. S. Ben-Porath (Eds.), *Memory and testimony in the child witness* (pp. 141–159). Thousand Oaks, CA: Sage.

Fivush, R., & Hamond, N. R. (1989). Time and again: Effects of repetition and retention interval on 2 year olds' event recall. *Journal of Experimental Child Psychology, 47,* 259–273.

Fivush, R., & Shukat, J. R. (1995). Content, consistency, and coherence of early autobiographical recall. In M. S. Zaragoza, J. R. Graham, G. C. N. Hall, R. Hirschman, & Y. S. Ben-Porath (Eds.), *Memory and testimony in the child witness* (pp. 5–23). Thousand Oaks, CA: Sage.

Geiselman, R. E., Saywitz, K. J., & Bornstein, G. K. (1993). Effects of cognitive questioning techniques on children's recall performance. In G. S. Goodman & B. L. Bottoms (Eds.), *Child victims, child witnesses: Understanding and improving testimony* (pp. 71–93). New York: Guilford.

Hardie, S. (1991). *Reducing suggestibility in children's eyewitness testimony: A training program to improve children's competence to resist.* Unpublished doctoral dissertation, University of California, Los Angeles.

Home Office. (1992). *Memorandum of good practice: On video recorded interviews with child witnesses for criminal proceedings*. London: Author.

Hunt, J. S., Komori, L. A. C., Kellen, L. M., Galas, J. R., & Gleason, T. R. (1995, July). Faulty and non-productive questioning techniques: Potential pitfalls of the child interview. In N. W. Perry (Chair), *Communicating with child witnesses: Current practices and future directions*. Symposium conducted at the meeting of the Society for Applied Research in Memory and Cognition, Vancouver, British Columbia.

Iowa Code, § 910A.14.4 (1994).

Jones, D. P. H. (1992). *Interviewing the sexually abused child: Investigation of suspected abuse*. London: Gaskell.

Jones, D. P. H., & McQuiston, M. G. (1988). *Interviewing the sexually abused child*. London: Gaskell.

Koehnken, G. (1993). *The Cognitive Interview: A step-by-step introduction*. Unpublished training materials, The University of Kiel, Germany.

Koehnken, G. (1995, July). A phased approach to interviewer training. In G. Koehnken (Chair), *Delivery of interviewing skills*. Symposium conducted at the meeting of the Society for Applied Research in Memory and Cognition, Vancouver, British Columbia.

Lamb, M. E. (1994). The investigation of child sexual abuse: An interdisciplinary consensus statement. *Expert Evidence, 2*, 151–156.

Lamb, M. E., Herschkowitz, I., Sternberg, K. J., Esplin, P. W., Hovav, M., Manor, T., & Yudilevitch, L. (1996). Effects of investigative utterance types on Israeli children's responses. *International Journal of Behavioral Development, 19*, 627–637.

Laws of New York, § 642-a (1996).

Leichtman, M. D., & Ceci, S. J. (1995). The effects of stereotypes and suggestions on preschoolers' reports. *Developmental Psychology, 31*, 568–578.

Lepore, S., & Sesco, B. (1994). Distorting children's reports and interpretations of events through suggestion. *Journal of Applied Psychology, 79*, 108–120.

Lunning, S., & Eilts, J. (1996, May). *Do children respond accurately to forced choice questions?: Yes or no*. Paper presented at the annual meeting of the Midwestern Psychological Association, Chicago.

Maryland v. Craig, 110 S. Ct. 5157, 111 L.Ed.2d 666 (1990).

McGough, L. S., & Warren, A. R. (1994). The all-important investigative interview. *Juvenile and Family Court Journal, 45*, 13–29.

Memon, A., Holley, A., Wark, L., Bull, R., & Koehnken, G. (1995, July). Reducing suggestibility in child witness interviews. In N. W. Perry (Chair), *Communicating with child witnesses: Current practices and future directions*. Symposium conducted at the meeting of the Society for Applied Research in Memory and Cognition, Vancouver, British Columbia.

Myers, J. E. B. (1992). *Legal issues in child abuse and neglect*. Newbury Park, CA: Sage.

Minnesota Statutes, § 592.02 (m) (1993).

New Mexico Statutes, § 32A-18-1.A (1993).

Perry, N. W. (1995, July). Interviewing child eyewitnesses: Ask, but you may not receive. In N. W. Perry (Chair), *Communicating with child witnesses: Current practices and future directions*. Symposium conducted at the meeting of the Society for Applied Research in Memory and Cognition, Vancouver, British Columbia.

Perry, N. W., McAuliff, B. D., Tam, P., Claycomb, L., Dostal, C., & Flanagan, C. (1995). When lawyers question children: Is justice served? *Law and Human Behavior, 19*, 609–629.

Perry, N. W., & Teply, L. (1984–1985). Interviewing, counseling, and in-court examination of children: Practical approaches for attorneys. *Creighton Law Review, 18*, 1369–1426.

Perry, N. W., & Wrightsman, L. S. (1991). *The child witness: Legal issues and dilemmas*. Newbury Park, CA: Sage.

Poole, D. A. (1995, May). *Repeated questioning and the child witness: A reevaluation*. Paper presented at the annual meeting of the Midwestern Psychological Association, Chicago.

Poole, D. A., & Warren, A. R. (1995, March). Recent challenges to three commonly held assumptions about children's eyewitness testimony. In D. P. Peters (Chair), *Children as witnesses: New research, new issues.* Symposium conducted at the biennial meeting of the Society for Research in Child Development, Indianapolis, IN.

Poole, D. A., & White, L. T. (1995). Tell me again and again: Stability and change in the repeated testimonies of children and adults. In M. S. Zaragoza, J. R. Graham, G. C. N. Hall, R. Hirschman, & Y. S. Ben-Porath (Eds.), *Memory and testimony in the child witness* (pp. 24–43). Thousand Oaks, CA: Sage.

Salmon, K., Bidrose, S., & Pipe, M. E. (1995). Providing props to facilitate children's event reports: A comparison of toys and real items. *Journal of Experimental Child Psychology, 60,* 174–194.

Saywitz, K., Jaenicke, C., & Camparo, L. (1990). Children's knowledge of legal terminology. *Law and Human Behavior, 14,* 523–535.

Saywitz, K., Moan, S., & Lamphear, V. (1991, August). *The effect of preparation on children's resistance to misleading questions.* Paper presented at the annual convention of the American Psychological Association, San Francisco, CA.

Saywitz, K., Nathanson, R., Snyder, L., & Lamphear, V. (1993). *Preparing children for the investigative and judicial process: Improving communication, memory, and emotional resiliency* (Final report to the National Center on Child Abuse and Neglect). Los Angeles: Authors.

State v. Michaels, 625 A.2d 489 (N.J. App. 1993), aff'd, 1994 WL 278424 (N.J. Sup. 1994).

Tobey, A., & Goodman, G. S. (1992). Children's eyewitness memory: Effects of participation and forensic context. *Child Abuse & Neglect, 16,* 779–796.

Utah Code, § 77-37-4(1-3) (1993).

Walker, A. G. (1993). Questioning young children in court: A linguistic case study. *Law and Human Behavior, 17,* 59–81.

Walker, A. G. (1994). *Handbook on questioning children: A linguistic perspective.* Washington, DC: American Bar Association Center on Children and the Law.

Walker, A. G., & McKinley-Pace, M. (1995, July). "Do you know the difference between the truth and a lie": An incompetent competency question. In N. W. Perry (Chair), *Communicating with child witnesses: Current practices and future directions.* Symposium conducted at the meeting of the Society for Applied Research in Memory and Cognition, Vancouver, British Columbia.

Warren, A. R., & Lane, P. (1995). Effects of timing and type of questioning on eyewitness accuracy and suggestibility. In M. S. Zaragoza, J. R. Graham, G. C. N. Hall, R. Hirschman, & Y. S. Ben-Porath (Eds.), *Memory and testimony in the child witness* (pp. 44–60). Thousand Oaks, CA: Sage.

Warren, A. R., & McGough, L. S. (1995). *Research on children's suggestibility: Implications for the investigative interview.* Unpublished manuscript, University of Tennessee – Chattanooga.

Warren, A. R., Perry, N. W., Nelson, D. H., Porter, C., Elliott, K., Komori, L., Hunt, J., Gleason, T., Galas, J., & Kellen, L. (1995, June). *Interviewing children: Questions of structure and style.* Poster presented at the Third National Colloquium of the American Professional Society on the Abuse of Children, Tucson, AZ.

Wisconsin Statutes, § 950.055(2)(b) (1995).

Wolfner, G., Faust, D., & Dawes, R. (1993). The use of anatomical dolls in sexual abuse evaluations: The state of the science. *Applied and Preventative Psychology, 2,* 1–11.

Yuille, J. C., Hunter, R., Joffe, R., & Zaparnuik, J. (1993). Interviewing children in sexual abuse cases. In G. S. Goodman & B. L. Bottoms (Eds.), *Child victims, child witnesses: Understanding and improving testimony* (pp. 95–115). New York: Guilford.

5

A Phased Approach to Interviewer Training

Günter Köhnken
University of Kiel

The interview is one of the most frequently used methods of obtaining information from people. It is indispensable whenever the relevant information cannot be observed directly and when the data cannot be collected by means of psychological tests or questionnaires. This is the case, for example, when a victim or witness of a crime is required to give a description of the incident. For the police, in particular, interviewing is one of the major tools of investigation. Research in Germany has shown, for example, that police officers spend approximately 70% to 80% of their total working time interviewing witnesses, victims, and suspects (Herren, 1976). However, interviewing is not an important tool only in criminal investigations. Wells, Benson, and Hoff (1985), for example, estimated that physicians spend at least 50% of their time with patients talking with them. Personnel selections are usually, at least in part, based on interviews with the job applicants. Furthermore, interviews play a central role in psychological assessment in general, therapeutic intervention, journalistic investigations, market research, and opinion polls, to name but a few examples. The aims of interviews can be divided into two categories: First, interviews are conducted to evaluate present moods, attitudes, and opinions, or to establish rapport with the interviewee. In all these cases retrieval of information from the interviewee's memory is of only minor importance.

Second, the individual may be questioned about past events or experiences that he or she now has to retrieve from memory. This is almost always the case when victims or witnesses of a crime are questioned as part of the legal proceedings, when physicians or clinical psychologists attempt to reconstruct the development of an illness or behavioral symptom. This chapter focuses on the training of skills for interviews that aim to retrieve information from memory; that is, investigative interviews.

AN INFORMATION-PROCESSING VIEW
OF INTERVIEWING

Conducting an investigative interview is a highly complex process that makes great demands on the interviewer. He or she constantly has to be aware of the overall interview strategy and adhere to general rules and guidelines for interviewing. The wording of questions has to be adapted to the intellectual capacity of the interviewee. At the same time the interviewer has to process the flow of verbal information, store it in memory, take notes, and decide on follow-up questions. In addition to this, the nonverbal and speech behavior of both the interviewee and the interviewer have to be monitored and evaluated. Figure 5.1 gives an overview of this process and shows the various stages of information processing (Köhnken, 1995).

Figure 5.1 shows where information may be lost and where incorrect or fabricated details (i.e., details that are mentioned by the interviewee but were not present in the original event) may creep in. The interviewee who experiences an event is unlikely to perceive and encode all available information. The information processing will be influenced by his or her general knowledge about this type of event. Such generic knowledge is called a *cognitive schema* (Alba & Hasher, 1983; Bartlett, 1932; Graesser & Nakamura, 1982). Cognitive schemata, social expectations, and current motivation guide perception and may filter out details to a lesser or greater extent. In a similar vein, what is processed and eventually stored in memory also depends on a number of factors. In addition to cognitive schemata, which guide the storage of information in memory, high stress or even panic may severely disturb information processing and often result in incomplete and/or distorted recollections (Deffenbacher, 1983).

Hence, when a person enters an interview he or she only has a limited amount of information about the event in memory. It is important to keep this in mind when we look at the sometimes low level of completeness of interview data. Loss of information is not always the interviewer's fault. No interview technique, however sophisticated, will be able to recover information that has never been stored in memory.

What has been encoded and stored in memory has to be recalled during the course of the interview. This involves another possible source of

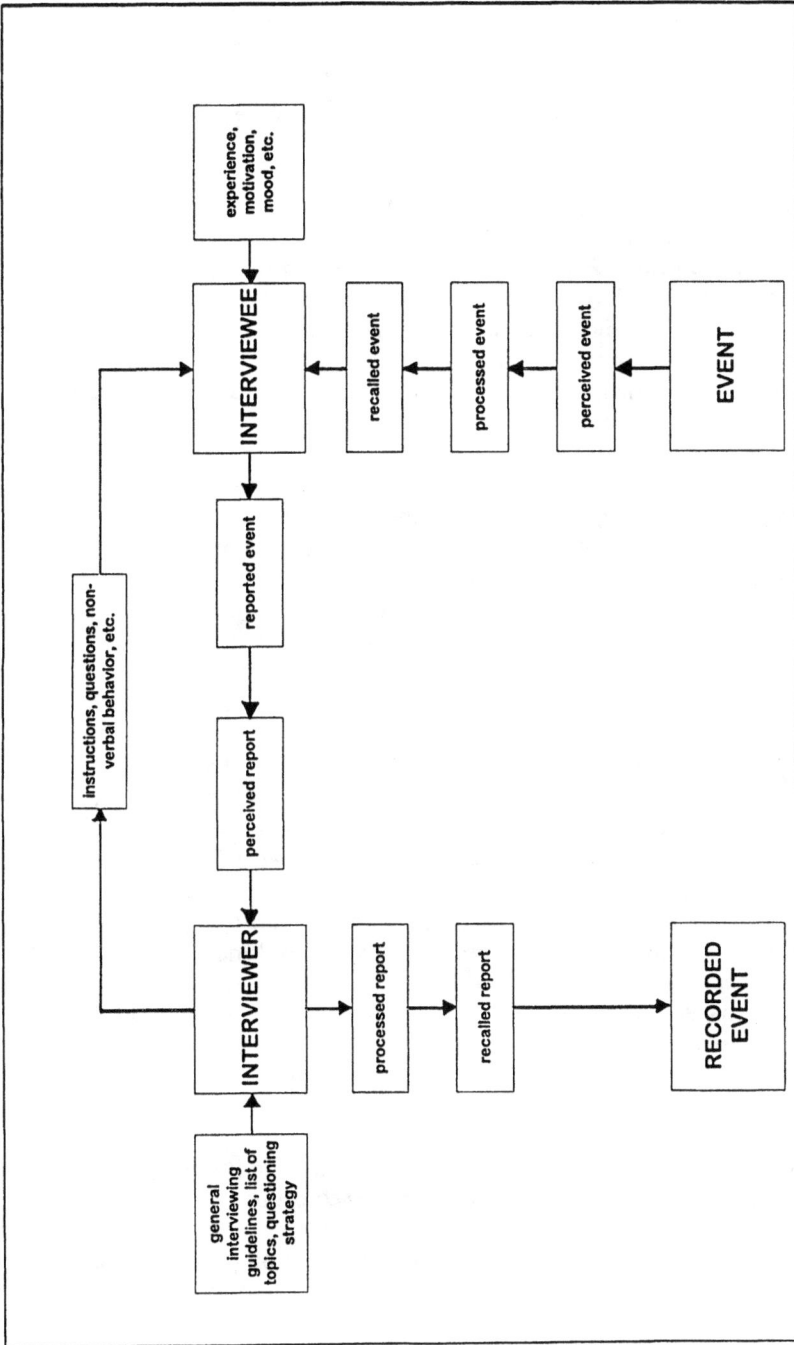

FIG. 5.1. Flow of information in an interview. From "Interviewing Adults" by G. Köhnken, 1995, in R. Bull & D. Carson (Eds.), *Handbook of Psychology in Legal Contexts* (p. 217). Copyright John Wiley & Sons Limited. Reprinted with permission.

incompleteness. Rarely is an interviewee able to retrieve all potentially available details from memory. Some information may be lost due to forgetting, whereas other details are difficult or even impossible to access without specific aids (Tulving, 1983; Tulving & Thomson, 1973). Furthermore, even details that have been successfully recalled to mind are not always overtly reported. The interviewee may suppress available information because he or she assumes it to be unimportant or because it is too embarrassing to be reported (Fisher & Geiselman, 1992). Furthermore, as Fisher and Geiselman (1992) pointed out, an event is represented simultaneously at several different levels of precision, ranging from the very general to the very detailed (see also Fisher & Chandler, 1984, 1991). The level the interviewee selects for reporting depends, among other things, on his or her immediate or past experiences with interviews, assumed communication rules, and assumptions about the interviewer's knowledge. For example, an interviewee who expects the interviewer to know what a blood donation event consists of may decide that merely mentioning that a blood donation took place may be sufficient and he or she may therefore not bother to describe it in detail. This would be an economic strategy in everyday communication but it may be inappropriate in an investigative interview because it results in incomplete information.

What is reported depends not only on the interviewee's internal state, but also to a large degree on the interviewer's instructions, questions, and general behavior. It is important to keep in mind that the interview is a learning situation. This is particularly the case if the interviewee has no or only very little previous experience with interviews in general or with this type of interview in particular. In such a situation any interviewer behavior (instructions, questions, interruptions, reinforcements, nonverbal behavior) will not only have an immediate effect (e.g., on an answer). The interviewee will also learn from this behavior what is expected and try to adjust his or her behavior according to these expectations. Interrupting a lengthy answer, for example, will stop this answer immediately and will make lengthy and detailed answers less likely in the further course of the interview. The interviewee has learned that the interviewer expects short answers. Finally, what has passed all these various "filters" has to be put into words and reported verbally to the interviewer. At this stage, limited linguistic abilities or a restricted vocabulary may add to the various filtering processes (e.g., Leibowitz & Guzi, 1990).

As far as the interviewer is concerned, the information processing passes through very similar stages. What the interviewee communicates verbally and nonverbally has to be perceived and encoded by the interviewer. Here, again, selective attention and schema-guided information processing act as first filters. The interviewer holds certain hypotheses about the event in question and probably has a schema about this type of event. Information that is consistent with the schema receives preferential treatment, whereas inconsistent details may be distorted to fit the schema or even filtered out completely (Schank & Abelson, 1977; Taylor & Crocker, 1981). Furthermore, the multitude of tasks (e.g., being aware of the general interviewing guidelines, the specific interviewing strategy, the list of topics to be investigated, the processing of verbal and nonverbal information, planning the next questions, etc.) place high demands on the interviewer. Because there are limited cognitive resources available to any human being at any one time, the quality of the interview may deteriorate (e.g., important topics may be left out, questions may be inappropriate) and/or there will be incomplete perception and encoding of the available information (Kahneman, 1973; Navon & Gopher, 1979).

The encoded information is then stored in the interviewer's memory and later recalled to produce a written protocol. Apart from ordinary forgetting, further filters may affect storage and retrieval. Among other factors, schema-guided processing, social perception, and a tendency to confirm existing hypotheses may determine what is stored and later retrieved. Finally, the written report is subject to further loss of information. Köhnken, Thürer, and Zoberbier (1994) found that even a report that is written by the interviewer immediately after completion of the interview contains only about two thirds of the information reported by the interviewee.

What can be done to improve the quality of interview data? Obviously, any information that has not been perceived and encoded by the interviewee can never be recovered later during an interview. However, the completeness and accuracy of interview data can be enhanced by appropriate measures in the remaining three of these areas.

First, because one of the main sources of loss of information on the side of the interviewer is cognitive overload, everything that reduces this load should improve his or her information-processing capacity. Recording the interview on tape, for example, would free the interviewer from detailed note taking. As a consequence, he or she has more resources available to concentrate on the process of interviewing and on the interviewee's report. Furthermore, careful preparation for an interview is likely to reduce the interviewer's cognitive load during the interview, thus leaving more capacity for the interviewing process.

However, apart from any mental, technical, and organizational preparation, the interviewing process is a highly complex task in itself, requiring a number of sophisticated skills on the part of the interviewers. Generally, the less automatized these skills are the more conscious attention is required on the part of interviewer. It is, therefore, of utmost importance that an interviewer is well trained in applying the respective interviewing strategy as well as the behavioral and communication skills that are part of the interviewing process.

TRAINING CONTENTS

In this section a procedure for interviewer training that has been used in a number of studies on the effectiveness of the cognitive interview is described (Köhnken, Schimossek, Aschermann, & Höfer, 1995; Köhnken et al., 1994; Mantwill, Köhnken, & Aschermann, 1995; Memon, Holley, Milne, Köhnken, & Bull, 1994; Memon, Wark, Bull, & Köhnken, in press). In these studies an identical training procedure was used for both the cognitive interview and the structured interview, with a control condition that resembled the cognitive interview except for the mnemonic retrieval aids. Although the focus of this chapter is on training procedures, a brief overview of the elements of the cognitive and the structured interview is necessary in order to give an impression of the training contents (for a detailed description of the cognitive interview see Fisher & Geiselman, 1992).

Figure 5.2 shows the basic components of the structured and the cognitive interview that are targeted in the training program. First, the interviewers are encouraged to prepare each interview mentally and orga-

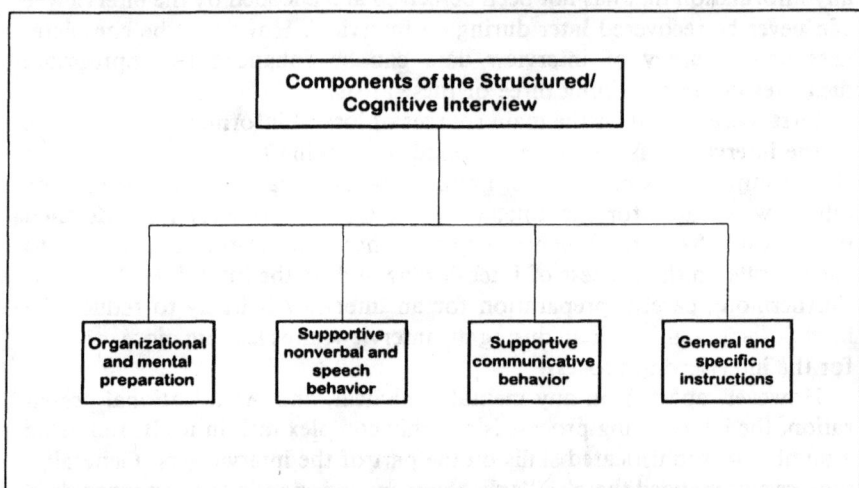

FIG. 5.2. Components of the structured and cognitive interview.

nizationally. This includes, among other things, setting up the context (room, equipment), preventing disturbances, rereading any information that may be available about the interviewee and the event in question, and anticipating potentially applicable topics for the rapport-building and neutralizing phases. The second component comprises supportive non-verbal and speech behavior (e.g., position, posture, gaze, speech rate, facial expression). Third, interviewers have to learn a number of communication skills. These include, for example, using verbal and nonverbal reinforcements ("active listening"), avoiding any interruptions, and allowing for pauses. The fourth component refers to the general and specific instructions that form the basic elements of the respective interviewing technique.

Table 5.1 shows the elements of the cognitive interview as applied in the previously mentioned experiments. The structured interview differs from a cognitive interview as described in Table 5.1 in six ways:

1. Interviewees are not explicitly instructed to report everything that comes to mind; instead, they are asked to give a detailed report.
2. No attempt is made to re-create the context of the event.
3. No attempt is made to activate a mental image in the questioning part; instead, interviewers are encouraged to ask open-ended questions first, followed by more detailed questions, and to avoid any form of leading questions.
4. No attempt is made to recall the events in reverse order; instead, another retrieval attempt is made by asking the interviewee to give a second free report.

TABLE 5.1
General Structure of the Cognitive Interview

1. Greeting and personalizing
2. Establishing rapport
3. Explaining the purpose of the interview
    Encouraging to describe everything
    Reminding not to guess or to fabricate
4. Recreating the context of the original event
5. Asking for a free report
6. Asking the interviewee if he or she can remember more
7. Questioning part
    Activating a picture
    Probing the picture
8. Asking the interviewee to recall the event in reverse order
9. Changing persepctive
10. Summarizing the description by the interviewer
11. Closure, thanking the interviewee for the cooperation

5. No attempt is made to recall details from a different perspective.
6. The interviewer does not summarize the information before closing the interview. All other elements are identical in both types of interview.

THE PHASED TRAINING PROCEDURE

Because of the complexity of both types of interview it was necessary to separate the various components and the required skills and to teach and practice each component individually in a predetermined sequence. The training program was, therefore, split into 12 phases (see Fig. 5.3).

Interviewer training is conducted in small groups, consisting of five to a maximum of eight participants. At the start of the training sessions each trainee receives two booklets, a brief step-by-step introduction that describes the components of the interview technique, and a practice booklet that is used for paper-and-pencil rehearsals. The cognitive interview introduction booklet is based on the description of the cognitive interview as provided by Fisher and Geiselman (1992).

Introduction and Overviews

Methods. The first part of the training program is dominated by lectures that are complemented by a set of transparencies. The participants have, however, the opportunity to ask questions and discuss whatever topic they like.

Aims. The aims are to provide the participants with a rationale for the interview technique, to explain their role as interviewers, to introduce supportive nonverbal behavior and communication skills, and to give an overview of the components of the interview technique and the training sequence.

Phase 1. The training begins with a general introduction to interviewing as an important tool in psychological assessment as well as various other fields (e.g., interviewing witnesses, opinion polls, market research, journalistic investigations). At this point, a distinction is made between therapeutic interviews, which aim to evaluate present moods, emotions, attitudes, and so forth, and investigative interviews, the purpose of which is to retrieve information from the interviewee's memory. The cognitive interview (or the structured interview, respectively) is introduced as a technique for helping the interviewee to retrieve more information from memory. A rationale for the respective technique is given by presenting selected research results and relevant theories of memory and retrieval.

Following this, the role of the interviewer is described and explained. In the cognitive interview training, the emphasis is on the transference of control to the interviewee (see Fisher & Geiselman, 1992), whereas in the structured interview the interviewers are instructed to follow the predetermined structure instead of being guided by ad hoc associations.

Phase 2. In this phase a set of generally supportive nonverbal behaviors and communication skills (see Table 5.2) are introduced and described, including demonstrations by the trainer.

Phase 3. In the third phase a brief overview is given of the components of the cognitive or structured interview, respectively, and the general sequence of the interview technique is described. This serves as a "cognitive map" for the sequential introduction of each individual component of the interview technique, which follows later.

Paper and Pencil Rehearsals

Methods. Phases 4 to 6 consist of a repeated sequence of introductory lecture (supported by a set of transparencies), paper-and-pencil rehearsals, and discussion of examples provided by the participants.

Aims. Participants are to develop a detailed concept of each component of the interview technique. Furthermore, the discussion of examples for each component is expected to broaden the spectrum of applicable

TABLE 5.2
Generally Supportive Nonverbal Behavior and Communication Skills

- Sit in a relaxed manner; turn your body somewhat toward the interviewee ("ten-to-two position")
- Express friendliness and support
- Use eye contact frequently but do not stare at the interviewee
- Speak slowly, use short sentences, and leave short pauses between sentences
- Express attention and interest frequently by nodding, "mhm," and so on, but avoid qualitative feedback" ("good," "right")
- Praise the interviewee for his or her effort in general
- Avoid hectic movements and hectic speech style
- Do not interrupt
- Allow pauses
- Express patience

Introduction and Overviews

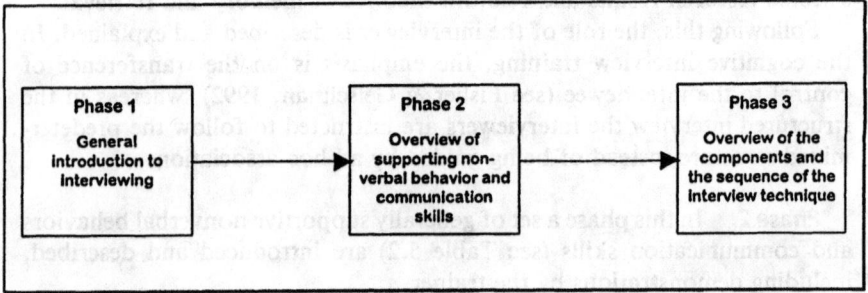

Phase 1	Phase 2	Phase 3
General introduction to interviewing	**Overview of supporting non-verbal behavior and communication skills**	**Overview of the components and the sequence of the interview technique**

Pencil and paper rehearsals

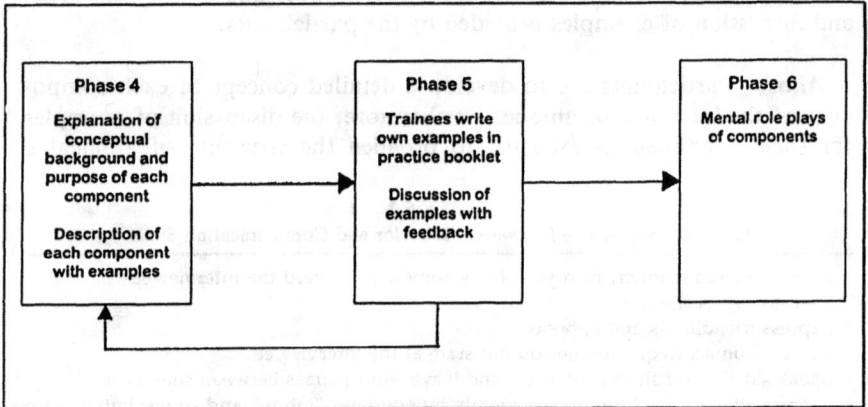

Phase 4	Phase 5	Phase 6
Explanation of conceptual background and purpose of each component **Description of each component with examples**	**Trainees write own examples in practice booklet** **Discussion of examples with feedback**	**Mental role plays of components**

FIG. 5.3. Overview of the phases of the interview training program.

Written and videotaped examples

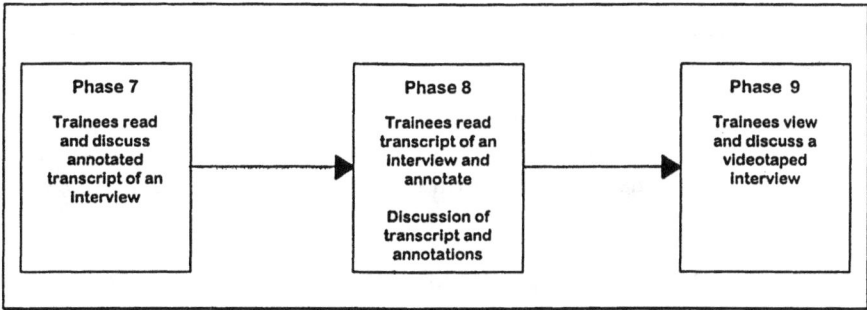

Role plays

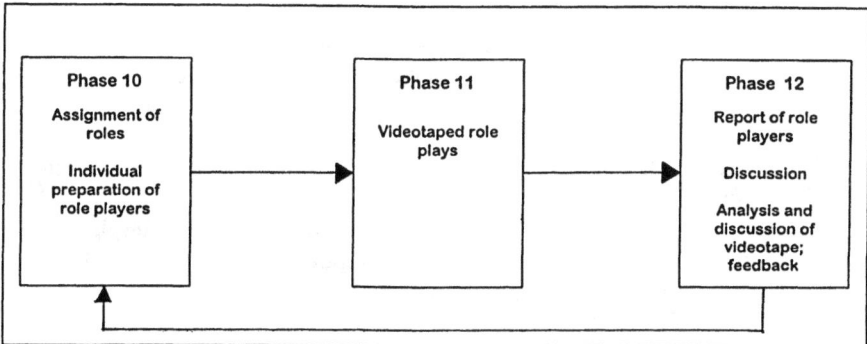

phrases. To have such a "toolbox" of potentially applicable phrases helps to reduce the interviewer's cognitive load during the interview itself. This is particularly important for interviewing children. Adults who have little or no experience in talking to children often have problems using appropriate wordings for their instructions and questions.

Phase 4. Each of the components of the interview technique is addressed in a lecture that gives the rationale for that component, describes the component in detail, and illustrates its practical use by a variety of examples.

Phase 5. After each component has been described, the participants are instructed to imagine that they are conducting an interview and to think what they could say to the interviewee in order (e.g., to explain the purpose of the interview. They are asked to write at least one example in their own words into the practice booklet they received at the onset of the training. This booklet contains a page with blank lines for each component. Using one's own words is considered important because the participants have to integrate the instructions into their own style of speaking. Otherwise it will remain an artefact in danger of being abandoned in stressful situations.

After several minutes of silent work each trainee reads aloud his or her example(s). The other participants are encouraged to comment on these examples. Depending on their appropriateness, the trainer suggests modifications, offers alternatives, or recommends the example to be included in the toolbox.

This sequence (introductory lecture with examples, followed by paper-and-pencil rehearsal, discussion, and feedback) is repeated for each component of the respective interview technique.

Phase 6. This phase is actually a homework assignment. The participants are instructed to read the introduction booklet carefully at home and then to mentally role play short sequences of an interview; for example, the opening phase up to the initiation of a free report or the first part of the questioning. However, if the time schedule allows, it is recommended to conduct brief role play during the training session in addition to the homework assignment.

Written and Videotaped Examples

Methods. Phases 7 to 9 use written and videotaped examples of the respective interview technique. Both the transcripts and the videorecorded interview are discussed in the training group. Because the videorecorded interview is intended to serve as a model it was designed with some principles of observational learning in mind (e.g., Bandura, 1976; Rachman, 1972). For example, it is not advisable to use a "perfect" interview because the trainees may have difficulties accepting a perfect interviewer as a realistic model for themselves. Furthermore, identification with the model should be facilitated if he or she is perceived as similar to the trainee (Flanders, 1968). As a consequence, the interviewer should be a student if students are to be trained. Similarly, a police officer would be a more appropriate model for training police officers, and so on.

Aims.   The purpose of Phases 7 to 9 is to provide participants with models of the respective interview technique and to facilitate observational learning.

Phase 7.   Together with the practice booklet the participants received two interview transcripts, one annotated, the other without comments. Both are transcripts of real interviews that have been edited for training purposes. The left column shows the transcripts with the annotations in the right column. Most of the annotations simply label the communication skill, component, or question type used. For the second transcript the right column is empty.

Reading the transcripts and commenting on the second transcript could be part of another homework assignment. Discussion and feedback would then take place at the beginning of the next session. However, if time allows this task should be included in a training session. In this case two trainees could role play the interview such that one participant reads aloud the interviewer's utterances and another trainee reads the interviewee's responses. The purpose of this exercise is to facilitate and prepare for the actual role plays that form the major part of the final section. Many trainees are not familiar with role playing as a learning technique and, as a consequence, they may feel uncomfortable and often tense being exposed to the group and a video camera. Such tension interferes with behavioral learning. Practicing role plays by reading an interview transcript aloud may help trainees to become familiar with this technique and thereby reduce possible tension.

Phase 8.   After the discussion of the annotated transcript has been completed the participants are asked to read another interview transcript without comments. They are assigned the task of naming the interview components, question types, and communication skills used by the interviewer. In addition, the trainees are encouraged to offer alternative or additional suggestions. After completion of this task the group works through the transcript step by step and discusses the participants' comments and suggestions.

Phase 9. In this phase the participants view a demonstration video of the respective interview technique that has been specifically designed for training purposes. The videotape is stopped whenever a trainee wishes to comment on the course of events or to ask a question. In addition, the trainer stops the tape for commenting or in order to offer alternative suggestions regarding the interviewer's behavior.

Role Plays

Methods. Role plays with subsequent discussions and feedback using the videorecording of the role play are the main methods used in Phases 10 to 12. These role plays form the core of the training program. They usually take more time than the previous three sections taken together. It is very important for the trainer to exhibit supportive and primarily nonnegative behavior in order to create an atmosphere that facilitates behavioral learning. He or she should frequently reinforce any positive approach and be sparing with criticism. This behavior also serves as a model of how to give feedback for the participants. The participants, assisted by the trainer, are encouraged to set their own goals for the role play.

Aims. The general aim of the training program is to modify behavior and to establish new behavior skills. Although it is important to provide the trainees with a conceptual background for the various components, behavior skills are best (and can probably only be) learned by acting. Role plays offer the opportunity to try out new behaviors without having to fear negative and perhaps irreversible consequences. At the same time the role players provide a model for the other group members who observe the role plays.

Phase 10. After the role-playing procedure has been explained to the participants, the trainer asks for two volunteers who are willing to perform the first (or next) role play. The roles of interviewer and interviewee are assigned in accordance with the role players' wishes and a topic for the interview (preferably an event that the interviewee has really experienced rather than a fictitious event) is chosen. If time allows for multiple role plays for each trainee, the interviewer is asked to pay special attention to certain behavior skills or interview components during the role play. In this case, the feedback is focused on these elements, whereas the remaining parts of the interview are simply treated as learning material for all participants. This strategy significantly reduces the perceived complexity of the interviewer's task and, as a consequence, helps to reduce tension. The interviewer is then granted as much time as he or she wishes to mentally prepare the interview.

Phase 11. The role-playing phase always begins by addressing certain segments of the entire interview. For example, the first series of role plays addresses the opening part of an interview up to the point where the interviewee would begin to deliver a free report. After each trainee has participated in one role play, the second series of role plays commences, and so on. As training proceeds individual parts are combined in more and more complex role plays until each participant eventually role plays a complete interview. Each role play is recorded on videotape.

Phase 12. Role playing is an exciting and often stressful experience for the trainees. This is especially the case if the group members are professionals who are supposed to be good at interviewing (e.g., police officers). It is, therefore, very important, before anything else happens, to give the role players, particularly the interviewer, the opportunity to report their experiences and impressions. In this context the trainer addresses the particular skills and components that the interviewer had intended to focus on. Following the interviewer's report the interviewee is asked to describe how he or she experienced the interviewer's behavior. Finally, the remaining group members are asked to report and discuss their observations. This discussion provides the material for the subsequent detailed analysis of the videotaped interview.

Eventually, the recorded interview is replayed. The tape is paused frequently in order to discuss the interview and to offer additional or alternative suggestions regarding the interviewer's behavior. This analysis usually requires three to five times the length of the interview itself.

If time allows, the same interviewer should perform another role play immediately after this discussion, preferably with a different participant in the role of the interviewee. This follow-up role play should focus particularly on those skills or components that the interviewer wants to improve further.

Following the role play(s) of one participant, the trainer asks for two more volunteers and the procedure restarts at Phase 10. On completion of the training sessions the interviewers are strongly encouraged to read through the manual at home and to frequently rehearse interviews mentally.

LENGTH OF TRAINING AND PERSISTENCE OF EFFECTS

The training procedure described here was initially developed for participants who served as interviewers in cognitive interview studies. The interviews usually commenced a few days after completion of the training and rarely lasted longer than 2 weeks. In some studies each interviewer only conducted a single interview shortly after the training. For this relatively short period, a 2-day training period has proved to be sufficient to generate the frequently reported effects of the cognitive interview compared with a structured interview. As an absolute minimum the training can be conducted in two 6-hour sessions, although this is very unsatisfactory. For some studies this was necessary due to time constraints on the part of the interviewers.

However, training participants for an experiment is one thing, whereas training professionals (e.g., police officers) and attempting to establish long-term effects in their interviewing behavior is an entirely different matter. It is quite inconceivable to expect persistent effects after just 2 days of training. One reason for this cautious view is the fact that in almost all of our studies the participants had no prior experience with interviewing. This was done in order to improve experimental control and reduce any error variance that might be due to preexisting interviewing habits. Professionals, on the other hand, often enter the training after several years of on-the-job interviewing experience. Over this time they have developed strong habits in their interviewing behavior that are much more difficult to modify than it is to learn new behavior skills.

Furthermore, interviewers in experimental studies usually conduct their interviews in a fairly relaxed and well-organized context and the event in question often remains the same in several interviews. In contrast, police officers are often under pressure. The events they are confronted with are always different and may be emotionally upsetting. They have to deal with interviewees who may be nervous or uncooperative, and there is no experimenter who has set up the time schedule, arranged rooms, and prepared the technical equipment. In short, their working conditions are often far less optimal than those in thoroughly prepared experimental studies. Under such less than optimal conditions it is much more difficult to maintain newly acquired behavior over a long period.

In order to achieve long-term effects in interviewing behavior it is, therefore, essential not only to conduct a longer initial training with weekly sessions. Even more important are regular follow-up sessions over a period of at least several weeks. For these sessions, trainees should bring their own tape-recorded interviews and discuss these with the trainer and the other group members. The follow-up sessions should also specifically address any problems that the trainees may have encountered in using the interview techniques. Such an extended training program has a far greater chance to achieve long-term effects in interviewing behavior than a single 2-day training program.

ACKNOWLEDGMENTS

A number of colleagues have significantly contributed to developing and modifying the interview training procedure described in this chapter. The author wishes to thank Ellen Aschermann, Ray Bull, Angela Holley, Mona Mantwill, Amina Memon, Rebecca Milne, Renee Tassler, Claudia Thürer, Imke Vieweg, Linsey Wark, and Dirk Zoberbier. Furthermore, the author gratefully acknowledges the helpful comments of Ron Fisher and Ed Geiselman.

REFERENCES

Alba, J. W., & Hasher, L. (1983). Is memory schematic? *Psychological Bulletin, 93*, 203-231.

Bandura, A. (1976). Effecting change through participant modelling. In J. D. Krumboltz & C. E. Thoresen (Eds.), *Counseling methods* (pp. 248-265). New York: Holt, Rinehart & Winston.

Bartlett, F. C. (1932). *Remembering: A study in experimental and social psychology.* Cambridge, UK: Cambridge University Press.

Deffenbacher, K. A. (1983). The influence of arousal on reliability of testimony. In S. M. A. Lloyd-Bostock & B. R. Clifford (Eds.), *Evaluating witness evidence: Recent psychological research and new perspectives* (pp. 235-251). Chichester, UK: Wiley.

Fisher, R. P., & Chandler, C. C. (1984). Dissociations between temporally-cued and theme-cued recall. *Bulletin of the Psychonomic Society, 22*, 203-210.

Fisher, R. P., & Chandler, C. C. (1991). Independence between recalling interevent relations and specific events. *Journal of Experimental Psychology: Learning, Memory and Cognition, 17*, 722-733.

Fisher, R. P., & Geiselman, R. E. (1992). *Memory-enhancing techniques for investigative interviewing.* Springfield, IL: Thomas.

Flanders, J. (1968). A review of research on imitative behavior. *Psychological Bulletin, 69*, 316-337.

Graesser, A. C., & Nakamura, G. V. (1982). The impact of a schema on comprehension and memory. In G. H. Bower (Ed.), *The psychology of learning and motivation* (Vol. 16, pp. 59-109). New York: Academic Press.

Herren, R. (1976). Das Vernehmungsprotokoll [The interview protocol]. *Kriminalistik, 7*, 313-317.

Kahneman, D. (1973). *Attention and effort.* Englewood Cliffs, NJ: Prentice-Hall.

Köhnken, G. (1995). Interviewing adults. In R. Bull & D. Carson (Eds.), *Handbook of psychology in legal contexts* (pp. 215-233). Chichester, UK: Wiley.

Köhnken, G., Schimossek, E., Aschermann, E. & Höfer, E. (1995). Statement validity analysis and the cognitive interview. *Journal of Applied Psychology, 80*, 671-684.

Köhnken, G., Thürer, C., & Zoberbier, D. (1994). The cognitive interview: Are the interviewers' memories enhanced, too? *Applied Cognitive Psychology, 8,* 13–24.

Leibowitz, H. W., & Guzi, L. (1990). *Can the accuracy of eyewitness testimony be improved by the use of non-verbal techniques?* Paper presented at the Conference of the American Psychology-Law Society, Williamsburg, VA.

Mantwill, M., Köhnken, G., & Aschermann, E. (1995). Effects of the cognitive interview on the recall of familiar and unfamiliar events. *Journal of Applied Psychology, 80,* 68–78.

Memon, A., Holley, A., Milne, R., Köhnken, G., & Bull, R. (1994). Towards understanding the effects of interviewer training in evaluating the cognitive interview. *Applied Cognitive Psychology, 8,* 641–659.

Memon, A., Wark, L., Bull, R., & Köhnken, G. (in press). Isolating the effects of the cognitive interview technique. *British Journal of Psychology.*

Navon, D., & Gopher, D. (1979). On the economy of the human information processing system. *Psychological Review, 86,* 214–255.

Rachman, S. (1972). Clinical application of observational learning, imitation and modeling. *Behavior Therapy, 3,* 379–397.

Schank, R. C., & Abelson, R. P. (1977). *Scripts, plans, goals and understanding.* Hillsdale, NJ: Lawrence Erlbaum Associates.

Taylor, S. E., & Crocker, J. (1981). Schematic basis of social information processing. In E. T. Higgins, C. P. Herman, & M. P. Zanna (Eds.), *Social cognition: The Ontario symposium* (Vol. 1, pp. 89–134). Hillsdale, NJ: Lawrence Erlbaum Associates.

Tulving, E. (1983). *Elements of episodic memory.* Oxford, UK: Clarendon.

Tulving, E., & Thomson, D. M. (1973). Encoding specificity and retrieval processes in episodic memory. *Psychological Review, 80,* 353–370.

Wells, K. B., Benson, M. D., & Hoff, P. (1985). A model for teaching the brief psychosocial interview. *Journal of Medical Education, 60,* 181–188.

6

The Relation Between Confidence and Accuracy in Eyewitness Identification Studies: Is the Conclusion Changing?

J. Don Read
University of Lethbridge

D. Stephen Lindsay
University of Victoria

Tonia Nicholls
Simon Fraser University

Few claims about eyewitness behavior have generated as much controversy as those concerning the relation between a witness' confidence in an identification decision and the objective accuracy of that decision (Penrod & Cutler, 1995; Sporer, Penrod, Read, & Cutler, 1995; Wells, 1993). On the one hand, beliefs about a positive confidence–accuracy (CA) relation have been expressed in survey research by members of the public (Brigham & Bothwell, 1983; Deffenbacher & Loftus, 1982; Noon & Hollin, 1987; Yarmey & Jones, 1983) and the legal profession (Brigham & Wolfskeil, 1983), as well as the judiciary through court decisions (e.g., *Neil v. Biggers*, 1972; Penrod & Cutler, 1995; see Brooks, 1983). On the other hand, psycholegal researchers have presented numerous research studies and meta-analyses of them in support of the conclusion that little or no statistical (or practical) CA relation exists (Bothwell, Deffenbacher, & Brigham, 1987; Deffenbacher, 1980; Lieppe, 1980; Wells, 1993; Wells & Lindsay, 1985; Wells & Murray, 1984). For example, Bothwell et al. (1987) obtained an average correlation coefficient of $r = .25$ across 35 field studies of person identification. This same position has been shown to characterize the majority of eyewitness testimony experts polled by Kassin, Ellsworth, and Smith (1989). Despite the seeming unanimity of these responses by the research community, it is worth noting that very strong CA relations have occasionally been obtained in forensically valid simulation research (e.g., Brigham, Maass, Snyder, & Spaulding, 1982; Krafka & Penrod, 1985; Malpass & Devine, 1981; Read, 1995) and several investigators have attempted to identify features that characterize situations producing meaningful or valid CA relations (Bothwell et al., 1987; Cutler & Penrod, 1989b; Deffenbacher, 1980; Fleet, Brigham, & Bothwell, 1987; Sporer et al., 1995). The earliest such attempt was by Deffenbacher (1980), who offered the *optimality hypothesis* as an explanatory principle, according to which the more optimal the encoding and retrieval opportunities for person identification, the greater the likelihood of a positive CA relation.

Nonetheless, the gulf between laypersons' beliefs and expert opinion regarding the CA relation remains large. Because the majority position represents that of the public, law enforcement, and the legal profession, researchers' claims of a nonrelation perhaps has been dismissed as an academic irrelevance and, as a result, seems to have won few converts. Despite the efforts of researchers to make known the scientific evidence demonstrating the lack of a CA relation, and despite their exhortations urging triers of fact, police, and prosecutors to be very cautious in their use of confidence as an indicator of accuracy (Cutler & Penrod, 1989b; Loftus, 1983), it is very clear from mock juror studies (as well as court cases — see Brooks, 1983) that the single most useful predictor of juror beliefs in the credibility of eyewitnesses is the confidence they express in their identification choices (e.g., Cutler, Penrod, & Dexter, 1990; Lieppe, Manion, & Romanczyk, 1992; Lindsay, 1994; Lindsay, Wells, & Rumpel, 1981; Penrod & Cutler, 1995; Wells, 1993).

Why is the claim of no relation between confidence and accuracy so difficult to convey convincingly to others? It may be that most people have had everyday experiences they take as support for the belief in a strong positive CA relation (as in Tversky & Kahneman's 1974 availability heuristic). Or, perhaps more likely, people may have failed to learn from experiences wherein this belief has been disconfirmed (see general and specific discussions of heuristics in regard to the CA relation by Deffenbacher, 1980; Lieppe, 1995; Wells, Lindsay, & Ferguson, 1979; Wells & Murray, 1984). As a result, we likely place more confidence in our ability to calibrate subjective confidence with accuracy than is deserved. An alternative explanation is that psycholegal researchers have, in fact, inaccurately summarized the real state of affairs regarding this relation because of the specific paradigms and identification procedures they have used. If true, a distinction is suggested between a general and a specific eyewitness CA relation (Luus & Wells, 1994a; Wells, 1993; Wells & Lindsay, 1985). For example, it is plausible that a general relation does hold across many arenas of our cognitive lives but that relation is difficult to detect in single-target eyewitness identification tasks. We lean toward this position for two reasons: First, research in cognitive domains from signal-detection to autobiographical memory does support a general CA relation and, second, because identification tasks used by psycholegal researchers contain features or peculiarities that distance them from real-world identification tasks.

On the first point, people often do demonstrate positive and strong CA relations. Without suggesting a thorough review of the relevant literature, it is the case that substantial and positive CA relations have been obtained in each of the following domains: signal detection and discrimination tasks (Murdock, 1974; Wells, 1993), recognition memory of verbal materials (Tulving & Thomson, 1971), decision making (Lichtenstein, Fischoff, & Phillips, 1982; Sharp, Cutler, & Penrod, 1989); autobiographical memory (Brewer, 1996), reading comprehension (Glenberg & Epstein, 1985), social influence (Maass & Clark, 1984), general knowledge questioning (Costerman, Lories, & Ansay, 1992; Perfect, Watson, & Wagstaff, 1993), and research on predictions of subsequent recognition and recall of verbal material (Costermans et al., 1992; Lovelace, 1984; Read & Bruce, 1982). Given the familiarity cognitive psychologists have with these topics, it is somewhat surprising that there has not been more resistance to the counterintuitive claim of no relationship (see Elliott, 1993; McCloskey & Egeth, 1983).

Second, several researchers have suggested a variety of task-specific or psychometric bases for the failure to document a positive CA relation in person identification. One factor considered has been the nature of lineup construction including the specifics of the similarity between target and foils (and among foils) and distinctiveness of the target (Brigham, 1990; Cutler & Penrod, 1989b; Lindsay, 1986), manipulations of which have altered the CA relations. Further, generalizing the results of face-recognition procedures to person identification paradigms has been questioned because the two tasks require different kinds of decisions: A familiarity judgment alone is required in a recognition task, but an identification task requires an episodic memory judgment as well (e.g., Davies, 1988; Read, 1994; Sporer et al., 1995). Although witnesses have made identifications of two targets rather than one in a few studies (Read, 1995, Exp 3; Read, Yuille, & Tollestrup, 1992), no researchers to date have published within-subjects estimates of the CA relation based on multiple person identifications (Wells, 1993).

A second group of critiques includes the view that subjective confidence is an inherently unreliable dependent measure because identification studies usually require only one decision from each participant and calibrations of accuracy with subjective confidence are likely to be highly dissimilar across people (see Cutler & Penrod, 1989b; Deffenbacher, 1980; Lichtenstein et al., 1982; Luus & Wells, 1994a; Sharp et al., 1989; Sporer et al., 1995; Wells, 1993; Wells & Murray, 1984), perhaps because they have little familiarity or expertise in identification tasks. Similarly, use of differential confidence levels by participants to mark a discrimination between accurate and inaccurate judgments ("resolution" in Cutler & Penrod's, 1989b, terms; Wells & Lindsay, 1985) further reduces the possibility of obtaining a reliable relation. Although both of these questions about individual differences are reasonable, there has been as yet virtually no success in establishing stable personality differences regarding the use of confidence judgments (Hosch, 1994; Sporer et al., 1995). To explore the latter issue, Deffenbacher, Leu, and Brown (1981) compared between- and within-subjects CA correlations on a face-recognition task but, surprisingly, found the between-subjects estimate of the CA relation to be higher than that of the average within-subjects estimate. Motivated by similar concerns, Smith, Kassin, and Ellsworth (1989) compared within- and between-subjects assessments of CA in the answering of questions about a witnessed event. Their results, however, only served to establish further the claim of no relation because both estimates of the relationship were weak and equivalent.

There have been other arguments that the common between-subjects technique for estimating CA relations, in addition to being psychometrically unreliable and insensitive, is forensically inappropriate (Wells, 1993; Wells & Lindsay, 1985). These researchers have emphasized the importance of obtaining estimates of forensically valid CA relations and have advocated the use of lineups in which there is but one suspect, a suspect who is replaced by a specific innocent foil when a target-absent lineup is used and, further, that calculations of the CA relation should be based only on those participants who choose one or the other of these two people (Luus & Wells, 1994a; Wells & Lindsay, 1985). Wells and colleagues argued that because any selection other than the suspect in a single-suspect lineup is a "known error," such selections would not lead to arrest of the person identified (but perhaps a discrediting of the witness) and, therefore, these responses should be omitted from the calculation of the CA relation. However, our interest is in determining whether there is a general CA relation, and this strategy may obstruct our attempts to find it. The fact that many, one, or none of the foils are "errors" known only to the investigating authorities is irrelevant to the general question of whether or not confidence is related to identification accuracy. By eliminating the identifications of known innocent foils we may systematically bias our estimate of a general CA relation (however, see Sporer et al., 1995, whose analyses were relatively unaffected by a partial removal of foil identifications). In any case, information as to the errors that witnesses made in identification would be forensically relevant to the assessments of the triers of fact of the credibility of those witnesses who do appear in court (Luus & Wells, 1994; Wells & Lindsay, 1985).

As Wells and Murray (1984) emphasized and as demonstrated in research by Luus and Wells (1994b), confidence itself is malleable and subject to variables different from those affecting accuracy, an argument eloquently made by Lieppe (1980, 1995). Depending on the length of the retention interval, many factors including postevent information, metamemory, and social influences can alter subjective confidence in one's decision. In this connection, laboratory (e.g., Lindsay et al., 1981) and field studies (e.g., Krafka & Penrod, 1985) have usually differed with much longer retention intervals (hours, days, or weeks) intervening between encoding and test in the latter. And, perhaps not unrelatedly, when strong CA relations have been obtained. it has been field studies that have produced them. Stronger CA relations with longer retention intervals run counter to the effects of retention interval outlined in Deffenbacher's (1980) optimality hypothesis; however, Deffenbacher's concern appeared to be with intervening events known to alter the tracking of confidence with accuracy.

For example, confidence expressed by a witness at trial or following interactions with counsel and other witnesses, or following repeated questioning, is known to be different from that assigned at the original identification (Luus & Wells, 1994a, 1994b; Shaw, 1996; Wells et al., 1979; Wells & Murray, 1984; Wells & Seelau, 1995). However, arguing against the optimality hypothesis, it is plausible that some intervening period of time between exposure or encoding and the identification task is critical to the observation of a substantial CA relation. That is, when there are few opportunities to experience losses in the availability of either the information about the eyewitness event or the target, appropriate calibration of confidence with accuracy may not occur. For instance, when participants are actively reminded of an exposure event across a 2-week retention interval, thereby presumably maintaining its availability in memory, and compared to those who are not so reminded, CA relations are significantly lower for the reminded than the nonreminded participants (Read, 1995, Exp. 2). Similarly, participants tested immediately after viewing, as is typical in identification studies, may easily retrieve the event and may mistakenly attribute familiarity for the event to familiarity for the target's physical characteristics (see Jacoby, Kelley, & Dywan, 1989; Whittlesea, 1993, for general discussions of such misattributions). As a consequence, these participants may provide higher and more uniform confidence ratings than they might when tested after a substantial retention interval. Further, real forensic situations usually do involve substantial delays between crime witnessing and person identification (see Shepherd, 1983; Wells, 1993).

There is another psychometric issue that does play an important role in the calculation of the magnitude of the CA relation: namely, the variability of accuracy measures and confidence ratings across participants. Because assessments of the CA relation are usually expressed as correlation coefficients, nontrivial coefficients can arise only if variation exists on both measures (Deffenbacher, 1980; Sporer et al., 1995; Wells & Lindsay, 1985; Wells & Murray, 1984). It is obvious that if a group's performance on an identification task is uniform at any level of accuracy, this restriction of range will preclude a nontrivial correlation coefficient. Similarly, if participants express uniform levels of confidence, no CA relation would be obtained. In other words, as one moves away from uniformity, the opportunities for obtaining a nonzero correlation increase, unless heterogeneity reflects chance variation alone (Wells & Murray, 1984). It stands to reason that some variables may enhance opportunities for variations in encoding and should, as a consequence, result in variations of accuracy and confidence at the time of identification (Deffenbacher, 1980; Gruneberg & Sykes, 1993; Schooler, Ryan, & Foster, 1995; Wells & Lindsay, 1985). Such was the logic of Lindsay et al. (1981) who manipulated witnessing conditions or optimality of information-processing and retrieval conditions (see Bothwell et al., 1987; Deffenbacher, 1980) in a staged-crime experiment to yield three rates of accurate identification. However, despite significantly different accuracy rates (33%, 50%, and 74%), the CA relations did not differ. Two factors may have precluded these researchers from obtaining an effect of witnessing condition: First, only a target-present lineup was used at test, and substantial differences in CA relations for target-present and target-absent lineups have been found previously (e.g., Malpass & Devine, 1981; Wells & Lindsay, 1985). Second, testing occurred immediately after the witnessed event, timing that may have caused metamemorial factors to predominate in the witnesses' decisions. Specifically, because participants were aware that the event had just occurred, the assignment of confidence ratings may have been influenced more by this knowledge than the relation of confidence to perceived accuracy. Consistent with this suggestion, the mean confidence ratings obtained were, across witnessing conditions, highly similar and of midscale values.

More recently, in their meta-analysis of field studies, Bothwell et al. (1987) reported that, in line with the optimality hypothesis, exposure duration was a significant moderating variable of the CA relation because it increased in magnitude with increases in target exposure duration (see also Cutler & Penrod, 1989a). Our own manipulations of exposure duration within two preliminary studies (to be discussed) produced similar results for face and voice identification. Manipulations of cue degradation in a face-recognition task, intended to reflect differential opportunity for optimal processing of faces, have also supported Deffenbacher's optimality hypothesis (Cutler & Penrod, 1989b).

To identify factors that contribute to strong CA relations in the present research we constructed paradigms and materials that would maximize the variability between participants in accuracy and confidence. At the heart of three experiments is our view that person identification studies have overcontrolled extraneous variables and, as a result, have failed in their attempts to match research identification tasks to actual forensic situations. Specifically, the natural variations in encoding and retrieval processes of participant witnesses observed in real-world forensic situations may have been restricted in ways that preclude detection of a CA relation. Two preliminary field studies (Read, 1995, Exp. 3; Read, McFadzen, Mensch, & Tollestrup, 1996) are first summarized to buttress this argument, followed by three experiments designed to manipulate encoding variability.

PRELIMINARY RESEARCH

Preliminary studies are reported herein to demonstrate the possibility of strong CA relations and the effects of two variables that have often been considered extraneous and in need of control by many researchers: postexposure cognitions and target exposure duration. In the first study (Read, 1995, Exp. 3), 192 retail store clerks participated in a "customer interaction" survey. Two researchers (one male, one female) interacted in person with the clerks, one in a sustained 10-min interaction (primary target) and the other in a brief 15-sec interaction (secondary target) with assignment of researchers to conditions counterbalanced across participants. Encoding of targets was assumed to be incidental because participants were not warned of the forthcoming identification tests. Over the course of a 2-week retention interval period, clerks were interviewed twice via telephone by a third researcher. Each clerk received one of three types of interview: a control condition in which no discussion or rehearsal of the primary target was encouraged, a "perceptual" condition in which they were asked to provide a detailed verbal description of the primary target, and a "contextual" condition that encouraged rehearsal of the clerk's interaction with the primary target. Two weeks following the interactions, identification decisions and confidence ratings on a 5-point scale ranging from 1 (*not at all sure*) to 5 (*very confident*) were collected for each target from each clerk.

Table 6.1 presents the CA correlation coefficients calculated across both targets and lineups (target-present, target-absent) in the study, as a function of target exposure (primary or secondary), experimental condition, and the basis of their calculation: whether all participants were included or only those who actually identified someone, hereafter referred to as "choosers" (see Sporer et al., 1995; Wells & Lindsay, 1985). Average accuracy levels across both target-present and target-absent lineups were 65.3% for primary targets and 34.9% for secondary targets. As may be seen, the between-subjects correlation coefficients do vary across targets, rehearsal condition, and type of decision.

TABLE 6.1
Correlation Coefficients for the Confidence–Accuracy Relations Observed
in the First Preliminary Study

	Experimental Condition			Total	
Decision Type	Control	Perceptual	Contextual	Primary	Secondary
All	.30	.65	.47	.47	.41
	(64)	(64)	(64)	(192)	(192)
Choosers	.79	.85	.60	.73	.60
	(30)	(26)	(32)	(88)	(130)

Note. Primary target coefficients are presented as a function of experimental condition and type of decision (all vs. identifications only). Experimental condition did not pertain to the secondary target. All coefficients are statistically reliable ($p < .05$). Sample ns are in brackets.

Briefly, the important points for our purposes are, first, the CA relations are frequently and impressively higher than those previously reported (as high as $r = .80$ in some conditions); second, somewhat lower CA coefficients were obtained following the short (secondary target) than the long (primary target) interactions; third, uniformly higher CA relations were observed among "choosers" than for all participants; and, finally, the magnitude of the CA relation was significantly affected by the postexposure rehearsal manipulation for the primary target. Most striking of these effects was that for choosers, relative to the control condition, there was an enhancement of the CA relation following perceptual rehearsal but a decrement following contextual rehearsal activities. One effect of contextual rehearsal procedures appears to be an increase in participants' willingness to identify someone, resulting in increased misidentifications and a lower CA relation (Read, 1995).

In a second study (Read et al., 1996), 256 members of the public were approached at their homes by two researchers seeking volunteers for a "telephone survey" research project. Participants phoned the laboratory once each day and maintained a diary in regard to the numbers and types of telephone calls received. To manipulate exposure duration, one researcher who served as the interviewer's assistant during the solicitation interview left the participant's home at one of three prearranged departure times. Fourteen days later, participants identified from photo lineups the researcher who had played a minor role and left the interview early.

The level of correct identification performance, collapsed over exposure durations, was low (36.5%) but similar to that obtained for the secondary target in the first experiment. The CA relation data revealed generally low correlations but their magnitudes were positively related to exposure duration with $r = .02$, at the shortest, $r = .28$, $p < .05$, at the intermediate, and $r = .30$, $p < .05$ at the longest interval.

From these preliminary studies it is clear that the CA relation can be impressively high but, more importantly, exposure duration can be a moderating variable. From our perspective, these gains in the CA relation with increased exposure reflect increased opportunity for differential encoding across participants, rather than simply enhanced encoding as is implied by some readings of Deffenbacher's optimality hypothesis (Bothwell et al., 1987; Cutler & Penrod, 1989b; Narby, Cutler, & Penrod, 1996). That is, the longer a target is available for incidental encoding, the more likely it is that participants will substantially differ in their encodings of that target. Rather than designing a technique by which incidental encoding might be manipulated on a between-subjects basis, we first constructed identification tests that capitalized on preexisting encoding variability within a sample of participants.

EXPERIMENT 1

To gain estimates of the CA relation on a within-subjects basis, 80 public figures were chosen as identification targets; that is, people who had achieved some fame or success within the domains of sports, politics, or entertainment and whose names would be familiar to most members of the public (e.g., Chris Evert, Nelson Mandela, and Sally Field). However, assuming differential interest by participants across domains, participants should differ substantially in the numbers of public figures with whom they are highly familiar and thereby demonstrate variation in their levels of accurate identifications. Other investigators have used familiar faces, sometimes celebrities (e.g., Davies, Ellis, & Shepherd, 1978; Fisher & Cox, 1975) and sometimes familiar people known to the participants such as school classmates (Goldstein & Mackenberg, 1966) and university colleagues (Valentine & Bruce, 1986) in face-recognition paradigms; however, lineup identification tasks were not used.

Of the complete set of public figures, 40 were assigned randomly to a lineup (multiple-photograph) and 40 to a showup (single-photograph) test condition (see, Gonzalez, Ellsworth, & Pembroke, 1993; Yarmey, chap. 7, this volume). Within each of these, one half were randomly assigned to target-present and one half to target-absent test conditions. Foils matching general descriptions of the 80 targets but who were unknown (at least to the experimenters) were also selected from print media in numbers that provided four foils for target-absent lineups (three of these to be used as foils for target-present lineups), and the one foil in each of the 20 target-absent showup conditions. All media photos were copied to match the approximate size of each photocopied, black-and-white, target photo. Standard identification instructions were provided (i.e., "the person may or may not be present") and a 5-point confidence rating (as in the earlier field studies) followed each decision. The 36 university student participants completed, at their own pace, booklets in which each of 80 pages presented an individual's name in either a lineup or showup test format. Complete details of other aspects of design and procedure including counterbalancing, timing, names of public figures, and instructions may be found in Read and Lindsay (1996).

An important departure from standard identification study procedures was the inclusion of a "don't know" option to be used by those participants who were unfamiliar with a named target. Although Wells (1993) reminded us that a forensic lineup identification is not a forced-choice test, the majority of identification studies have not allowed "don't know" responses. Wells speculated that the inclusion of participants who know that they do not know the target in question would likely have had the effect of raising the CA relation in these studies. It could as easily be anticipated that their inclusion had reduced the CA relation (see Sporer et al., 1995) such that the weak correlations previously reported reflect, in part, the forced-choice nature of those tests.

Results

As our initial interest was a within-subjects estimate of the CA relation, we calculated for each participant separate CA correlations, first, across all types of identification decisions and, second, CA correlations based only on targets for which participants actually made an identification; that is, when a photo was chosen. Comparison of this latter group of "choosers" with the data collected across all lineup and showup decisions provides an indication of the impact of the moderating variable of choosing on the CA relation (Fleet et al., 1987; Sporer et al., 1995). All calculations excluded those items for whom a "don't know" response had been given to a lineup or showup.

Histograms of the distribution of the 36 within-subjects CA relations are presented in Figs. 6.1 and 6.2. Presented in the upper panels of Figs. 6.1 and 6.2 are the distributions of the CA coefficients calculated over the 40 targets (all decision types). In the lower panels are the distribution of the participants' CA coefficients based on targets for which an identification was made by each participant ("choosers"). Overall, accuracy levels were fairly high with 72.6% in lineups (Fig. 6.1) and 73.7% in showups (Fig. 6.2). As target ns varied from participant to participant, the indicated statistical reliability in the distributions is based on the fewest degrees of freedom appropriate (i.e., the lowest number across participants).

As may be seen for the lineup data in the upper panel of Fig. 6.1, average

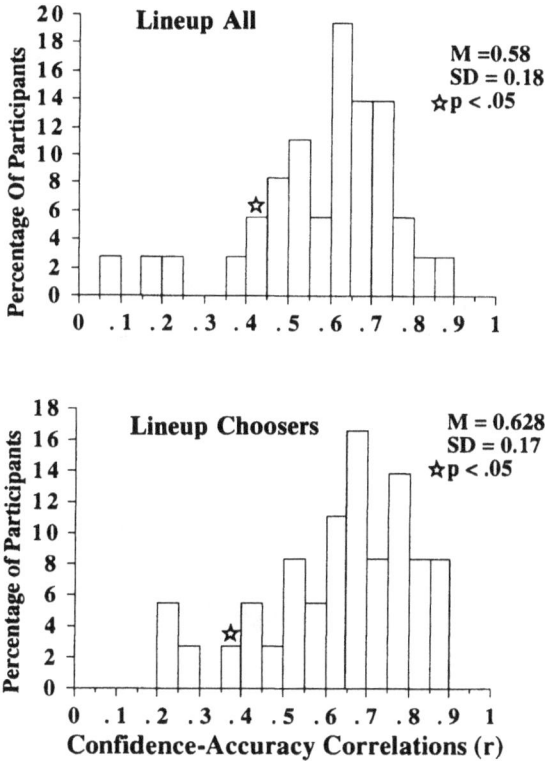

FIG. 6.1. Frequency distribution of participants' correlation coefficients for the confidence–accuracy relation in the lineups of Experiment 1. The distributions differ with all lineup decisions in the upper panel (includes "not present" choices) and identifications only (choosers) in the lower panel.

CA values are substantially higher than the $r = .25$ reported in Bothwell et al.'s (1987) meta-analysis of field studies. Further, when choosers alone are considered (lower panel), the values are higher still. Indeed, the distributions are negatively skewed such that median values ($rs = .64$ and $.68$) exceed mean values ($rs = .57$ and $.63$). Surprisingly, regardless of the type of decision, 72% of the participants gained CA values in excess of $r = .50$. In the case of choosers alone, 81% of participants gained CA values in excess of $r = .50$.

The CA relations for showups are provided in the two panels of Fig. 6.2. Overall, the mean CA values are much lower ($rs = .36$ and $.31$) than for lineups, are sometimes negative in direction, and only 25.0% in either panel exceeded the value of $r = .50$. The finding of a lower CA relation for showups suggests greater unreliability of the showup procedure and may be in part responsible for the generally lower acceptance it has gained with

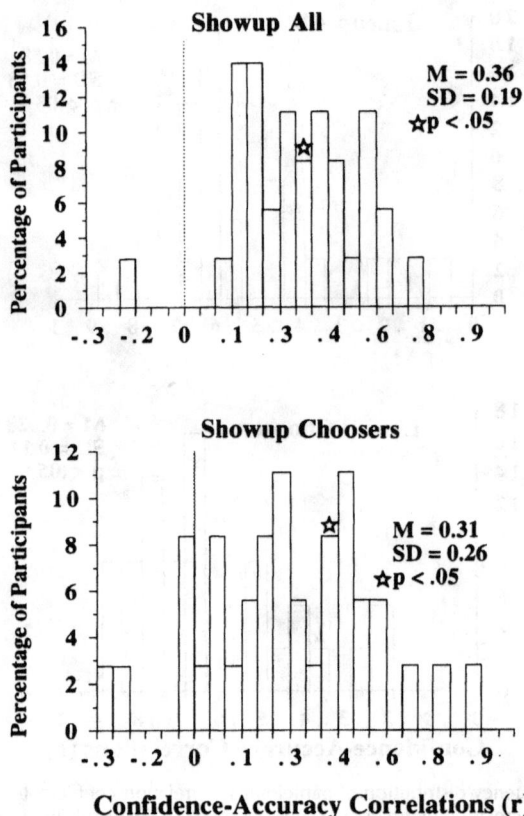

FIG. 6.2.   Frequency distribution of participants' correlation coefficients for the confidence–accuracy relation in the showups of Experiment 1. The distributions differ with
all showup decisions in the upper panel (includes "not present" choices) and identifications only (choosers) in the lower panel.

psycholegal experts (Kassin et al., 1989; Yarmey, chap. 7, this volume).
Further, although we had anticipated a substantial within-subjects correlation between the participants' CA relations calculated for lineups and for
showups, this relationship was, in fact, weak ($r = .21$) and statistically
unreliable, perhaps because of the contribution of the unreliable showup
CA relations.

To summarize, the within-subjects correlations based on lineups reveal
markedly higher values than are normally seen in eyewitness research.
Showups, on the other hand, demonstrated lower CA relations but also
slightly greater than the average reported by Bothwell et al. (1987). At a
minimum, it is clear that when confronted with multiple identifications
from lineups, most research participants do demonstrate a relation between

accuracy and confidence that reflects the reliable assignment of higher rated confidence to correct than incorrect decisions. These results are consistent with those found in the wide variety of cognitive research domains cited earlier in this chapter.

EXPERIMENT 2

We next asked whether the same mean CA magnitudes would characterize specific targets in the between-subjects manner of estimating the CA relation in most psycholegal research (see Luus & Wells, 1994a; Smith et al., 1989). Doing so was precluded in Experiment 1 because we had not constructed both target-present and target-absent lineup and showup versions for each target person. Experiment 2 remedied this deficiency.

Based on the results of Experiment 1, a subset of 24 targets was selected to reflect a broad range of familiarity or performance accuracy but for whom the rates of "don't know" responses were low and approximately equivalent. Targets for whom performance accuracy was extreme were eliminated from Experiment 2 because such performance may reflect very low or very high familiarity or, alternatively, their performances may reflect particularly difficult or easy test constructions. Overall, the 24 targets we selected achieved 62.5% accuracy in lineups and 62.0% in showups and allowed an assignment to three levels of familiarity (high, moderate, low) with mean accuracy levels of 78.7%, 61.5%, and 46.7%, respectively. Examples of targets within the high, moderate, and low levels of familiarity were Meryl Streep, Lorena Bobbitt, and Michael Eisner, respectively. A total of 12 targets were assigned to either lineup or showup test formats in a quasi-random manner such that the three levels of familiarity were equivalent across subsets of four targets in each format.

For each target 16 university student participants received a target-present and 16 received a target-absent test form (lineup or showup). Instructions followed those of Experiment 1 with one exception: We manipulated the response options available to the participants at the time of test. Specifically, as a between-subjects variable, 16 participants were provided, in addition to the options of choosing a photo or not, a "don't know" option, on both lineups and showups (DK condition). The remaining 16 participants (control condition) did not have the same opportunity, leaving them but two options: identify someone or choose "not present."

Results

Overall, participants were correct 53.9% of the time on lineups and 68.2% of the time on showups; however, the DK condition in both test formats obtained higher accuracy scores than the control conditions (61.3% vs. 47.8% for lineups and 71.0% vs. 66.2% for showups, respectively). Table 6.2 provides the mean CA coefficients achieved by the 12 targets in each of the lineup and showup conditions as a function of level of familiarity, experimental condition (DK vs. control), and type of decision made (all vs. choosers). Each tabled value represents the mean of the CA correlations for the relevant subset of targets and as expressed by 16 participants. Several features of these data should be noted. First, inspection of the coefficients indicates again that the majority are above the mean value of $r = .25$ reported by Bothwell et al. (1987). The CA values for lineup targets (all decisions) varied substantially with 16.7% and 50% obtaining coefficients in excess of $r = .50$ in the control and DK conditions, respectively. Considering lineup choosers alone, these values rose to 25.0% and 66.7%, respectively. For showups, percentages of targets with CAs above $r = .50$ were 8.3% and 16.7% in the control and DK conditions, respectively. Considering showup choosers alone, these values rose to 16.7% and 25.0%, respectively.

Second, CA magnitudes vary with type of test, available response options, and type of decision made. Lineups revealed, as they did in Experiment 1, overall higher CA relations than did showups. Choice responses again produced higher CA relations than all decisions considered

TABLE 6.2
Mean Correlation Coefficients Achieved for Target Public Figures
for the CA Relation in Experiment 2, Presented as a Function
of Experimental Condition, Test Type (Targets = 12), and Level
of Target Familiarity (Targets = 4)

| | Familiarity | | | |
	Low	Moderate	High	Total
Lineup format				
DK condition				
All	.49**	.50**	.50**	.50** (.223)
Choosers	.54**	.56**	.56**	.56** (.193)
Control condition				
All	.13	.35*	.33*	.27 (.186)
Choosers	.23	.33*	.34*	.30 (.173)
Showup format				
DK condition				
All	.24	.38*	.33*	.33* (.214)
Choosers	.34*	.50**	.34*	.39* (.228)
Control condition				
All	.00	.26	.11	.13 (.232)
Choosers	.18	.15	.12	.15 (.296)

Note. Standard deviations of the targets' coefficients are presented in parentheses.
$*p < .05.$ $**p < .01.$

together; and finally, CA values were highest when participants had a "don't know" option available to them at test. Indeed, for DK condition lineups the average CA coefficients across all levels of familiarity were $r = .50$ (all decision types) and $r = .56$ for choice decisions alone. The latter value is very similar in magnitude to the value of r reported for comparable lineup conditions of Experiment 1, but which were based on substantially greater numbers of targets and calculated on a within-subjects basis. Comparable values for the showup tests with a DK option included were $r = .33$ and $r = .39$, respectively.

Inspection of the familiarity data in Table 6.2 suggests an inverted U-shaped relation between rated familiarity and CA magnitude such that targets of either low or high familiarity often yield lower magnitudes than do targets of moderate familiarity. This finding is, of course, consistent with our hypothesis regarding encoding variability because we would expect a restriction of encoding variability at the ends of the continuum where targets would be more consistently unknown or known across participants. However, in contrast, the lineup data of the DK condition are remarkably stable across levels of familiarity and this pattern strongly suggests that lineups with a "don't know" option are impervious to the effects of target familiarity. Our interpretation of this finding is that the DK option removes those participants whose identifications and assignments of confidence are likely to be based on guessing and thereby contribute random variation to the CA relation.

Considering Experiments 1 and 2 together, it is clear that the CA relation can be substantial and useful for predicting accuracy from confidence when public figures are identified. The strength of the CA relations observed in the experiments is supportive of the concept of encoding variability reflected by the natural variations in participants' knowledge of the public figures. It is also possible, however, that because each participant received many identification tests, their calibrations of accuracy with confidence could have developed during rather than existed before the experiment (see Kassin, 1985; Lichtenstein et al., 1982; Lieppe, 1980; Sharp et al., 1989, for discussion of the consequences of training on the CA relation). If true, the results of Experiments 1 and 2 would be applicable only to multiple-identification tasks, not to the single-suspect identifications typical of real-world forensic situations.

Although one-time-only viewings of a target characterize much eyewitness research, many forensically relevant identifications are required when a single perpetrator has been seen on multiple occasions (Bekerian, 1993). Nonetheless, it is also reasonable to question whether the data of Experiments 1 and 2 may be readily generalized to a single target seen but once because it is likely that participants typically have more encoded information available about a public figure than about a person seen but once. The third experiment investigates encoding variability in regard to a single target and a single identification test.

EXPERIMENT 3

In the final experiment, research participants were asked to identify a single male target either 3, 6, or 9 months after a single exposure. Participants were 125 retail store clerks who participated in a customer interaction survey (as in the preliminary research study) that required their communication via telephone with researchers over a 2-week period. The experiment was constructed to provide two levels of encoding variability. We reasoned as follows: If observers of a target person believe that they will later be challenged with an identification test for the target, they will attempt to prepare for the test, perhaps resulting in relatively homogeneous encoding of the target in comparison to the encoding variability of a group of participants who are unaware that an identification test is forthcoming. In other words, with expectation of test, encoding will be intentional; with no such expectation, encoding will be incidental and will demonstrate greater variability than the former group. Extended to the issue of CA relations, coefficients would be predicted to be lower following intentional than incidental conditions because of reduced encoding variability among members of the intentional encoding group. This prediction stands in direct contrast to Deffenbacher's comments relating intentional versus incidental encoding to optimality of processing. Because the optimality hypothesis focuses on absolute levels of encoding, rather than the variability of encoding, Deffenbacher (1980) argued that the CA relation should be higher for intentional than incidental learning conditions.

To create such encoding differences, clerks were randomly assigned to either a prewarned or nonwarned condition. In the prewarned condition participants were informed, at the approximate halfway point during a 10-min interview with the target, that at a later time they would be recontacted for a final interview and at that time, among other questions, they would also be tested on their ability to identify the interviewer from a picture. Participants in the nonwarned condition, on the other hand, were informed about the future interview but received no information about the identification test.

Because we assumed participants would lose access to information about the target and the interaction over time, we anticipated time-dependent changes in the CA relation. Hence, the final interviews with a female research assistant occurred approximately 3, 6, or 9 months later. The identification tests consisted of an eight-person lineup accompanied by the "not present" option. Approximately one half of the participants received a target-present lineup and the remaining clerks received a target-absent lineup. Two male targets were used and counterbalanced across the two encoding conditions.

Results and Discussion

Identification Accuracy. Overall performance accuracy was significantly higher for the prewarned (69.0%) than the nonwarned participants (55.4%) and although both declined significantly with retention interval, this decline interacted significantly with encoding condition. Specifically, whereas the nonwarned condition declined precipitously from the 3- to the 9-month interval, the prewarned participants suffered only moderate losses and demonstrated long-term advantages of encoding in preparation for an identification test (see Read & Lindsay, 1996, for a complete description of this experiment's results).

CA Relations. As in Experiment 2, correlation coefficients were calculated on a between-subjects basis whereby each participant contributed data in regard to one target. These data are presented in Fig. 6.3. As may be seen, a striking interaction between encoding condition and retention interval was obtained. To understand the nature of this interaction, consider first the 3-month retention interval data. We had predicted that the prewarned condition would least favor interparticipant variability in encoding because these participants all would have understood that an identification test would occur in the future and, as a result, they would

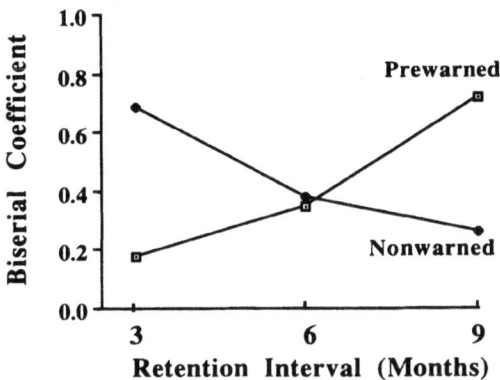

FIG. 6.3. CA correlation coefficients obtained in the prewarned and nonwarned conditions of Experiment 3, presented as a function of retention interval.

prepare themselves for it in a relatively homogeneous manner. In contrast, the nonwarned participants had no such expectation and likely encoded a target in accordance with idiosyncratic levels of interest or disinterest in him. As may be seen, with rs of .18 and .69, respectively, in the prewarned and nonwarned conditions at this first retention interval, our expectations were met.

Figure 6.3 also shows that the magnitudes of the two conditions' overall CA relations change over time, increasing and decreasing in symmetrically opposing directions. As a result, by the 9-month retention interval rs of .26 and .72 now characterize the nonwarned and prewarned conditions, values diametrically opposite those observed at the 3-month interval. Inspection of the two panels of Fig. 6.4 provides a parallel but somewhat different look at the relation between confidence ratings and decision accuracy over time. In the left panel the prewarned condition participants' confidence ratings are plotted for correct and incorrect decisions over time. As may be seen, mean confidence ratings for correct and incorrect decisions are similar in value at 3 months but have diverged substantially by 9 months with the major change being a reduction in mean confidence for incorrect decisions. Of course, to obtain a positive CA relation of any magnitude, a difference like that seen at 9 months is required On the other hand, the right panel presents the opposite pattern of change over time for the nonwarned condition participants. At the 9-month interval these participants appear to be unable to discriminate correct from incorrect decisions. No doubt all participants are losing access to target knowledge over time and, according to the accuracy data, at a more rapid rate for the nonwarned than prewarned participants. At 9 months following the interaction, the non-warned participants no longer have sufficient information to discriminate

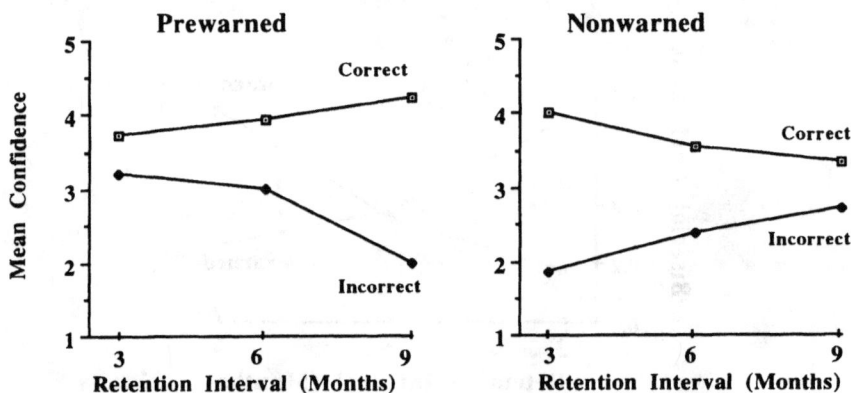

FIG. 6.4. Mean confidence ratings assigned correct and incorrect decisions by the prewarned (left panel) and nonwarned (right panel) conditions of Experiment 3.

correct from incorrect decisions. We suggest that at this same point in time the availability of target information to the prewarned participants is at approximately the same level as it was for nonwarned participants after but 3 months.

As in the previous studies the CA relations were stronger for choosers than those based on all decisions for both the prewarned ($rs = .46$ vs. $.37$) and nonwarned participants ($rs = .71$ vs. $.47$), respectively.

GENERAL DISCUSSION

The studies reported make a number of points that are relevant to the controversy surrounding CA relations in person identification. First, whether we look at the within-subjects data of Experiment 1 or the between-subjects data of Experiments 2 and 3, it is clear that the CA relation can be very strong; such strength often characterizes the majority of participants and targets in these studies; and it provides for reliable predictions of accuracy from rated confidence. Conclusions like these have not been presented to the courts because empirical research has previously failed to provide consistent support for such claims. Although much more work and replication is required before these data would appear in a court presentation, we think it is clear that they seriously undermine the generality of much of the previous research. McCloskey and Egeth (1983; Egeth, 1993) and others (Elliott, 1993) have argued that eyewitness testimony research has not yet developed a sufficient corpus of relevant and applicable knowledge on which courtroom presentations may be made. We disagree with their position because, like Loftus (1983), we believe that as one could always make the argument that the information base is as yet insufficient, psycholegal researchers may never be prepared to contribute to the legal system. Instead, it becomes a matter of what weight the court will assign such information, given its limitations; at a minimum, courtroom presentation may have the salutary effect of countering strong claims made by other participants in the legal system, claims that are completely without empirical foundation (see also Lieppe, 1995).

Second, a consistent finding obtained in Experiments 1 and 2 was the substantially lower average CA relation gained from showups than lineups. Previous researchers have often concluded that the showup procedure is potentially more suggestive and/or can increase misidentifications of innocent suspects (e.g., Kassin et al., 1989), perhaps particularly so at longer retention intervals (Yarmey, chap. 7, this volume). On the other hand, some research has demonstrated that the two procedures can be equivalent in terms of correct and incorrect (false positive) identifications

(Gonzalez et al., 1993). Our data support the former position because with comparable targets the showups yielded consistently weaker CA relations than lineups. One explanation for these differences may reside in the notion of better or enhanced opportunities for calibration of accuracy and confidence by eyewitnesses within lineups than showups. That is, because the lineups of Experiments 1 and 2 provided four options rather than one, it seems likely that participants may become more aware of their differential levels of confidence across the four lineup choices for a target. As a result, perhaps greater consideration was given by these participants to the confidence judgment they assigned to a lineup than a showup decision. The confidence data of Experiment 2 do support this possibility because across all decision types showup targets attracted significantly higher mean confidence ratings (3.49) than did lineup targets (2.95) and did so within the context of significantly less variability ($SD = 1.37$) than the lineup targets ($SD = 1.49$).

Third, the magnitude of the CA relation is moderated by the type of decision made and the response options available to the eyewitness. Stronger CA relations were found among choosers (in all three experiments) and among participants provided an opportunity to respond with "don't know" (Experiments 1 and 2). Finally, as observed in the final experiment with retail store clerks, the magnitude of the CA relation may depend heavily on the orientation of witnesses to the target during exposure and the delay between exposure and test. Unlike other changes in rated confidence over time (e.g., Luus & Wells, 1994a, 1994b), the changes observed in Experiment 3 were not the effect of explicit experimental manipulations. Instead, within either the prewarned or nonwarned conditions, retail clerks all experienced the identical encoding conditions but demonstrated markedly different CA relations depending on the length of the retention interval between encoding and test. It is possible that the immediate testing procedure of many laboratory and field studies of both face recognition and person identification has been an insensitive choice of retention interval for the estimation of CA relations.

We emphasized at the outset that our goal was to better understand the nature and magnitude of the CA relation at the time of identification. A first step toward the application of the present findings to forensic situations would be the development of standardized methods by which confidence ratings could be collected and identification decisions initially made. Whatever position researchers take about the CA relation there seems no disagreement that, to the extent confidence ratings can be diagnostic of accuracy, they are most likely to be so when assigned at the time of identification, not weeks or months later in court (e.g., Penrod & Cutler, 1995; Wells & Seelau, 1995). Additional standardization might also include the collection of information about potentially relevant variables such as the eyewitness' orientation to the target and the length of the retention interval. If such procedures were available and if, in further testing, other researchers support the CA relations observed in our studies, police, prosecutors, and courts may ultimately be able, with knowledge of the circumstances of encoding and retrieval, to place some reliance on the confidence with which witnesses make identifications. For the moment, our results suggest that expert psychological witnesses should be somewhat cautious in pronouncements about the CA relation: False identifications are sometimes made with great confidence, but our results suggest that, on average, real-world identifications made with confidence are more likely to be accurate than those made without confidence.

ACKNOWLEDGMENTS

Research described in this chapter was supported by grants from the Alberta Law Foundation and the Natural Sciences and Engineering Research Council of Canada. The authors thank Eileen McFadzen, Matthew Davidson, Julie Greer, Tanya Payne, Grant Tingley, and Wayne Ormond, who served as researchers or targets in Experiment 3. Portions of this research were presented at the Meeting of the American Psychology-Law Society, Hilton Head, SC, March 1996.

REFERENCES

Bekerian, D. A. (1993). In search of the typical eyewitness. *American Psychologist, 48*, 574–576.

Bothwell, R. K., Deffenbacher, K. A., & Brigham, J. C. (1987). Correlation of eyewitness accuracy and confidence: Optimality hypothesis revisited. *Journal of Applied Psychology, 72*, 691–695.

Brewer, W. (1996). What is recollective memory? In D. C. Rubin (Ed.), *Remembering our past: Studies in autobiographical memory* (pp. 19–66). Cambridge, UK: Cambridge University Press.

Brigham, J. C. (1990). Target person distinctiveness and attractiveness as moderator variables in the confidence-accuracy relationship in eyewitness identifications. *Basic and Applied Social Psychology, 11*, 101–115.

Brigham, J. C., & Bothwell, R. K. (1983). The ability of prospective jurors to estimate the accuracy of eyewitness identifications. *Law and Human Behavior, 7*, 19–30.

Brigham, J. C., Maass, A., Snyder, L. D., & Spaulding, K. (1982). Accuracy of eyewitness identifications in a field study. *Journal of Personality and Social Psychology, 42*, 673–681.

Brigham, J. C., & Wolfskeil, M. P. (1983). Opinions of attorneys and law enforcement personnel on the accuracy of eyewitness identifications. *Law and Human Behavior, 7*, 337–349.

Brooks, N. (1983). *Police guidelines: Pretrial identification procedures*. Ottawa, Ontario: Law

Reform Commission.

Costermans, J., Lories, G., & Ansay, C. (1992). Confidence level and feeling of knowing in question answering: The weight of inferential processes. *Journal of Experimental Psychology: Learning, Memory, and Cognition, 18*, 142–150.

Cutler, B. L., & Penrod, S. D. (1989a). Forensically relevant moderators of the relation between eyewitness identification accuracy and confidence. *Journal of Applied Psychology, 74*, 650–652.

Cutler, B. L., & Penrod, S. D. (1989b). Moderators of the confidence–accuracy correlation in face recognition: Role of information processing and base rates. *Applied Cognitive Psychology, 3*, 95–107.

Cutler, B. L., Penrod, S. D., & Dexter, H. R. (1990). Juror sensitivity to eyewitness identification evidence. *Law and Human Behavior, 14*, 185–191.

Davies, G. M. (1988). Faces and places: Laboratory research on context and face recognition. In G. M. Davies & D. M. Thomson (Eds.), *Memory in context: Context in memory* (pp. 35–53). London: Wiley.

Davies, G. M., Ellis, H., & Shepherd, J. (1978). Face recognition accuracy as a function of mode of representation. *Journal of Applied Psychology, 63*, 180–187.

Deffenbacher, K. A. (1980). Eyewitness accuracy and confidence: Can we infer anything about their relationship? *Law and Human Behavior, 4*, 243–260.

Deffenbacher, K. A., Leu, J. R., & Brown, E. L. (1981). Memory for faces: Testing method, encoding strategy, and confidence. *American Journal of Psychology, 94*, 13–26.

Deffenbacher, K. A., & Loftus, E. F. (1982). Do jurors share a common understanding concerning eyewitness behavior? *Law and Human Behavior, 6*, 15–30.

Egeth, H. (1993). What do we not know about eyewitness identification? *American Psychologist, 48*, 577–580.

Elliott, R. (1993). Expert testimony about eyewitness identification. *Law and Human Behavior, 17*, 423–437.

Fisher, G. H., & Cox, R. L. (1975). Recognizing human faces. *Applied Ergonomics, 6*, 104–109.

Fleet, M. L., Brigham, J. C., & Bothwell, R. K. (1987). The confidence–accuracy relationship: The effects of confidence assessment and choosing. *Journal of Applied Social Psychology, 17*, 171–187.

Glenberg, A. M., & Epstein, W. (1985). Calibration of comprehension. *Journal of Experimental Psychology: Learning, Memory & Cognition, 11*, 702–718.

Goldstein, A. G., & Mackenberg, E. J. (1966). Recognition of human faces from isolated facial features: A developmental study. *Psychonomic Science, 6*, 149–150.

Gonzalez, R., Ellsworth, P. C., & Pembroke, M. (1993). Response biases in lineups and showups. *Journal of Personality and Social Psychology, 64*, 525–537.

Gruneberg, M. M., & Sykes, R. N. (1993). The generalisability of confidence–accuracy studies in eyewitnessing. *Memory, 1*, 185–190.

Hosch, H. (1994). Individual differences and eyewitness identification. In D. F. Ross, J. D. Read, & M. P. Toglia (Eds.), *Adult eyewitness testimony: Current trends and developments* (pp. 328–347). New York: Cambridge University Press.

Jacoby, L. L., Kelley, C. M., & Dywan, J. (1989). Memory attributions. In H. L. Roediger & F. I. M. Craik (Eds.), *Varieties of memory and consciousness: Essays in honor of Endel Tulving* (pp. 391–422). Hillsdale, NJ: Lawrence Erlbaum Associates.

Kassin, S. M. (1985). Eyewitness identification: Retrospective self-awareness and the accuracy-confidence correlation. *Journal of Personality and Social Psychology, 49*, 878–893.

Kassin, S. M., Ellsworth, P. C., & Smith, V. L. (1989). The "general acceptance" of psychological research on eyewitness testimony: A survey of the experts. *American Psychologist, 44*, 1089–1098.

Krafka, C., & Penrod, S. D. (1985). Reinstatement of context in a field experiment on eyewitness identification. *Journal of Personality and Social Psychology, 49*, 58–69.

Lichtenstein, S., Fischoff, B., & Phillips, L. D. (1982). Calibration of probabilities: The state of the art to 1980. In D. Kahneman, P. Slovic, & A. Tversky (Eds.), *Judgments under uncertainty: Heuristics and biases* (pp. 306–334). New York: Cambridge University Press.

Lieppe, M. R. (1980). Effects of integrative memorial and cognitive processes on the correspondence of eyewitness accuracy and confidence. *Law and Human Behavior, 4*, 261–274.

Lieppe, M. R. (1995). The case for expert testimony about eyewitness memory. *Psychology, Public Policy, and Law, 1*, 909–959.

Lieppe, M. R., Manion, A. P., & Romanczyk, A. (1992). Eyewitness persuasion: How and how well do fact finders judge the accuracy of adults' and childrens' memory reports? *Journal of Personality and Social Psychology, 63*, 181–197.

Lindsay, R. C. L. (1986). Confidence and accuracy of eyewitness identification from lineups. *Law and Human Behavior, 10*, 229–239.

Lindsay, R. C. L. (1994). Expectations of eyewitness performance: Jurors' verdicts do not follow from their beliefs. In D. F. Ross, J. D. Read, & M. P. Toglia (Eds.), *Adult eyewitness testimony: Current trends and developments* (pp. 362–384). New York: Cambridge University Press.

Lindsay, R. C. L., Wells, G. L., & Rumpel, C. M. (1981). Can people detect eyewitness-identification accuracy within and across situations? *Journal of Applied Psychology, 66*, 79–89.

Loftus, E. F. (1983). Silence is not golden. *American Psychologist, 38*, 564–572.

Lovelace, E. A. (1984). Metamemory: Monitoring future recallability during study. *Journal of Experimental Psychology: Learning, Memory & Cognition, 10*, 756–766.

Luus, C. A. E., & Wells, G. L. (1994a). Eyewitness identification confidence. In D. F. Ross, J. D. Read, & M. P. Toglia (Eds.), *Adult eyewitness testimony: Current trends and developments* (pp. 348–361). New York: Cambridge University Press.

Luus, C. A. E., & Wells, G. L. (1994b). The malleability of eyewitness confidence: Co-witness and perseverance effects. *Journal of Applied Psychology, 79*, 714–723.

Maass, A., & Clark, R. D., III. (1984). Hidden impact of minorities: Fifteen years of minority influence research. *Psychological Bulletin, 95*, 428–450.

Malpass, R. S., & Devine, P. G. (1981). Eyewitness identification: Lineup instructions and the absence of the offender. *Journal of Applied Psychology, 66*, 482–487.

McCloskey, M., & Egeth, H. E. (1983). Eyewitness identification: What can a psychologist tell a jury? *American Psychologist, 38*, 550–563.

Murdock, B. B. (1974). *Human memory: Theory and data.* New York: Wiley.

Narby, D. J., Cutler, B. L., & Penrod, S. D. (1996). The effects of witness, target, and situational factors in eyewitness identifications. In S. L. Sporer, R. S. Malpass, & G. Koehnken (Eds.), *Psychological issues in eyewitness identification* (pp. 23–52). Mahwah, NJ: Lawrence Erlbaum Associates.

Neil v. Biggers, 409 U.S. 188 (1972).

Noon, E., & Hollin, C. R. (1987). Lay knowledge of eyewitness behavior. *Applied Cognitive Psychology, 1*, 143–153.

Penrod, S., & Cutler, B. (1995). Witness confidence and witness accuracy: Assessing their forensic relation. *Psychology, Public Policy, and Law, 1*, 817–845.

Perfect, T. J., Watson, E. L., & Wagstaff, G. F. (1993). Accuracy of confidence ratings associated with general knowledge and eyewitness memory. *Journal of Applied Psychology, 78*, 144–147.

Read, J. D. (1994). Understanding bystander misidentifications: The roles of familiarity and contextual knowledge. In D. F. Ross, J. D. Read, & M. P. Toglia (Eds.), *Adult eyewitness testimony: Current trends and developments* (pp. 56–79). New York: Cambridge University Press.

Read, J. D. (1995). The availability heuristic in person identification: The sometimes misleading consequences of enhanced contextual information. *Applied Cognitive Psychology, 9*, 91–121.

Read, J. D., & Bruce, D. (1982). Longitudinal tracking of difficult memory retrievals. *Cognitive Psychology, 14*, 280–300.

Read, J. D., & Lindsay, D. S. (1996). *Identification accuracy and confidence: Have we misled the courts?* Unpublished manuscript, University of Lethbridge and University of Victoria.

Read, J. D., McFadzen, E., Mensch, L., & Tollestrup, P. (1996). *Strangers at the door: Memory for brief encounters in a natural context.* Unpublished manuscript, University of Lethbridge.

Read, J. D., Yuille, J. C., & Tollestrup, P. (1992). Recollections of a robbery: Effects of arousal and alcohol upon recall and person identification. *Law and Human Behavior, 16*, 425–446.

Schooler, J. W., Ryan, R. S., & Foster, R. A. (1995, July). *How accurate are witnesses who are certain in their identifications?* Paper presented at the Society for Applied Research in Memory and Cognition, Vancouver, British Columbia.

Sharp, G. L., Cutler, B. L., & Penrod, S. D. (1989). Performance feedback improves the resolution of confidence judgments. *Organizational Behavior and Human Decision Processes, 42*, 271–283.

Shaw, J. S., III. (1996). Increases in eyewitness confidence resulting from postevent questioning. *Journal of Experimental Psychology: Applied, 2*, 126–146.

Shepherd, J. W. (1983). Identification after long delays. In S. Lloyd-Bostock & B. R. Clifford (Eds.), *Evaluating witness evidence* (pp. 173–188). London: Wiley.

Smith, V. L., Kassin, S. M., & Ellsworth, P. C. (1989). Eyewitness accuracy and confidence: Within- versus between-subjects correlations. *Journal of Applied Psychology, 74*, 356–359.

Sporer, S. L., Penrod, S. L., Read, D., & Cutler, B. (1995). Choosing, confidence, and accuracy: A meta-analysis of the confidence–accuracy relation in eyewitness identification studies. *Psychological Bulletin, 118*, 315–327.

Tulving, E., & Thomson, D. M. (1971). Retrieval processes in recognition memory: Effects of associative context. *Journal of Experimental Psychology, 87*, 116–124.

Tversky, A., & Kahneman, D. (1974). Judgments under uncertainty: Heuristics and biases. *Science, 185*, 1124–1131.

Valentine, T., & Bruce, V. (1986). Recognizing familiar faces: The role of distinctiveness and familiarity. *Canadian Journal of Psychology, 40*, 300–305.

Wells, G. L. (1993). What do we know about eyewitness identifications? *American Psychologist, 48*, 553–571.

Wells, G. L., & Lindsay, R. C. L. (1985). Methodological notes on the accuracy-confidence relation in eyewitness identification. *Journal of Applied Psychology, 70*, 413–419.

Wells, G. L., Lindsay, R. C. L., & Ferguson, T. J. (1979). Accuracy, confidence, and juror perceptions in eyewitness identifications. *Journal of Applied Psychology, 64*, 440–448.

Wells, G. L., & Murray, D. (1984). Eyewitness confidence. In G. L. Wells & E. F. Loftus (Eds.), *Eyewitness testimony: Psychological perspectives* (pp. 155–170). Cambridge, UK: Cambridge University Press.

Wells, G. L., & Seelau, E. P. (1995). Eyewitness identification: Psychological research and legal policy on lineups. *Psychology, Public Policy, and Law, 1*, 765–791.

Whittlesea, B. W. A. (1993). Illusions of familiarity. *Journal of Experimental Psychology: Learning, Memory, & Cognition, 19*, 1235–1253.

Yarmey, A. D., & Jones, H. P. T. (1983). Is eyewitness identification a matter of common sense? In S. M. A. Lloyd-Bostock & B. R. Clifford (Eds.), *Evaluating witness research: Recent psychological research and new perspectives* (pp. 13–40). New York: Wiley.

7

Person Identification in Showups and Lineups

A. Daniel Yarmey
University of Guelph

The major objective of eyewitness researchers is to provide the general community of psycholegal scholars, the police, the courts, and policymakers with information that can further their understanding and explanation of person identification. Some of this information has come from controlled laboratory experiments, whereas other knowledge is based on incident studies and field investigations, or drawn from case studies and archival records (see Clifford, 1995). Each of these different sources of information is important in its own right and, when compared and contrasted with each other, each addresses the issue of convergent validity (see Davies, 1992; Ellsworth, 1991; Yuille, 1993).

In this chapter I present the results of four recently conducted investigations. Studies 1 and 2 involved a field investigation of eyewitness memory that examined three major issues: (a) a comparison of the accuracy of interrogative (cued) recall and narrative (free) recall descriptions of a culprit's physical appearance; (b) witnesses' accuracy in retrospective duration estimates of an event; and (c) the accuracy of identification in one-person versus six-person lineups as a function of changes in clothing and a 24-hour retention period. Study 3 involved a laboratory investigation of eyewitness and earwitness identification for both voice and movement information. Finally, Study 4 investigated witnesses' collaborative recall and collaborative recognition for a staged videotaped bank robbery. Although collaborative recall and recognition typically are not permitted in

North American courts, existing rules of evidence should not prevent psychological research from being conducted on issues that are inadmissible. It is possible, of course, that the courts and policymakers may be enlightened by the results of such research, and may choose to consider the relevancy of this information at some future time.

STUDY 1: EYEWITNESS RECALL AND DURATION ESTIMATES IN FIELD SETTINGS (YARMEY & YARMEY, 1997)

Witnesses to a crime typically are asked by the police to state what happened and provide descriptions of the culprit(s). These descriptions usually are elicited first by a free narrative followed by cued recall in which witnesses are asked a series of specific questions such as, "What was the person's height? What was his or her weight?" and so on. We know from research done in the first part of the 1900s that witness descriptions of actions and perpetrator's characteristics are generally inaccurate, vague, and incomplete (e.g., Muensterberg, 1908; Stern, 1910). Contemporary findings gathered from laboratory experiments (e.g., Deffenbacher & Horney, 1981; Yarmey, 1986), staged-crime research (e.g., Lindsay, Martin, & Webber, 1994; Wells, Lindsay, & Ferguson, 1979), and case studies (Yuille & Cutshall, 1986) have confirmed this historical evidence. However, except for the few studies that have examined eyewitness reports of actual crimes (e.g., Kuehn, 1974; MacLeod & Shepherd, 1986), and a field study of cued recall (Yarmey, 1993), there is a relative lack of information on descriptive recall of culprits in naturalistic settings (Sporer, 1996). This investigation was part of a program on field experiments in eyewitness identification (see Yarmey, 1993; Yarmey, Yarmey, & Yarmey, 1994).

Age and gender differences in eyewitness descriptions have been found by several investigators (e.g., Kuehn, 1974; MacLeod & Shepherd, 1986; Powers, Andriks, & Loftus, 1979; Yarmey, 1993). In the Yarmey (1993) study, young people between the ages of 18 and 29 were superior to persons between the ages of 30 and 44, who in turn were superior to individuals between the ages of 45 and 65 in cued recall for physical characteristics of a young adult woman. Women proved superior to men on average and, in particular, were superior in recall for the target's weight, hair color, and hair length. One likely reason for gender differences and age differences in recall is the fact that gender-related and age-related stimuli draw attention to different aspects of an event (Powers et al., 1979). Although gender differences in eyewitness recall occur for selected characteristics of culprits and other events, overall general performance is similar for men and women (Powers et al., 1979; Yarmey & Jones, 1983).

Information regarding the accuracy of time-estimation durations can be of particular importance to trial deliberations because it allows for placing of incidents into general and specific periods of time. Furthermore, jurors may attach greater reliability to eyewitness reports of events that last for relatively long periods of time than events that are relatively short. However, the actual duration of most criminal events is seldom known and witnesses' accuracy of duration estimates must be inferred. Except for one staged-crime study (Pigott, Brigham, & Bothwell, 1990) and one field investigation (Yarmey, 1993), most eyewitness studies testing duration estimations have been conducted in laboratory settings using film or videotape (e.g., Loftus, Schooler, Boone, & Kline, 1987; Marshall, 1966), or role playing (e.g., Orchard & Yarmey, 1995; Yarmey & Matthys, 1990). Nevertheless, these different types of investigations have found similar results; that is, duration estimations of simulated crimes lasting approximately 1 minute or less are routinely overestimated, often approaching an overestimation factor of 2.5 to 1, or greater. Furthermore, women have been found to give significantly longer duration estimates than men (Loftus et al., 1987; Yarmey, 1993). The present field investigation attempted to replicate the staged-crime findings of Pigott et al. (1990) who found that witnesses were more accurate in duration estimations when they reconstructed the event first with mental imagery in contrast to simply giving a free response.

Method

Two young White women were used as targets (culprits) and presented in counterbalanced order of presentation across witnesses ($N = 603$). An opportunity sampling method was employed. Targets approached the first White person between the ages of 18 and 65 years to appear in designated areas in public places and asked for directions or for assistance in finding some lost jewelry. The culprits interacted with each witness for approximately 15 seconds while attempting to maintain as much eye contact as possible. Two minutes later, the witness was approached by an investigator and asked to participate in a study on person perception and memory. The two culprits always wore the same color and type of top clothing but varied in other clothing. Both targets had blond, shoulder-length hair, and were similar in weight (115 pounds), height (5 feet 2 inches), and complexion (fair), but differed in eye color (blue vs. green), hair style (straight vs. wavy), and age (23 years old vs. 26 years old).

Half of the witnesses were given a 15-question interrogative test for the target's physical appearance and clothing, and the remainder were asked to freely describe what the target looked like (narrative recall). Participants were asked to rate their overall confidence in their recall on a 7-point scale. Half of each group then was asked to estimate the duration of time spent between the target first speaking to them and turning away to leave. The remainder of witnesses were told to mentally rehearse this same period by imagining the total interaction in their mind's eye as if it were on a videotape, and then to estimate the duration of this event. Finally, all witnesses were asked to rate their confidence in their duration estimation on a 7-point scale.

Results and Discussion

Correct recalls for age of the targets were scored as ± 3 years of actual age, height, ± 2 inches (5.08 cm); weight, ± 5 pounds (2.27 kg); complexion as fair or fair-tan, hair blond and shoulder-length. Target A had wavy hair and blue eyes, and Target B had straight hair and green eyes. Clothing characteristics were scored for accuracy in recall for type of footwear; type, color, and design on top clothing; and type and color of lower clothing. (All significant differences in this study and the other studies reported in this chapter were reliable at $\alpha = .05$.)

Recall for the two targets differed significantly on hair color, hair style, hair length, eye color, age, and weight . These differences suggest that specific target characteristics, even those that were highly similar such as hair color, hair length, and weight can be differentially recalled. All recall differences between targets were for physical characteristics rather than for clothing characteristics.

A comparison of interrogative recall and narrative recall showed no significant differences between men and women. Older persons were inferior to younger persons in recall. Significant negative correlations were found between age and correct interrogative recalls, and age and correct narrative responses. As expected, interrogative recall was substantially more complete than narrative recall. Significantly more correct responses were given with interrogative recall than narrative recall, however, interrogative recall also produced significantly more errors. When scores were combined to give an accuracy index (the total number of correct recalls/total number of responses attempted) narrative recall ($M = 67\%$) proved significantly superior to interrogative recall ($M = 59\%$). Person characteristics were more accurately recalled than clothing characteristics in both types of recall.

Men were significantly more confident than women and narrative responses were given with reliably greater confidence than interrogative reports. No significant correlations were found between age and interrogative recall, or age and narrative recall.

Both men and women overestimated the duration of the 15-second interaction with the culprit, with women (M = 50.48 seconds) giving significantly longer estimates than men (M = 41.77 seconds) in the no-rehearsal condition. However, there were no reliable differences between men (M = 18.30 seconds) and women (M = 13.75 seconds) when duration estimates were preceded by imagery rehearsal. Despite the fact that duration estimates with imagery were relatively accurate, witnesses were significantly less confident in their estimations with imagery rehearsal than they were with no rehearsal. Men were more confident than women in the accuracy of their duration estimates. No significant relations were found between age of witnesses and accuracy of duration estimates, or confidence in accuracy of duration estimates.

In sum, the well-documented finding showing greater accuracy in narrative reports over interrogative reports (e.g., Deffenbacher, 1991) was supported by the present field investigation. Some of the characteristics shared by the two targets were very similar, such as both having blond hair and the same weight. It is possible that witnesses differed in their recall of these characteristics because of differences in stimulus saliency for specific characteristics. It is also possible that differences in social exchanges between targets and witnesses accounted for recall differences. Targets may differ in paralanguage cues and other nonverbal cues that could influence attention. The fact that age of witnesses correlated negatively with accuracy of recall supports the findings of Yarmey (1993). This study also showed that overall levels of recall were comparable for men and women; however, men were more confident in their recall than women. Finally, the results for the no-rehearsal condition were consistent with previous studies that show that short duration events are substantially overestimated (e.g., Loftus et al., 1987). However, the use of imagery-rehearsal strategies appears to facilitate more accurate reports of duration (see Pigott et al., 1990). Witnesses' duration estimates of criminal events can be important to the courts because they permit placing of incidents into time sequences with specific periods of time. Nevertheless, the veridicality of witnesses' estimated durations may be challenged, and the courts must be cautious in their reliance on witnesses' duration estimates.

STUDY 2: ACCURACY OF EYEWITNESS IDENTIFICATIONS IN SHOWUPS AND LINEUPS (YARMEY, YARMEY, & YARMEY, 1996)

One-person lineups or showup confrontations are considered to be highly prejudicial to suspects because the identity of the suspect, regardless of his or her guilt, is obvious (Brooks, 1983; Kassin, Ellsworth, & Smith, 1989; Yarmey et al., 1994). The police may implicitly indicate to the witness that they believe the individual being viewed is the perpetrator. If witnesses believe that police are authorities, and would not conduct a showup unless they were sure that the guilty suspect was present, pressure to validate the showup encounter may be difficult to resist. Furthermore, because the identity of the suspect is obvious, it is difficult to determine whether an identification is made from memory, or merely by deducing which person is believed by the police to be the suspect.

Although these arguments appear persuasive, Gonzalez, Ellsworth, and Pembroke (1993) failed to find greater suggestiveness in showups than in six-person simultaneous lineups. Witnesses were less likely to identify a suspect from a showup than from a lineup even when the culprit was absent from the showup and lineup. The fact that witnesses were more ready to pick a suspect from a lineup than from a showup may suggest that the presence of distracters in lineups encourages identification responses even though they are inaccurate. In contrast, showups may promote greater caution in choosing anyone such that guilty persons are more likely to be missed.

These results do not suggest, however, that showups should be preferred over lineups. Whereas showups have a 50% chance of a misidentification, fair lineups of six or more persons allow false positive responses to be distributed across persons selected to be distracters (Wagenaar & Veefkind, 1992). Furthermore, greater accuracy of identification has been found in six-person simultaneous photo lineups in contrast to photo showups when choices were corrected for guessing (Yarmey et al., 1994). This study also showed that the diagnosticity ratio for identifications was higher in lineups than in showups, suggesting that lineups have more probative value than showups. However, this investigation and that of Gonzalez et al. (1993) tested identification only minutes after the original observation of the culprit.

Judicial attention is given to the length of retention intervals and high credibility is attributed to showup identifications that occur soon after the occurrence of a crime. At least two U.S. courts have indicated that showup confrontations that occur within 30 minutes of an incident contribute to the accuracy of identification (*People v. Brnja*, 1980; *Singletary v. United States*, 1978). Although some showups take place only minutes after a crime, many showups are conducted hours or even days later (Gonzalez et al., 1993). One purpose of this investigation (Part A) was to test photo showup and photo lineup identifications over a 24-hour retention interval.

If police officers locate an individual who fits the general description of the perpetrator in the same geographical area where the crime was committed, eyewitnesses may be brought to a showup confrontation in an "in-field identification" or a "drive-by." The danger, of course, in this type of situation is the chance that an innocent person with similar clothing and similar body build and facial characteristics could be readily misidentified as the guilty suspect. Thus, a second purpose of this investigation was to test whether or not an innocent look-alike suspect dressed in similar or different clothing to that of the culprit is at undue risk for being misidentified in a photo showup in contrast to a photo lineup.

Finally, a separate study (Part B) was conducted investigating accuracy of showup identifications with live suspects. The same research design used in Part A was followed in Part B; however, because of budgetary constraints an investigation of live lineups was not conducted.

Part A: Photo Showups and Lineups

Method. Following the recall stage described in Study 1, identification was tested either immediately (5 minutes), or 30 minutes, or 2 hours, or 24 hours after the initial encounter. Witnesses were assigned randomly to a retention condition with the qualification that testing appointments would be changed to a more convenient time if necessary. Five hundred and sixty-five witnesses were given either a photographic showup or a six-person sequential photographic lineup, and rated their confidence in their decision on a 7-point scale. Witnesses were not told about the total number of photographs they would judge, and the stack of photographs was concealed from the witness' view. If a witness asked to see one or more photographs a second time, all six photographs were presented again in the same sequential order as originally presented. Half of the participants were presented with a target-present lineup and the remainder with a target-absent lineup. In the target-absent condition, the culprit was replaced by a photograph of an innocent look-alike suspect; that is, a woman judged to be highly similar in appearance to the target. At the identification test, half of the witnesses were shown photographs of suspects and distracters wearing exactly the same sweater worn by the culprit during the initial encounter. The remainder were shown photographs of the suspects and distracters dressed in the same sweater, but one that was distinctly different from that worn by the culprit (see Lindsay, Wallbridge, & Drennan, 1987).

In summary, the research design consisted of a 2 (Target 1, Target 2) × 2 (one-person, six-person lineup) × 2 (target-present, target-absent) × 2 (same clothing, different clothing) × 4 (immediate, 30-minute, 2-hour, 24-hour retention interval) between-subjects factorial, with approximately 17 witnesses per cell.

Results and Discussion. No significant differences in identification decisions were found as a function of the two targets and their results were combined in the statistical analysis.

Confidence scores and accuracy scores were combined into a 14-point confidence–accuracy index and analyzed by a 2 (type of lineup) × 2 (target availability) × 2 (clothing) × 4 (retention) analysis of variance (ANOVA). Confidence–accuracy scores were significantly higher in showups than in lineups, and confidence–accuracy declined over time. A significant interaction effect between Lineup × Clothing × Retention Interval revealed that when suspects wore different clothing in the showup from that originally worn by the culprit, confidence–accuracy scores were highest on the immediate test and declined significantly after 2 hours and 24 hours. A significant interaction effect also was found between Target Availability × Clothing × Retention. Confidence–accuracy scores declined significantly over time when the target was present and wore different clothing at the test.

These analyses did not take into account that chance responding in a showup is .50 and in a six-person lineup chance is .17. When identification scores were adjusted for chance, showup identifications (hits) differed significantly from chance on the immediate test (.70), but not on the 30-minute (.64), 2-hour (.54), and 24-hour (.55) retention tests. In contrast, hit scores on the six-person lineups were significantly better than chance at each of the four retention periods (.49, .39, .36, and .32, respectively). Witnesses correctly rejected the innocent suspect in the target-absent showup condition significantly better than chance only on the immediate test (.82, .56, .42, and .47, respectively). In contrast, except for the 30-minute condition, witnesses correctly rejected the six-person target-absent lineup significantly better than chance at each of the other three retention stages (.38, .28, .31, .29, respectively). Clothing of lineup members had no significant effect on decisions in either the target-present or target-absent six-person lineups. In contrast, in the showup condition, an innocent suspect in the target-absent condition was more readily rejected when she was shown in different clothing than that worn by the culprit.

Perhaps one of the most important issues involving showup encounters is whether or not an innocent suspect is at greater risk of being falsely identified in a showup than in a lineup. No significant differences were found in false identifications between showups and lineups on the immediate test (.18 vs. .16), or on the 30-minute test (.44 vs. .33). However, showups, in contrast to lineups, were four times as likely to lead to false identifications of the innocent suspect at the 2-hour (.58 vs. .14) and 24-hour (.53 vs. .14) tests. Furthermore, when results were collapsed across the retention stage, an innocent suspect wearing the same clothing as the culprit was significantly more likely to be falsely identified in a showup than in a lineup.

For showups, a significant correlation between confidence and performance was found only in the target-present condition, $r = .21$. For lineups, significant confidence–performance relations were found in both the target-present ($r = .33$) and target-absent ($r = .30$) conditions. According to Wells and Lindsay (1985), the most appropriate confidence–accuracy relation from a forensic perspective is the correlation between differences in the confidence of witnesses who accurately identified the target in the culprit-present lineup, and those who falsely identified the innocent suspect in the culprit-absent lineup. In the showup the correlation was $r = .17$ (significant), and in the six-person lineup the correlation was $r = .18$ (*ns*). Thus, in both lineups, but significantly so in showups, witnesses were likely to be equally confident in their correct choices of targets and false identifications of innocent suspects.

These results offer no support for the use of showups. This conclusion is further supported by the *diagnosticity index*; that is, the ratio of correct choices when the target's photograph is present versus the incorrect choices when the target's photograph is absent. The higher the diagnosticity ratio, the greater the probative value of identification decisions. The diagnosticity indexes indicated little differences between showups and lineups at or under the 30-minute retention period. However, identification decisions from six-person lineups in contrast to showups were twice as likely to have probative value after a 2-hour retention interval.

Earlier it was stated that witnesses who requested another look at suspects were allowed a "second chance" to review the successive six-person lineup. No significant differences in identification decisions were found on the target-absent lineup ($n = 24$) or the target-present lineup ($n = 22$) for witnesses who had a second look versus those who took only a single opportunity to look at suspect photographs.

In Study 1 witnesses were asked to give either a free description of the culprit or answer 15 questions about her height, weight, and so on. Witnesses were categorized by a median split of accuracy scores into "good" describers and "poor" describers for both narrative and interrogative recall. No significant differences were found between these two categories of witnesses on showup or lineup decisions. These results suggest that identification decisions in showups and in lineups are independent of whether or not witnesses are good or poor in cued recall or free descriptions (see Wells, 1985; Wolfskiel & Brigham, 1985).

In sum, the totality of these findings indicates that eyewitness identification errors following nontraumatic encounters are more likely to occur when police use showups rather than lineups. Furthermore, innocent suspects are put at greater risk of misidentification in showups than in lineups, especially if they are wearing similar clothing to that of the culprit.

Part B: Live Showups

Most showup identifications, especially drive-by identifications, involve witness decisions about a live person rather than a photograph of a suspect. It is possible that witnesses would be more accurate in showups if they were asked to make a decision about a live suspect than a photographed suspect, especially if testing was done soon after the encounter, and clothing was the same at both observation and identification (Cutler & Fisher, 1990).

Method. The procedure for the live study was similar to that used in Part A with two exceptions. Lineups were not conducted. And, in addition to presenting an innocent look-alike suspect, some witnesses were given a target-absent showup involving a dissimilar innocent suspect. This person differed in complexion, hair color, hair style, and facial features from the culprits, but was comparable in age, height, weight, and clothing. If the clothing of a suspect is of primary importance in showup choices, it is possible that an innocent suspect dissimilar to the culprit but dressed in similar clothing could be misidentified, especially after a delay in identification of a few hours.

A 2 (Target 1, Target 2) × 2 (target-present, target-absent) × 2 (same clothing, different clothing) × 4 (immediate, 30-minute, 2-hour, 24-hour retention interval) between-subjects factorial design was employed. Half of the participants saw one of two targets as the culprit. Two types of suspects were used in the target-absent condition, an innocent look-alike suspect and a dissimilar innocent suspect. On signal from the investigator the suspect, who had been hidden from view, walked to within 1.5 m of the witness but did not speak.

Results. Witnesses were extremely accurate (99%) in rejecting the dissimilar innocent suspect at each of the four retention periods. The similarity or difference in clothing worn by this foil compared to the culprit had no effect on decisions. Because performance was nearly perfect with the dissimilar suspect, the remaining analyses focused only on the target and look-alike suspect.

Confidence–accuracy scores were analyzed by a 2 (target availability) × 2 (clothing) × 4 (retention interval) ANOVA. No significant differences were found in the target-present condition. Witnesses in the target-absent condition gave significantly higher scores when the suspect wore different clothing than the same clothing. Witnesses also gave significantly higher confidence–accuracy scores in the target-absent condition than in the target-present condition, but this superiority was restricted to the immediate test.

Significant confidence–accuracy correlations were found in both the target-present ($r = .30$) and target-absent showups ($r = -.23$). The confidence–accuracy correlation between the confidence of witnesses who accurately identified the culprit in the target-present showup and those who falsely identified the innocent look-alike suspect was $r = .34$. Thus, confidence in identification choices of the live culprit and the live innocent suspect were reliably associated.

No significant differences were found in hit scores over the 24-hour retention period. However, in contrast to the immediate test, correct rejections of the innocent look-alike suspect were significantly poorer at the 30-minute, 2-hour, and 24-hour retention tests. Clothing facilitated performance only in the target-absent condition; that is, the innocent suspect was more readily rejected when she wore clothing different from that of the culprit. Witness confidence in performance showed a significant decrement after the immediate test.

The two individuals used as culprits in the photograph portion of this study also were used as the culprits in the live sessions. No significant differences were found in hit scores or in confidence–accuracy scores as a function of the target being presented live or in a photograph. Because different women played the role of innocent look-alike suspect in the live showup and the photographic showup, false identification scores for the two presentation conditions could not be compared with each other.

Conclusion. The use of showup identifications, in contrast to lineups, conducted within a 24-hour retention period following a relatively short low-impact encounter cannot be supported on empirical grounds. Accuracy of identifications from photo lineups was superior to photo showups. Innocent suspects were significantly less likely to be falsely identified in lineups than in the showups, especially over 2-hour and 24-hour retention intervals. Furthermore, false identifications of innocent look-alike suspects were found to be more probable in showups when the suspect was dressed in similar clothing to that worn by the culprit. Accuracy of showup identifications are similar when suspects are presented live or in photographs. Furthermore, witnesses are likely to show similar confidence in their correct choices of targets and incorrect choices of innocent suspects in both live and photo showups.

STUDY 3: PERSON IDENTIFICATION:
MOVEMENT AND VOICE (YARMEY, BERARDI,
& JAKOBI, 1995)

In crimes involving poor lighting or disguise, attention and memory for facial information may be minimal but a perpetrator may still be heard and/or observed moving about. Although voice identification has been studied in both laboratory and field settings (Yarmey, 1994), little attention has been given to person identification as a function of movement (MacLeod, Frowley, & Shepherd, 1994; Yarmey, 1995a). Furthermore, no attention has been given to person identification when the primary perceptual cues are a combination of voice and movement information. The purpose of this experiment was to investigate the effectiveness of bimodal lineup identification based on body movement (gait) and voice information.

Individual differences in gait occur because of the rotation of the shoulders, pelvis, and lower leg, and the motion of the arms (Inman, Ralston, & Todd, 1981). In addition, anthropomorphic features such as body mass, thigh length, calf length, knee diameter, foot length, and foot breadth influence body motion (Vaughan, Davis, & O'Connor, 1992). A series of studies by Cutting and his colleagues (Barclay, Cutting, & Kozlowski, 1978; Cutting & Kozlowski, 1977; Kozlowski & Cutting, 1977) indicate that participants are able to recognize friends and recognize the gender of strangers by their walk. Similarly, the age of a walker can be accurately estimated from his or her movement (Montepare & Zebrowitz-McArthur, 1988). Because body movement remains relatively stable across time and settings (Frey & von Cranach, 1973, cited in Clifford & Bull, 1978), it should be possible to identify individuals as a function of body movement. However, it is still unclear how gait would play a role in lineup identifications of specific unfamiliar individuals.

Witnesses' testimony about the sound of a culprit's voice and identification of that person's voice in a lineup is regarded as direct evidence of identity, and is admissible in courts of law. Consequently, voice identification testimony alone is enough to convict an accused (Hollien & Klepper, 1984; Yarmey, 1995b). In their review of the literature, Bull and Clifford (1984) concluded that "under *ideal* conditions maximal earwitness performance can be quite high (but rarely as high as optimal eyewitness performance)" (p. 123). Contrary to logic, when witnesses can both see a culprit and hear his or her voice, they do not give greater attention to and have better memory for voice information as lighting gets poorer (Yarmey, 1986). Although voice identification has been studied in a variety of contexts such as telephone conversations (Yarmey, 1991) and complex environmental situations involving different amounts of light (Yarmey,

1986), it has not been investigated in conjunction with perpetrators' gait and posture. To my knowledge, this study is the first investigation to address this issue.

Memory has been conceptualized as the reconstruction of fragments of information into organized wholes: As the number of elements are increased at retrieval, memory for that particular event is enhanced (Underwood, 1969; Wickens, 1970). The encoding process involved in eyewitness memory for a perpetrator includes the storage of sensory information, feature and holistic characteristics, and relational information. Both item and relational information are involved in recognition (Humphreys, 1976). Providing witnesses with multiple retrieval cues may promote the reestablishment of the original context and thereby facilitate retrieval (Melara, DeWitt-Rickards, & O'Brien, 1989). Melara et al. (1989) demonstrated that a lineup in which suspects are visually and auditorily observed yielded superior identification than lineups containing only voice information, or only visual information. Similarly, Cutler and Penrod (1988) concluded that lineups containing cues to gait, posture, voice, and full-body views of suspects provide context cues that benefit identification accuracy. However, research on bimodal lineups has explored visual cues mainly in terms of facial information. This investigation investigated eyewitness and earwitness identification in sequential lineups for suspect voices, suspect movement, and bimodal lineups involving suspect voices and movement.

Method

A total of 144 men and women were shown a videotape of one of two culprits committing a 30-second armed robbery in a dimly lit apartment. Participants were instructed to assume the role of victim in the videotape. The perpetrator carried a handgun and wore dark clothing with a hooded sweater and nylon over his face as a disguise. The culprit spoke continuously throughout the episode in a normal conversational tone of voice, and was observed moving with a limp in full view, side view, and back view. A small AA battery was placed in the right shoe of each culprit to cause a limp.

Thirty men served as potential lineup foils. The perpetrators and foils were White and were similar in age, height, weight, and body build. A separate group of 15 judges gave free recall descriptions of the culprits' movement characteristics. The most characteristic descriptions of each of the targets' movements were read to the potential foils. Six foils that were rated moderately similar in movement to each of the targets by a separate group of 10 judges were selected as foils for the target-absent and target-present conditions. The judges also rated 30 voices for their similarity to the targets and six voices rated moderately similar to each of the target's voices were selected as foils.

Twenty-four hours after observing the videotaped crime, witnesses were given a videotape of one of three sequential six-person lineup conditions: a movement lineup in which each individual walked with a limp for 20 seconds giving front, profile, and rear views; a six-person voice lineup in which speakers gave the same neutral passage approximately 20 seconds in length; or a bimodal lineup consisting of both the voice and movement conditions. Test stimuli were presented once and only once in sequence, and witnesses were not told how many stimuli would be given (see Lindsay & Wells, 1985). Witnesses were not forewarned as to the type of lineup modality (target-present or target-absent) they would receive.

Thus, the experiment consisted of a 3 × 2 × 2 between-subjects groups factorial. The independent variables were lineup modality (voice, movement, voice and movement), lineup availability (target-present, target-absent), and target (Perpetrator A, Perpetrator B).

Results

The analysis of results revealed a main effect for targets in both the target-present and target-absent lineups. Ratings from a separate group of judges indicated that Perpetrator B was a more distinctive walker than Perpetrator A. Consequently, separate 2 × 3 analyses with 12 witnesses per cell were conducted for Target A and for Target B. Results were analyzed in terms of hit scores, correct recognitions and misidentifications.

Perpetrator A (Nondistinctive Walker). Accuracy of identification (hits) was significantly better in the bimodal (movement and voice) lineup ($M = .67$) than in the voice lineup ($M = .33$), or in the movement lineup ($M = .08$). There was no significant difference between the latter two lineup conditions. Although the highest number of correct rejections of the target-absent lineup occurred with the bimodal condition, no significant differences were found among the three lineup conditions (overall $M = .61$). Significant positive and negative confidence-accuracy correlations were found but only in the movement condition for the target-present, $r = .59$, and the target-absent, $r = -.59$, lineups. The bimodal lineup also proved to be more diagnostic of identification (2.68) than the voice lineup (1.00) and the movement lineup (0.14).

Perpetrator B (Distinctive Walker). Accuracy of identification was significantly superior in the movement lineup (.50) than in the voice (.08), or in the bimodal (.08) lineups. No significant effects were found in the target-absent lineups. Significant negative confidence–accuracy correlations were found in the target-absent voice lineup, $r = -.63$, and the target-absent bimodal lineup, $r = -.62$. None of the other confidence–accuracy correlations proved significant. The movement condition with Perpetrator B also was more diagnostic of identification (1.50) than the voice condition (0.17) and the bimodal condition (0.14).

Discussion

Identification accuracy of the culprit with a slight but not distinctive limp was relatively high (67% accuracy) when he was both seen and heard in the lineup. However, identification of this individual was relatively low when based only on voice information, and was at chance level of performance when associated with movement alone. These results support the hypothesis that the encoding process involves the storage of relational information over and above individual item information (Humphreys, 1976). If the encoding and storage stages of memory are involved in the storage of relational information, the best retrieval cues are multiple sensory modality cues that operate to reinstate the original context of the event. In contrast, identification decisions for the culprit with a relatively distinctive gait were accurate when identification was based solely on the suspect's movements. This finding supports Smith's (1988) "outshining" hypothesis, which suggests that if a stimulus is very salient its memorial representations will outshine any additional contextual cues presented. The fact that bimodal presentation of the voice and movement of a person with a relatively distinctive gait produced a very high number of misidentifications suggests that the auditory modality (voice information) may interfere with the visual modality (movement information) when the visual channel is preferred in eyewitnessing (see McAllister, Dale, Bregman, McCabe, & Cotton, 1993; Yarmey, 1986). It should also be noted that confidence was not related to accuracy of identification for a culprit with a distinctive gait.

This study suggests that police must consider the distinctiveness of a suspect's movements when deciding to conduct bimodal or single-modality lineups. Support was found for both the interaction and the interference hypotheses of memory, depending on the presence or absence of distinctive movement in the perpetrator. The issue of perpetrator distinctiveness of movement appears to be an important factor in identification involving disguise and poor observation conditions. If the results of the present investigation are general, it is recommended that when suspects have distinctive gaits that identification be limited to presentations of single-modality lineups.

STUDY 4: THE EFFECTS OF DYADIC DISCUSSION ON RECALL AND RECOGNITION (YARMEY & MORRIS, 1995)

Prior to the arrival of police at the scene of a traffic accident or crime, it is highly probable that witnesses discuss the incident and /or perpetrator characteristics. Once police arrive at the scene they may fail to separate witnesses prior to gathering evidence, they may fail to instruct witnesses to refrain from discussing the event with each other, or they may interview a witness in the presence of other witnesses.

Because many people will discuss an interesting event if given an opportunity, eyewitness testimony in many cases cannot have an independent basis free of possible contamination from others. If this is the case, are there any benefits in allowing witnesses to give collaborative testimony; that is, the cooperative preparation of a single record of what was observed by two or more persons? This study attempted to answer this question by an investigation of collaborative dyadic recall and collaborative dyadic recognition memory for a simulated bank robbery.

In most adversarial systems of law it is argued that identification evidence should have an independent basis in perception and memory in order for due process to occur. However, in England, collaborative reports are allowed providing the court is warned that testimony is based on collaboration (Heaton-Armstrong, 1987). This practice most frequently occurs with police officers who may jointly prepare an evidentiary report of an incident. One officer will give evidence at trial on behalf of all the officers involved in the case.

A series of studies by Stephenson and his colleagues indicated that when two or more people jointly recall and discuss an event they have witnessed, groups were more accurate, more complete, and more consistent in their testimony than individuals. Groups also made fewer evaluative comments regarding the principle actors involved in an incident. However, groups were more prone to have a misplaced overconfidence in inaccurate recall than individuals. Although collaborative testimony from a dyad will be more comprehensive and factually correct than from a single individual, Stephenson concluded that witnesses should be interrogated separately after joint recall and discussion in order to maximize the information available to the interrogator and to minimize misplaced overconfidence (Clark & Stephenson, 1989; Clark, Stephenson, & Kniveton, 1990; Stephenson, 1990; Stephenson, Brandstaetter, & Wagner, 1983; Stephenson, Clark, & Kniveton, 1989; Stephenson, Clark, & Wade, 1986; Stephenson & Wagner, 1989).

Other studies on collaborative testimony have yielded inconsistent findings regarding the effects of collaboration on eyewitness reports (Alper,

Buckhout, Chern, Harwood, & Slomovits, 1976; Hollin & Clifford, 1983; Underwood & Milton, 1993; Warnick & Sanders, 1980). An investigation of the effects of collaborative recall for information overheard from a telephone conversation during a simulated kidnapping study showed that accuracy of recall following dyadic discussion and joint recall was not significantly different from individuals' reconstructions of the incident (Yarmey, 1992). However, joint recall was more consistent and concise, and produced more conventional accounts than that of individual recalls. Also, significantly more fabrications were found in dyadic discussion groups with individual recall than in the recalls of dyadic discussion groups with joint recall, and participants giving individual recall. Yarmey (1992) concluded that the deleterious effects on recall of dyadic discussion between witnesses are minimized by a collaborative response.

With the exception of a study by Warnick and Sanders (1980), there has been no published research on collaborative recognition memory for criminal events. Warnick and Sanders (1980) failed to find any significant differences on hit scores in a simultaneous target-present lineup between a group–individual condition (participants discussed the incident and then responded individually), a group–consensus condition, and an individual condition. In order to further address the issue of collaborative recall and recognition memory a laboratory experiment involving a videotaped staged crime was conducted. The videotape was produced by John Yuille at the University of British Columbia.

Method

A total of 164 female introductory psychology students watched a 27-second videotape of a simulated bank robbery in groups of up to six persons. After watching the tape, witnesses were randomly divided into four experimental conditions and assigned to separate cubicles for 10 minutes (filler task). The four treatment conditions consisted of: (a) collaborative dyads; that is, two witnesses who discussed the criminal incident for 10 minutes and gave joint responses; (b) dyadic crime discussion–individual responses; that is, two witnesses who discussed the criminal incident but gave individual responses; (c) dyadic neutral discussion–individual responses; that is, two witnesses who were instructed to discuss anything but the criminal incident during their interaction and responded individually; and (d) individual witnesses who were instructed to privately think about the incident for 10 minutes and, of course, responded individually. Following the filler task, half of the participants in each condition were excused and asked to return 7 days later for some related tasks. The remaining participants (immediate recall condition) were asked to write a report on everything they could remember about the perpetrator's characteristics, actions, and statements as if they were giving a statement to the police. These participants were then excused and asked to return in 7 days for some related tasks. All participants were asked to refrain from discussing the crime with anyone during the retention interval. When participants returned to the laboratory, the two crime-dyadic conditions discussed the incident for 5 minutes, the neutral-dyad groups discussed neutral topics, and participants in the individual condition sat alone and were asked to think about the crime. Participants in the delayed recall condition then completed their written description of the culprit. All participants were then given a six-person target-absent photographic lineup presented either simultaneously in a photospread or presented individually in a sequential order (Lindsay & Wells, 1985). Witnesses also rated their confidence in recognition on a 5-point Likert scale. The lineup consisted of six innocent suspects. Five of the suspects were rated by 10 independent judges to be moderately similar in appearance to the culprit, and one was rated to be highly similar in appearance to the culprit.

Results

Recall.   Participants' written narrative recalls of the perpetrator's characteristics, actions, and statements were compared against a standard coding system established by 10 independent judges who repeatedly viewed the videotape. An independent judge blind as to treatment condition scored each report in terms of number of words written; number of accurate propositions (i.e., descriptions of suspect characteristics, actions, and statements); conciseness, or number of words divided by the number of correct propositions; fabrications or errors of commission; and metastatements, or propositions that attributed motives or intentions to the suspect that were not specified in the incident.

The longest reports, regardless of their accuracy, were written by participants in the dyadic crime discussion–individual response condition. These reports were significantly longer than the reports written by the neutral-discussion dyads who wrote individual responses. The collaborative dyads and the crime discussion–individual response groups were significantly superior to both the neutral-discussion dyads and the individual responders in the number of correct propositions recorded. Significantly more correct propositions were given on the immediate test in contrast to the 1-week delayed test, but there was no significant interaction between the treatment conditions and retention period. No significant differences were found among the four experimental groups in the conciseness of their reports, or on the number of fabrications produced. However, all groups were more concise on the immediate test than on the delayed test. Finally, significantly more metastatements were made by collaborative dyads and crime-discussion dyads in contrast to the neutral-discussion dyads and individuals who did not discuss the crime. Metastatements refer to witness-derived attributions of the culprit's motives or intentions and are a type of error that could have implications for subsequent testimony and confidence.

Recognition. All witnesses were given a target-absent lineup 1 week after observing the bank robbery. Responses were scored in terms of correct rejections of the lineup, false identifications of the innocent suspect, and foil identifications of the five other distracters. An analysis of correct rejections revealed that the collaborative dyads were significantly more accurate ($M = 0.84$) in their joint rejections of the lineup than the other three groups who gave individual recognition responses (crime-discussion dyads, $M = 0.56$; neutral-discussion dyads, $M = 0.50$; and single witnesses, $M = 0.50$). Reliably more correct rejections were found with successive lineups than with simultaneous lineups, but the interaction between treatment groups and lineup presentations was not significant. Very few false identifications were made of the innocent suspect, and no significant differences were found across group conditions or lineup presentations. However, simultaneous lineups, in contrast to successive lineups, produced significantly more foil identifications of distracters.

Confidence. None of the correlations between confidence scores and correct rejections was significant as a function of experimental groups on either the successive or simultaneously presented lineups.

Discussion

The results of this study support the conclusion that discussion between witnesses can facilitate performance in some circumstances. Both the collaborative dyads and the crime-discussion dyads were significantly more accurate in recall of perpetrator characteristics than dyads who did not discuss the incident, and individual participants. Furthermore, the claim that witnesses who discuss an incident invariably produce more fabrications than those who do not discuss an event was not supported. Note, however, unlike studies of the misinformation effect (e.g., Loftus, 1992), participants were not misled; that is, they were not exposed to erroneous postevent misinformation, or interviewed with leading questions. It is possible that because participants were encouraged to be as accurate as possible, and were prepared to attend closely to the bank robber in a nonthreatening social situation, that fabrications were minimized across experimental conditions. Also, recall was tested either immediately or 1 week after observation of the crime, which would minimize the opportunity for related events to have intervened between observation and recall. Nevertheless, collaborative dyads and crime-discussion dyads did produce a greater number of metastatements than the other two conditions.

Collaborative dyads were superior to the three other conditions in their correct rejections of the target-absent lineup. However, this performance was not associated with higher confidence in recognition decisions. If these findings are general, and are considered in association with the results of Warnick and Sanders (1980), collaborative dyads do not produce greater accuracy in lineup identifications but, at the same time, they minimize the likelihood of false alarms relative to the other experimental conditions.

Following Bartlett (1932), the advantage of dyadic discussion of an incident may rest in the fact that memory is a social activity, and witnesses can anchor their constructions against mutual checks and balances. Dyadic recalls are semipublic constructions that are actively examined for misrepresentations. Dyadic individuals may feel accountable to their partner immediately after the incident and at the test, and may use each other for purposes of validation, refutation, and elaboration, as well as to supplement what each other already knows about such incidents (Clark & Stephenson, 1989; Meudell, Hitch, & Boyle, 1995; Meudell, Hitch, & Kirby, 1992).

Should evidence gathered by collaborative recall and recognition be considered by the police, and should it be admissible in court? This study suggests that collaborative testimony may be beneficial to the police in some circumstances. For example, collaborative dyads may be useful to criminal investigations if, as this study showed, pairs of witnesses are highly likely to correctly reject a target-absent lineup. However, it is inappropriate to generalize the results of a single laboratory-based study without testing the limits of such generalizations. Other research, for example, suggests that dyads tend to give schematic or conventional accounts that lead to the loss of other potentially important details (Yarmey, 1992). Joint recall also has been found to produce misplaced witness confidence that may lead to misrepresentations of evidence (Stephenson, 1990). In my opinion, joint testimony should be regarded at this time as an investigative tool rather than as evidence of proof.

CONCLUSION

Empirical and theoretical understandings of proper procedures for gathering identification evidence should continue to occupy the attention of eyewitness researchers. Although front-line researchers do not need to be reminded of the obvious, empirical evidence and theoretical explanations for all types of person memory including faces, actions, clothing, voices, movement, and other individual, relational, and situational characteristics are far from complete. Psycholegal research on eyewitness evidence should not be limited only to those factors that are admissible in courts of law. As Study 4 indicated, discussion between witnesses can facilitate the accuracy of eyewitness recall and recognition in some circumstances. It is likely that most North American courts would consider such identification evidence to be inadmissible at the present time because it lacked "independent basis" in perception. Nevertheless, what the courts allow or admit as evidence in the future may be influenced by the replicable, empirical findings of contemporary research.

ACKNOWLEDGMENT

This research was supported by a grant from the Social Sciences and Humanities Research Council of Canada (#410-94-1546).

REFERENCES

Alper, A., Buckhout, R., Chern, S., Harwood, R., & Slomovits, M. (1976). Eyewitness identification: Accuracy of individual vs. composite recollections of a crime. *Bulletin of the Psychonomic Society, 8,* 147–149.

Barclay, C. D., Cutting, J. E., & Kozlowski, L. T. (1978). Temporal and spatial factors in gait perception that influence gender recognition. *Perception and Psychophysics, 23,* 145–152.

Bartlett, F. C. (1932). *Remembering: A study in experimental and social psychology.* Cambridge, UK: Cambridge University Press.

Brooks, N. (1983). *Police guidelines: Pretrial eyewitness identification procedures.* Ottawa, Ontario: Law Reform Commission of Canada.

Bull, R., & Clifford, B. R. (1984). Earwitness voice recognition accuracy. In G. L. Wells & E. F. Loftus (Eds.), *Eyewitness testimony: Psychological perspectives* (pp. 92–123). New York: Cambridge University Press.

Clark, N. K., & Stephenson, G. M. (1989). Group remembering. In P. B. Paulus (Ed.), *Psychology of group influence: New perspectives* (pp. 357–391). Hillsdale, NJ: Lawrence Erlbaum Associates.

Clark, N. K., Stephenson, G. M., & Kniveton, B. H. (1990). Social remembering: Quantitative aspects of individual and collaborative remembering by police officers and students. *British Journal of Psychology, 81,* 73–94.

Clifford, B. R. (1995). Psychology's premises, methods and values. In R. Bull & D. Carson (Eds.), *Handbook of psychology in legal contexts* (pp. 13–27). Chichester, UK: Wiley.

Clifford, B. R., & Bull, R. (1978). *The psychology of person identification.* London: Routledge & Kegan Paul.

Cutler, B. L., & Fisher, R. P. (1990). Live lineups, videotaped lineups, and photoarrays.

Forensic Reports, 3, 439–448.

Cutler, B. L., & Penrod, S. D. (1988). Improving the reliability of eyewitness identification: Lineup construction and presentation. *Journal of Applied Psychology, 73,* 281–290.

Cutting, J., & Kozlowski, L. T. (1977). Recognizing friends by their walk: Gait perception without familiarity cues. *Bulletin of the Psychonomic Society, 9,* 353–356.

Davies, G. M. (1992). Influencing public policy in eyewitnessing: problems and possibilities. In F. Loesel, D. Bender, & T. Bliesener (Eds.), *Psychology and law: International perspectives* (pp. 265–274). Berlin: de Gruyter.

Deffenbacher, K. A. (1991). A maturing of research on the behaviour of eyewitnesses. *Applied Cognitive Psychology, 5,* 377–402.

Deffenbacher, K., & Horney, J. (1981). Psycho-legal aspects of face identification. In G. Davies, H. Ellis, & J. Shepherd (Eds.), *Perceiving and remembering faces* (pp. 221–226). London: Academic Press.

Ellsworth, P. C. (1991). To tell what we know or wait for Godot? *Law and Human Behavior, 17,* 77–90.

Gonzalez, R., Ellsworth, P. C., & Pembroke, M. (1993). Response biases in lineups and showups. *Journal of Personality and Social Psychology, 64,* 525–537.

Heaton-Armstrong, A. (1987). Police officers' notebooks: Recent developments. *Criminal Law Review,* 470–472.

Hollien, H., & Klepper, B. (1984). The speaker identification problem. *Advances in Forensic Psychology and Psychiatry, 1,* 87–111.

Hollin, C. R., & Clifford, B. R. (1983). Eyewitness testimony: The effects of discussion on recall accuracy and agreement. *Journal of Applied Social Psychology, 13,* 234–244.

Humphreys, M. S. (1976). Relational information and the context effect in recognition memory. *Memory and Cognition, 4,* 221–232.

Inman, V. T., Ralston, H. J., & Todd, F. (1981). *Human walking.* Baltimore: Williams & Wilkins.

Kassin, S. M., Ellsworth, P. C., & Smith, V. L. (1989). The "general acceptance" of psychological research on eyewitness testimony: A survey of the experts. *American Psychologist, 46,* 1089–1098.

Kozlowski, L. T., & Cutting, J. E. (1977). Recognizing the sex of walkers from a dynamic point-light display. *Perception and Psychophysics, 21,* 575–580.

Kuehn, L. L. (1974). Looking down a gun barrel: Person perception and violent crime. *Perceptual and Motor Skills, 39,* 1159–1164.

Lindsay, R. C. L., Martin, R., & Webber, L. (1994). Default values in eyewitness descriptions: A problem for the match-to-description lineup foil selection strategy. *Law and Human Behavior, 18,* 527–541.

Lindsay, R. C. L., Wallbridge, H., & Drennan, D. (1987). Do the clothes make the man? An exploration of the effect of lineup attire on eyewitness identification accuracy. *Canadian Journal of Behavioural Science, 19,* 463–478.

Lindsay, R. C. L., & Wells, G. L. (1985). Improving eyewitness identifications from lineups: Simultaneous versus sequential lineup presentation. *Journal of Applied Psychology, 70,* 556–564.

Loftus, E. F. (1992). When a lie becomes memory's truth: Memory distortion after exposure to misinformation. *Current Directions in Psychological Science, 1,* 121–123.

Loftus, E. F., Schooler, J. W., Boone, S. M., & Kline, D. (1987). Time went by so slowly: Overestimation of event duration by males and females. *Applied Cognitive Psychology, 1,* 3–13.

MacLeod, M. D., Frowley, J. N., & Shepherd, J. W. (1994). Whole body information: Its relevance to eyewitnesses. In D. Ross, J. D. Read, & M. P. Toglia (Eds.), *Adult eyewitness testimony: Current trends and developments* (pp. 125–143). Cambridge, UK: Cambridge University Press.

MacLeod, M. D., & Shepherd, J. W. (1986). Sex differences in eyewitness reports of criminal assaults. *Medical Science and Law, 26,* 311–318.

Marshall, J. (1966). *Law and psychology in conflict.* New York: Bobbs-Merrill.

McAllister, H. A., Dale, R. H. I., Bregman, N. J., McCabe, A., & Cotton, C. R. (1993). When eyewitnesses are also earwitnesses: Effects on visual and voice identifications. *Basic and Applied Social Psychology, 14,* 161–170.

Melara, R. D., DeWitt-Rickards, T. S., & O'Brien, T. P. (1989). Enhancing lineup identification accuracy: Two codes are better than one. *Journal of Applied Psychology, 74,* 706–713.

Meudell, P. R., Hitch, G. J., & Boyle, M. M. (1995). Collaboration in recall: Do pairs of people cross-cue each other to produce new memories? *Quarterly Journal of Experimental Psychology, 48A,* 141–152.

Meudell, P. R., Hitch, G. J., & Kirby, P. (1992). Are two heads better than one? Experimental investigations of the social facilitation of memory. *Applied Cognitive Psychology, 6,* 525–543.

Montepare, J. M., & Zebrowitz-McArthur, L. (1988). Impressions of people created by age-related qualities of their gaits. *Journal of Personality and Social Psychology, 55,* 547–556.

Muensterberg, H. (1908). *On the witness stand.* Garden City, NY: Doubleday.

Orchard, T. L., & Yarmey, A. D. (1995). The effects of whispers, voice-sample duration, and voice distinctiveness on criminal speaker identification. *Applied Cognitive Psychology, 9,* 249–260.

People v. Brnja, 70 A.D.2d. 17, 419 N.Y.S.2d 591 (1979), aff'd, 50 N.Y.2d 366, 40 N.E.2d 1066, 429 N.Y.S.2d 173 (1980).

Pigott, M. A., Brigham, J. C., & Bothwell, R. K. (1990). A field study on the relationship between quality of eyewitnesses' descriptions and identification accuracy. *Journal of Police Science and Administration, 17,* 84–88.

Powers, P. A., Andriks, J. L., & Loftus, E. F. (1979). Eyewitness accounts of females and males. *Journal of Applied Psychology, 64,* 339–347.

Singletary v. United States, 383 A.2d 1064 (D.C. 1978).

Smith, S. (1988). Environment context-dependent memory. In G. Davies & D. Thompson (Eds.), *Memory in context: Context in memory* (pp. 13–34). Chichester, UK: Wiley.

Sporer, S. L. (1996). Psychological aspects of person descriptions. In S. L. Sporer, R. S. Malpass, & G. Koehnken (Eds.), *Psychological issues in eyewitness identification* (pp. 53–86). Mahwah, NJ: Lawrence Erlbaum Associates.

Stephenson, G. M. (1990). Should collaborative testimony be permitted in courts of law? *Criminal Law Review,* 302–314.

Stephenson, G. M., Brandstaetter, H., & Wagner, W. (1983). An experimental study of social performance and delay on the testimonial validity of story recall. *European Journal of Social Psychology, 13,* 175–191.

Stephenson, G. M., Clark, N. K., & Kniveton, B. H. (1989). Collaborative testimony by police officers: A psycho-legal issue. In H. Wegener, F. Loesel, & J. Haisch (Eds.), *Criminal behavior and the justice system: Psychological perspectives* (pp. 254–270). New York: Springer-Verlag.

Stephenson, G. M., Clark, N. K., & Wade, G. S. (1986). Meetings make evidence? An experimental study of collaborative and individual recall of a simulated police interrogation. *Journal of Personality and Social Psychology, 50,* 1113–1122.

Stephenson, G. M., & Wagner, W. (1989). Origins of the misplaced confidence effect in collaborative recall. *Applied Cognitive Psychology, 3,* 227–236.

Stern, L. W. (1910). Abstracts of lectures on the psychology of testimony on the study of individuality. *American Journal of Psychology, 21,* 270–282.

Underwood, B. J. (1969). Attributes of memory. *Psychological Review, 76,* 559–573.

Underwood, G., & Milton, H. (1993). Collusion after a collision: Witnesses' reports of a road accident with and without discussion. *Applied Cognitive Psychology, 7,* 11–22.

Vaughan, C. L., Davis, B. L., & O'Connor, J. C. (1992). *Dynamics of human gait*. Champaign, IL: Human Kinetics.

Wagenaar, W. A., & Veefkind, N. (1992). Comparison of one-person and many-person lineups: A warning against unsafe practices. In F. Losel, D. Bender, & T. Bliesener (Eds.), *Psychology and law: International perspectives* (pp. 275-285). Berlin: de Gruyter.

Warnick, D. H., & Sanders, G. S. (1980). The effects of group discussion on eyewitness accuracy. *Journal of Applied Social Psychology, 10,* 249-259.

Wells, G. L. (1985). Verbal descriptions of faces from memory: Are they diagnostic of identification accuracy? *Journal of Applied Psychology, 70,* 619-626.

Wells, G. L., & Lindsay, R. C. L. (1985). Methodological notes on the confidence-accuracy relationship in eyewitness identifications. *Journal of Applied Psychology, 70,* 413-419.

Wells, G. L., Lindsay, R. C. L., & Ferguson, T. J. (1979). Accuracy, confidence, and juror perceptions in eyewitness identification. *Journal of Applied Psychology, 64,* 440-448.

Wickens, D. D. (1970). Encoding categories of words: An empirical approach to meaning. *Psychological Review, 77,* 1-15.

Wolfskiel, M. P., & Brigham, J. C. (1985). The relationship between accuracy of prior descriptions and facial recognition. *Journal of Applied Psychology, 70,* 547-555.

Yarmey, A. D. (1986). Verbal, visual, and voice identification of a rape suspect under different levels of illumination. *Journal of Applied Psychology, 71,* 363-370.

Yarmey, A. D. (1991). Voice identification over the telephone. *Journal of Applied Social Psychology, 21,* 1868-1876.

Yarmey, A. D. (1992). The effects of dyadic discussion on earwitness recall. *Basic and Applied Social Psychology, 13,* 251-263.

Yarmey, A. D. (1993). Adult age and gender differences in eyewitness recall in field settings. *Journal of Applied Social Psychology, 23,* 1921-1932.

Yarmey, A. D. (1994). Earwitness evidence: Memory for a perpetrator's voice. In D. Ross, J. D. Read, M. P. Toglia (Eds.), *Adult eyewitness testimony: Current trends and developments* (pp. 101-124). Cambridge, UK: Cambridge University Press.

Yarmey, A. D. (1995a). Earwitness and evidence obtained by other senses. In R. Bull & D. Carson (Eds.), *Handbook of psychology in legal contexts* (pp. 262-273). Chichester, UK: Wiley.

Yarmey, A. D. (1995b). Earwitness speaker identification. *Psychology, Public Policy, and Law, 1,* 792-816.

Yarmey, A. D., Berardi, N., & Jakobi, A. C. (1995). *Person identification: Movement and voice* Unpublished manuscript, University of Guelph, Guelph, Ontario, Canada.

Yarmey, A. D., & Jones, H. P. T. (1983). Accuracy of memory of male and female eyewitnesses to a criminal assault and rape. *Bulletin of the Psychonomic Society, 21,* 89-92.

Yarmey, A. D., & Matthys, E. (1990). Retrospective duration estimates of an abductor's speech. *Bulletin of the Psychonomic Society, 28,* 231-234.

Yarmey, A. D., & Morris, S. (1995). *The effects of dyadic discussion on eyewitness recall and recognition.* Unpublished manuscript, University of Guelph, Guelph, Ontario, Canada.

Yarmey, A. D., & Yarmey, M. J. (1997). Eyewitness recall and duration estimates in field settings. *Journal of Applied Social Psychology, 27,* 330-344.

Yarmey, A. D., Yarmey, A. L., & Yarmey, M. J. (1994). Face and voice identifications in showups and lineups. *Applied Cognitive Psychology, 8,* 453-464.

Yarmey, A. D., Yarmey, M. J., & Yarmey, A. L. (1996). Accuracy of eyewitness identifications in showups and lineups. *Law and Human Behavior 20,* 459-477.

Yuille, J. C. (1993). We must study forensic eyewitnesses to know about them. *American Psychologist, 48,* 572-573.

Yuille, J. C., & Cutshall, J. (1986). A case study of eyewitness memory of a crime. *Journal of Applied Psychology, 71,* 291-301.

8

The Impact of Traumatic Events on Eyewitness Memory

John C. Yuille
Judith Daylen
University of British Columbia

The effect on memory of experiencing a traumatic event is of great import to researchers interested in studying eyewitness memory in the forensic context. Individuals who witness criminal events or who are themselves victims of criminal activity, such as robbery or sexual assault, are often traumatized by these experiences, and there is evidence to suggest that their trauma may have memorial consequences. In this chapter, we explore the complexities of the relationship between trauma and memory. We begin with an overview of the literature that examines the impact of stress on memory. We suggest that a fuller understanding of the effects of traumatic events on a victim/witness's memory can be gained by increasing cooperation between eyewitness researchers and those working more directly with actual victims of crime (e.g., clinicians). We also present a proposed framework for the study of the impact of trauma on eyewitness memory. The framework deals with (a) how the nature of the original event affects memory and (b) changes in memory over time. This framework yields a taxonomy of the varying qualities of eyewitness recall that includes six behavioral/emotive/cognitive patterns of eyewitness memory.

EYEWITNESS RESEARCH OF THE IMPACT
OF STRESS ON MEMORY[1]

The relationship between witnessing a traumatic event and reporting one's memory of that event has been of interest to numerous eyewitness researchers since the study of eyewitness memory began almost a century ago in Europe. The early spate of eyewitness research has been labeled the *Aussage Period* (e.g., Cutshall, 1985), reflecting the German dominance of the field early in this century. *Aussage* (a German word for testimony) research demonstrated twin emphases on the experimental method and the application of its results to the "real world" (in this case, the courts). The characteristic *Aussage* study was the so-called "reality experiment" in which a striking event, often patterned after a crime, was staged before a group of people. For instance, in one study, conducted in 1902 by von Listz (reported in Munsterberg, 1908), a university lecture was interrupted by an argumentative student (actually a stooge of the experimenter) who drew a gun and fired a shot into the air. The observers (students in the classroom) were immediately asked to recount all that they could remember about the incident. In the *Aussage* period and in later research, trauma was typically manipulated in this fashion, not by directly threatening the subjects but by manipulating the stress level presumed to be induced by the event.

Although very little *Aussage* research dealt directly with the effects of stress, results from the von Listz "reality experiment" just recounted, showed that the second part of the written reports, which pertained to the more strongly emotional aspects of the event, contained 15% more errors than the first part of the report. Whipple (1915) reported that research conducted by Kobler in 1914 suggested that excitement improved observation and memory of witnesses up to a given point (which varied for different persons) and impaired performance beyond that point. From such scanty research findings, *Aussage* psychologists were unable to make any conclusive statements about the impact of stress on testimony; however, stress was

---

[1]Most of the eyewitness literature has used the term *stress* to refer to an aroused emotional state presumably engendered by particular stimuli (e.g., viewing an enacted crime). *Stress* is a very broad category that encompasses a wide range of responses, including mild arousal, low-level anxiety, and abject terror (although the latter is rarely, if ever, generated in laboratory studies). Not surprisingly, the wide ranging degrees of arousal encompassed by the term *stress* have resulted in conceptual confusion in the eyewitness literature. To address this issue, in this chapter we use the term *trauma* to refer to a more narrow range of responses—those representing extreme stress—that are presumably engendered by high intensity or catastrophic events (see discussion below). Although the conceptual problems inherent in the study of stress responses are not solved by this shift in terminology, they become somewhat more circumscribed and, in our opinion, more relevant to the forensic context.

generally considered by *Aussage* researchers to have a negative rather than a positive effect on witness' testimony.

The mixed pattern of results found in the *Aussage* research concerning the impact of stress on eyewitness memory has proven to be an enduring characteristic of this area of eyewitness research. For example, consider the confusing pattern of results found in a review of more recent studies of the relationship between stress and eyewitness memory. In Deffenbacher's (1983) review of 21 studies examining the impact of stress on eyewitness memory, he found that the results of 10 of the studies suggested that stress either increases eyewitness accuracy or has no effect, whereas the findings from 11 studies led to the conclusion that stress decreases eyewitness accuracy.

One possible explanation for these contradictory results relates to differences in the methodology employed in these studies. Of the 10 studies that reported a facilitative or neutral effect of stress on memorial accuracy, the majority involved staged live events similar to that pioneered by von Listz. Of the 11 studies suggesting that arousal or stress decreases memorial accuracy, only 1 study employed a live event. The remainder of these studies manipulated stress indirectly or vicariously; for example, by exposing the "witness" to white noise during the to-be-remembered event. Thus, the diversity of findings pertaining to the relationship between stress and eyewitness memory may reflect, at least in part, differences in the types of stressors employed by various experimenters to manipulate subjects' experience of "stress."

To further illustrate this problem, consider the following examples of two specific types of stressors used in eyewitness studies to generate stress in subjects performing memorial tasks. One type of study induced arousal in the witnesses by applying white noise (a loud hiss presented via earphones) or an electric shock. When "stress" is generated by these means, the source of the stress is completely independent of the event to be remembered. One of the things we have learned about stress is that it tends to focus attention (e.g., Easterbrook, 1959; Eysenck, 1982; Loftus, 1979; Mandler, 1975). That is, as one becomes stressed, his or her attention tends to narrow to focus on either the cause of the stress and/or on the effects of the stress. Thus, studies that use a stressor that is external to the eyewitness event are actually studies of unpleasant distracters rather than studies of the effects of witnessing or experiencing a stressful event such as a criminal act.

Another example of the stressor problem in the eyewitness literature is found in the many studies that have employed films as stimuli (e.g., Clifford & Hollin, 1981; Clifford & Scott, 1978; Loftus & Burns, 1982). In this type of research a witness's stress is assumed to be manipulated by the content of the film. Thus, some subjects may be shown a film with a gun shooting at the end of the film (stressful condition), whereas others view the same film without the shooting scene (control condition). It is astonishingly naive of psychologists to believe that most undergraduates would find the content of such films stressful. Most North Americans see so many shootings and other violence in movies and on television that they become inured to filmed violence. Myers (1990) reported that by high school graduation the average American has witnessed about 25,000 violent deaths on television and in films. Studies that employ such films as stimuli generally bear no relationship to the impact of real-life violence or threatened violence on victims of crime. As Christianson (1992a) noted in a recent review, "it may be that inconsistencies in empirical findings reflect differences in the to-be-remembered (TBR) detail information and testing circumstances" (p. 308).

The foregoing examples underscore one of the central problems in research attempting to study the memorial effects of witnessing a traumatic event: How do we conceptualize, define, and operationalize the stress experienced by eyewitnesses of traumatic events? Defining stress on the basis of presentation of relatively innocuous stimuli, such as white noise or filmed violence, has not been effective. Subjects' self-reports of stress may not correlate with the experimenters' manipulation of arousal (e.g., Brigham, Maass, Martinez, & Whittenberger, 1983). Attempts at providing more objective measurements of stress, such as physiological measures, have also met with little success (e.g., Brigham et al., 1983). Perusal of the research literature in related, relevant fields of psychology indicate that these types of difficulties are not unique to the eyewitness literature. In the voluminous stress and coping literature, there is an ongoing debate about how to measure stress. One approach focuses on the objective measurement of specific stressors or life events (e.g., divorce, birth of a child, death of a loved one) that are assumed to engender significant degrees of stress in those who experience them (e.g., Dohrenwend & Shrout, 1985; Holmes & Rahe, 1967). The other, more dominant approach in the current literature proposes a more subjective, cognitive-relational view of stress: The stress engendered by a particular event is cognitively mediated and differs according to the appraised significance of the event and the person's coping resources and styles (e.g., Lazarus, 1966; Lazarus & Folkman, 1984; see *Psychological Inquiry*, 1990, Vol. 1, pp. 3–51, for a lively discussion of these issues, with a lead article by Richard Lazarus and responses by prominent researchers in the field). The former view defines stress as a reaction to objective, environmental events; the latter view defines stress as a subjective appraisal of a misfit between environment demands and personal resources. Interestingly, eyewitness researchers, schooled in cognitive psychology, have generally adhered to a variant of the more objective, life-events approach to stress rather than focusing on the cognitively mediated aspects of the stress process emphasized by Lazarus and his colleagues. From our reading of the literature, it is clear that subjective appraisals of stressors (based on beliefs, values, past experience, personality traits, coping capacity, etc.) affect a person's experience of stress and should, therefore, be taken into account in studies pertaining to stress (even supporters of life-event measurement acknowledge the importance of taking into account individual differences; e.g., Dohrenwend & Shrout, 1985). In particular, subjective appraisals seem to be especially relevant in regard to less catastrophic, more every day kind of stressors or hassles (e.g., arguments) that are often employed in laboratory eyewitness research.

On the other hand, there do appear to be categories of events that are almost universally experienced as being stressful. For example, there is now a large PTSD (Post Traumatic Stress Disorder) literature that links certain types of catastrophic events (e.g., life-threatening events) with the development of stress-related symptomology, including increased anxiety, intrusive imagery, numbing, and loss of memory. These stress-inducing events are external events, outside of individual control, that are "capable of eliciting extreme fear and the perception of absolute helplessness" (March, 1993, p. 39). These high-intensity events have been characterized as "subject to the least transactional models" (March, 1993, p. 40). In other words, these types of events are less susceptible to the vagaries of individual appraisals; they are most often appraised as stressful across a wide range of individuals. Characteristic high intensity PTSD stressors include combat, criminal assault, rape, witnessing homicide or sexual assault, hostage taking, natural disasters, and human disasters (March, 1993). Thus, for researchers interested in the relationship between stress and eyewitness memory, there are several types of criminal events that are highly likely to be perceived and experienced as being very stressful. As we discuss more fully later, it is our contention that these are the types of events that we need to study more directly if we are to understand the effects that trauma has on eyewitness memory.

Given the relatively innocuous types of stressors employed in the extant eyewitness literature, we believe that it must be emphasized that an understanding of the impact of trauma on eyewitness memory is unlikely to be found from an examination of the existing eyewitness literature. Studies that claim to examine the impact of stress or trauma on eyewitness memory may be misleading. Virtually none of the studies that have been conducted to date reflect the nature or degree of impact on witnesses that, for example, a sexual assault is likely to have on the victim.

It should also be noted that the weak foundation of empirical studies relating effects of stress to eyewitness memory is not solely of academic concern. Several psychologists, following the lead of the *Aussage* period, have advocated the extension of research findings to the courtroom (e.g., Loftus, 1983, 1986). Thus, in spite of the problems associated with the current state of this research, some psychologists have been comfortable instructing the courts that the effects of stress on memory are understood. For example, some psychologists have evoked the Yerkes–Dodson law to encapsulate what they believe to be the effect of arousal on eyewitness memory (Mandler, 1992; for a critical review see Christianson, 1992b). This "law" was proposed early in this century to describe the relationship between arousal and performance in rats in simple learning tasks (Yerkes & Dodson, 1908). The relationship, an inverted U-shape, summarized the fact that animals' performance improves on learning tasks as arousal increases until an optimum level of arousal is reached. After this point, increases in arousal have a detrimental effect on performance. The application of this principle to eyewitness performance is unwarranted and without empirical foundation (Christianson, 1992b). Psychologists need a firmer empirical foundation if their knowledge is to be of use to triers of fact in criminal matters. In particular, as noted earlier, there is a need for research that studies the impact of stress or trauma on memory in actual criminal contexts. Naturally occurring trauma is the only context that will permit the ethical study of the impact of trauma on eyewitness memory.

Recent studies of those who have experienced high levels of stress as victims or witnesses of actual crimes (e.g., victims of armed robbery; see Tollestrup, Turtle, & Yuille, 1994) suggest that the impact of trauma is very complex. Some victims of stressful events may have vivid and detailed memories of the events, whereas others may only remember their subjective feelings of stress or may even suffer amnesia for the events (Yuille & Tollestrup, 1992). Individual differences in responses to stressful events must, therefore, be taken into account. This was dramatically illustrated in a study we conducted of a gun-shooting incident (Yuille & Cutshall, 1986) in which a key witness, who was in close proximity to the gun shooting, reported significantly less stress than other witnesses who were more distant from the action and in less physical danger. The key witness' lower stress response appeared to be related to his appraisal of the situation from the perspective of a gun aficionado and a person with a military background. The event was likely less extraordinary to him, and he likely felt more in control and less helpless than other bystanders. On the basis of these studies of real-life criminal incidents, it appears appropriate to echo Christianson's (1992b) conclusions that "(g)eneral statements (concerning the relation between memory and stress) seem unwarranted both in the literature and in practical settings" (p. 303).

A FRAMEWORK FOR STUDYING THE EFFECTS OF TRAUMA ON MEMORY

The purposes of this chapter are twofold: (a) to encourage more empirical research on the impact of trauma or stress on eyewitness memory, where a substantial part of that research is conducted in situ; and (b) to provide a framework for research in this field.

The preceding review suggested that stress has varied effects on memory. However, very little eyewitness research has focused on the effects of more severe stress, or trauma, on memory. Thus, drawing from case studies and related research from other areas, we propose a framework outlining some of the potential, diverse effects that trauma may have on memory in order to provide a foundation for research and thinking in this area. Before explicating our framework, we begin by specifying some of the assumptions underlying our approach.

First, this framework focuses on the impact of trauma on episodic or narrative memory. Although other types of memory may be involved in recall of a traumatic event (for example, "body memories" in the recall of trauma), our focus is on episodic memory. It appears to us that episodic memory is more amenable to empirical study. Furthermore, episodic memory is of central forensic interest.

Second, we assume, together with most of those who research memory, that memory is a reconstructive activity. Memories are not literally stored or retrieved; instead, they are recreated or reconstructed at the time of recall. Individuals generally have the ability to recognize whether the reconstruction is familiar or not. It is further assumed that most of the time the reconstruction/recognition of an episodic memory is accurate, although the process is prone to error under certain conditions (some of which are specified later).

Our third assumption refers to the impact of trauma on perception. Consistent with Easterbrook (1959), we assume that trauma drastically narrows the focus of attention (for a review see Steblay, 1992). Many of the diverse effects of trauma on memory, we believe, are a result of the focus of narrowed attention during stress.

As discussed previously, one of the major difficulties central to this area of research is that of defining or operationalizing trauma. Given the large body of literature relating to post-traumatic responses to traumatic events, we have turned to this literature, in particular to the criteria for PTSD and Acute Stress Disorder set forth in the Diagnostic and Statistical Manual (DSM–IV; American Psychiatric Association [APA], 1994), for a definition of the type of events that can be traumatic. We recognize that there are problems with this approach. In particular, a "traumatic event," as defined in the DSM–IV, (e.g., a natural disaster) may be traumatic for one witness and not for another, or the experienced trauma may be extreme for one witness and minimal for another. As noted previously, high-intensity events are likely to be less subject to individual differences in appraisal of trauma. For example, in a study of 64 rape victims, 2-weeks post-rape, 94% of the victims met the criteria for PTSD, indicating very high levels of stress among the victims of rape (Rothbaum, Foa, Riggs, Murdock, & Walsh, 1992). However, when 51 victims of assault and robbery were assessed 1 week post-crime, only 65% exhibited PTSD symptoms (Rothbaum et al., 1992). These findings do not indicate the degrees of stress experienced by these various crime victims at the time of the criminal event, but they do suggest that the magnitude of stress differed significantly between these two groups. Thus, while some types of events (e.g., rape) are likely to be almost universally stressful, individual differences in experiences of trauma will likely be evident across most types of events. Subjective measures of stress (e.g., Impact of Event Scale—Horowitz, Wilner, & Alvarez, 1979; Subjective Stress Scale—Kerle & Bialek, 1958) should therefore be included in studies relating to the effects of trauma on memory.

Based on a large body of research, the stressor criterion in relation to the potential development of post-traumatic stress symptomology has been explicated for the diagnosis of PTSD and Acute Stress Disorder (e.g., Breslau & Davis, 1987; Davidson & Foa, 1993; Green, 1990). The DSM–IV defines traumatic events as:

> (E)xperience of an event that involves actual or threatened death or serious injury, or other threat to one's physical integrity; or witnessing an event that involves death, injury, or a threat to the physical integrity of another person; or learning about unexpected or violent death, serious harm, or threat of death or injury experienced by a family member or other close associate. (APA, 1994, p. 424)

The examples of events that are given to illustrate this definition in the DSM–IV include the following:

> (M)ilitary combat, violent personal assault (sexual assault, physical attack, robbery, mugging), being kidnapped, being taken hostage, terrorist attack, torture, incarceration as a prisoner of war or in a concentration camp, natural or manmade disasters, severe automobile accidents, or being diagnosed with a life-threatening illness. For children, sexually traumatic events may include developmentally inappropriate sexual experiences without threatened or actual violence or injury. Witnessed events include, but are not limited to, observing serious injury or unnatural death of another person due to violent assault, accident, war, or disaster or unexpectedly witnessing a dead body or body parts. (APA, p. 424)

Based on the preceding assumptions and using the foregoing definition of traumatic events, we provide a model of how experiencing a traumatic event may affect eyewitness memory. The first section that follows provides an outline of the presumed effects of trauma on the initial nature of representation of the event. That is, we examine the various ways witnesses may encode an event depending on the degree of trauma they experience. The subsequent section outlines the manner in which the memory for an event may change with the passage of time. Finally, we outline the different patterns of recall that may be the consequences of the initial encoding and the passage of time.

THE QUALITY OF THE INITIAL
REPRESENTATION OF A TRAUMATIC EVENT

Figure 8.1 provides an outline of the assumed effect of trauma on the initial representation of the event for the witness. As noted earlier, it is assumed that a traumatic event (designated as an event of impact in Fig. 8.1) will result in a narrowing of the focus of attention. The critical concern is where the consequent narrowing beam of attention will focus. If the focus is external, it is likely that attention will be on the perceived threat. In this circumstance, a witness may focus on a weapon, on his/her attacker or some other core aspect of the threatening event. Given this focus of attention, the witness's memory for those core details that were the object of focus should be excellent. Memory for peripheral details should be poor

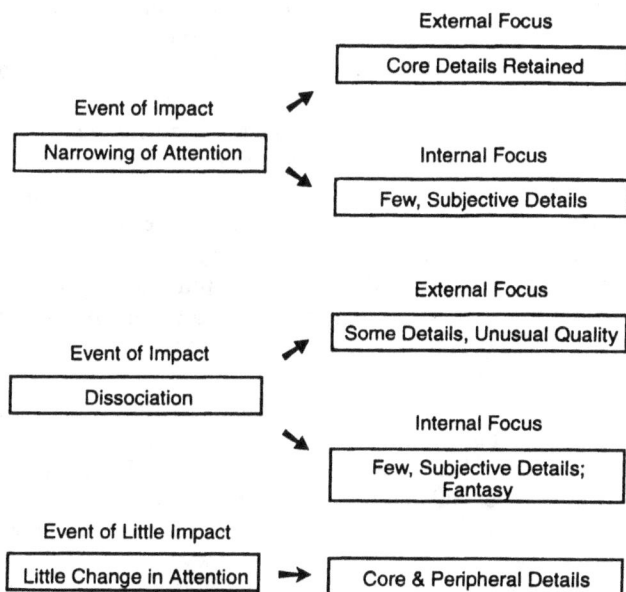

FIG. 8.1.   Quality of initial memory.

or absent. Alternatively, the narrowed focus of attention may be on the victim's own subjective responses. Thus, a victim of a sexual assault may focus on his or her own fear, or on the physical pain. Consequently, the victim would be able to recall little detail about the external aspects of the event; recall would be characterized by the presence of subjective details (i.e., about the victim's subjective state at the time of the attack).

The external versus internal focus of attention should be a topic of future research. We need to understand the combination of circumstance and psychological characteristics that result in one or the other focus of attention. Among the factors that may increase the likelihood of an external focus of attention are:

1. Previous experience with similar trauma;
2. A tendency to focus externally as a personality trait;
3. A lower degree of threat;
4. The type of threat (perhaps some traumas are more likely to demand an external focus);
5. Training in responding to traumatic situations.

There is a need for eyewitness research on these and other factors that will assist us in better understanding qualitative differences in eyewitness recall.

Some individuals may respond to trauma not merely by narrowing attention but by dissociating. That is, the witness may experience a separation of normally integrated psychological functions or an alteration in consciousness that may affect memory and/or identity.[2] The form that dissociation takes for the witness will typically depend on the focus of attention during the event. Like the narrowing of attention, dissociation can also result in either an internal or external focus of attention. An external focus occurs when the victim or witness experiences the event as if he or she were detached from it; for example, as if she or he were watching it on television. This type of witness subsequently would likely be able to recall some details of the event, although in contrast to the non-dissociating witness with an external focus the details would have an unusual quality. For example, the details may be characterized by an unusual perspective; the witness may report the event as if he or she observed it from a different perspective than his or her physical location (i.e., an out-of-body experience in which the victim describes the event as though seeing it from the ceiling).

A witness who dissociated and had an internal or subjective focus would have few memories for the external aspects of the event and would generally

---

[2]An in-depth discussion about dissociation is beyond the scope of this paper; however, the interested reader is referred to Kihlstrom, Tataryn, and Hoyt (1993) and Lynn and Rhue (1994).

recall only subjective details that would have unusual or idiosyncratic qualities. For example, this type of dissociation may include a distracting visualization during which the individual "travels" to another place and time, perhaps as a means of temporarily "escaping" the traumatic event. The memory would then relate primarily to these internal images and feelings.

The foregoing discussion of dissociation is based on the assumption that witnesses would be able to recall something about the traumatic event, whether primarily subjective or external information. However, when dissociation occurs a possible sequel is amnesia for the traumatic event. Thus, a witness who dissociates may have no memory at all for the event. Amnesia is discussed in more detail later.

This discussion raises another focus for research. Are there particular traumatic circumstances that are more likely to result in dissociation than others? What personality characteristics and what experiences are related to a susceptibility to dissociation? Some have suggested that dissociation can be a learned response to repeated trauma. Are the memory consequences, external vs. internal focus vs. amnesia, also learned?

The bottom entry in Fig. 8.1 refers to an event of little impact. This is the control condition for determining the impact of trauma on memory. This is the type of eyewitness memory that psychologists have studied for so many years. For obvious ethical reasons, the situations that researchers employ in controlled settings cannot have any traumatic impact. Thus, while valuable for control and comparison purposes, this type of research, as noted earlier, can yield no knowledge about the effect of traumatic events on eyewitness memory.

CHANGES IN MEMORY OVER TIME

The previous section dealt with how trauma can effect a witness's initial memory for an event. In this section we examine how the initial memory may change with the passage of time. Figure 8.2 presents a schematic of the assumed changes that occur in the quality of memory between the event and subsequent attempts to recall the event. It is assumed that the changes outlined in this section increase in their likelihood of occurrence with the longer passages of time. Thus, these changes would be absent or minimal if recall is attempted immediately after the event.

A decade ago we proposed the concept of *remarkable memory* to account for some of the observed differences in patterns of eyewitness recall (Yuille & Cutshall, 1986). This arose out of a comparison of the recall of undergraduate students, who have been the traditional focus of eyewitness

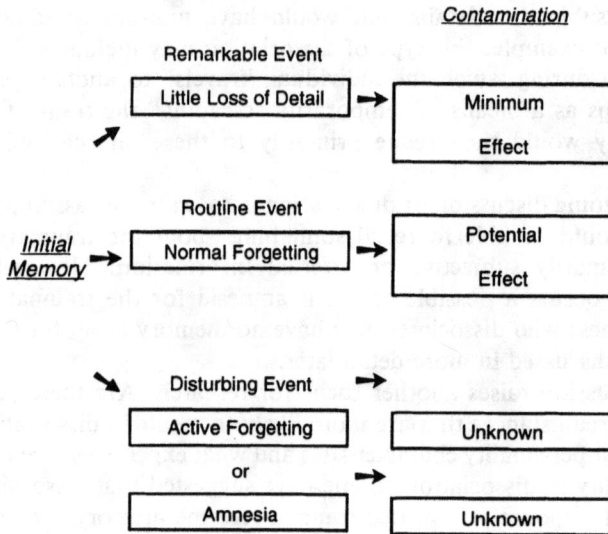

FIG. 8.2.   Changes in memory over time.

research, to that of actual witnesses to certain types of real crimes. As noted previously, most eyewitness research has employed undergraduate volunteers and has tested their memory for relatively innocuous events. This research has typically found that forgetting is relatively rapid and that eyewitness memory is malleable. In contrast, some of our early studies of actual eyewitness memory (that is, memory of witnesses to actual crimes, typically murders and robberies) found that forgetting was minimal and that these memories were resistant to suggestibility (e.g., Cutshall & Yuille, 1989). The term *remarkable memory* was coined to refer to the memory of witnesses in some actual crime contexts. The term was employed to reflect the multiple factors that appear to make some eyewitness memories persistent over time.[3] These are usually, if not always, memories for unique or very unusual events in the person's life. That is, the event itself is remarkable in the sense of its uniqueness. These events are also usually remarkable in the other sense of that word: The witnesses repeatedly recall the event, either to themselves or to others. For example, witnesses to a

---

[3]The term *remarkable memory* should not be confused with *flashbulb memory*. The latter term refers to a memory of the context in which one learned of a historic event (e.g., an assassination of a political figure). Flashbulb memories do not refer to personally traumatic experienced or witnessed situations of the type of concern in this chapter. Although flashbulb memories can be quite accurate, they are subject to loss of detail over time and to inaccuracies. Thus, flashbulb memories differ in both context and characteristics from remarkable memories.

shooting who we interviewed (Yuille & Cutshall, 1986) reported that they told almost anyone they met about this remarkable event. As noted in Fig. 8.2, the repeated recall or remarking on the event has two consequences for memory: (a) there is relatively little loss of detail, especially central details, over time; and (b) the memory is more resistant to suggestion or contamination.

The fact that the type of memory studied in the laboratory is for routine or innocuous events greatly affects the extent of assumed memory loss over time. The experimenter may show the witness a videotape or a slide sequence, or the research witness may observe a staged event. Although these events may be amusing or diverting, they are not of a nature to be remarkable events. Indeed, the ethical considerations that guide experimental work make it very unlikely that a laboratory-based event can be remarkable. Consequently, with the passage of time, normal forgetting will occur for these events. That is, there will be a considerable loss of detail over time. It is possible that the witness may have lost all memory for the event with a sufficient delay. Also, with the loss of details comes an increased susceptibility to suggestion and contamination.

It is important to note that normal forgetting is not relegated to the laboratory. Many witnesses of criminal events will show a similar pattern of loss of detail over time. This will typically occur when the crime constitutes a routine event in the life of the witness. There are several circumstances in which this will occur. First, the witness may not know that a crime is being committed at the time. For example, victims of fraud are typically unaware of the fraud at the time, otherwise the fraud would not be successful. For the witness, the event is simply another routine check cashing or processing of a credit card. Thus, fraud victims may behave much like the undergraduate witness in the laboratory. In contrast, victims of a robbery are much more likely to display remarkable memories. A detailed comparison of the memory of fraud victims with those of robbery victims is provided by Tollestrup et al. (1994).

A second circumstance in which a criminal event may be routine is where a victim has repeatedly experienced an event. For example, in informal discussions with bank tellers who have been the repeated victims of robberies, the first author found that the tellers reported detailed memory for the first robbery but they often had difficulty distinguishing subsequent robberies. Similarly, if a child is a victim of repeated sexual assaults, she or he may have difficulty remembering many specific episodes. Although any one assault would be a remarkable memory for a victim, the repeated nature of the assaults makes them blend together. In this circumstance one would expect the witness to have a memory of the general form of the assaults rather than for each episode. One useful idea in this context is the concept of *script memory* (e.g., Nelson, 1986). A script is an abstracted or generalized form of a memory drawn from repeated experiences of a similar nature. A victim of repeated sexual assaults is likely to remember the script. If any specific episodes are remembered they are likely to be script violations. That is, an episode may become a remarkable memory because it is a significant change or departure from the usual pattern or script of the event.

A third context in which witnesses may have a routine forgetting response to criminal events is similar to those just mentioned: Police officers may so frequently view a particular criminal act that they are unable to recall a single episode without the aid of detailed notes (Yuille, 1984).

Figure 8.2 contains a third type of event, other than remarkable or routine events, that can effect the pattern of retention over time. If the event is particularly disturbing to the witness, the impact on memory may be different from the other two types of events. A disturbing event is one that involved trauma to the witness at the time. It is also possible that an event that is perceived post hoc as a traumatic event would fall into this category; however, the lack of research on trauma and memory makes this possibility only speculative. A disturbing event may lead to three possible effects on memory over time. First, the witness may be unable to stop thinking about the event. That is, the witness may experience intrusive, repeated recall in the form often labeled as flashbacks or as nightmares. Intrusive thoughts and feelings, and re-experiencing of the event through nightmares and flashbacks are considered to be the cardinal symptoms of PTSD (e.g., Davidson & Foa, 1993; Peterson, Prout, & Schwarz, 1991). The repeated, vivid re-experiencing of the event could have the same memorial consequences as a remarkable event: detailed memory, little forgetting, resistance to contamination. However, it also should be noted that the veridicality of these intrusive memories is not often established. Instead, because these memories (i.e., flashbacks) are extremely vivid and recalled with great affect, the accuracy of the content is often unquestioned. Therapists and clinicians appear to be particularly unlikely to question the validity of these types of memories when recounted by their clients. This assumption of accuracy may be misplaced, however. In particular, when the content of intrusive imagery changes over time, as is often reported, which details are accurate and which details are a product of changes in the way in which the individual has come to think and feel about the trauma? These questions remain unanswered.

A second possibility with a disturbing event is that the witness may engage in active forgetting: that is, he or she may try to keep the event out of consciousness. Although active forgetting may not succeed (perhaps having the unintended consequence of making the memory a remarkable one), if the strategy is successful there should be memorial consequences.

However, there is no empirical research even to speculate what those consequences might be. Are the consequences of active forgetting the same or different from normal forgetting? We simply do not know.

A third possible course of memory for a disturbing or traumatic event is amnesia. Psychologically based amnesia, or dissociative amnesia, [also referred to at various times as psychogenic amnesia (DSM-III-R), and functional amnesia (Schacter & Kihlstrom, 1989)] is defined in the DSM-IV by the following diagnostic criteria:

A. The predominant disturbance is one or more episodes of inability to recall important personal information, usually of a traumatic or stressful nature, that is too extensive to be explained by ordinary forgetfulness.

B. The disturbance does not occur exclusively during the course of Dissociative Identity Disorder, Dissociative Fugue, Posttraumatic Stress Disorder, Acute Stress Disorder, or Somatization Disorder and is not due to the direct physiological effects of a substance (e.g., a drug of abuse, a medication) or a neurological or other general medical condition (e.g., Amnestic Disorder Due to Head Trauma).

C. The symptoms cause clinically significant distress or impairment in social, occupational, or other important areas of functioning. (APA, 1994, p. 481).

For the purposes of this chapter, Dissociative Amnesia or amnesia that occurs in the course of PTSD are not distinguishable; either context involves inability to recall a significant part of or all of a traumatic event.

Trauma-induced amnesia is at the center of a current controversy. The controversy often focuses on the term *repression* rather than *amnesia*. This is unfortunate, because *repression* is a term that carries considerable psychodynamic baggage in addition to the concept of psychologically based amnesia. In any event, the heated debate within psychology and psychiatry concerns the very existence of trauma-induced amnesia. Two opposing camps of opinion have emerged. One group, mostly comprised of therapists and counselors, claims that trauma-induced amnesia is commonplace among survivors of childhood sexual abuse, particularly incest. It is assumed by this group that childhood abuse is traumatic, and therefore, may result in amnesia for the abusive events (e.g., Bass & Davis, 1988). A second group, mostly comprised of academic researchers, asserts that there is no such thing as trauma-based amnesia (e.g., Loftus & Ketcham, 1994). It is assumed by this group that the memories of childhood abuse "recovered" by individuals in therapy are often the product of suggestion and pressure by therapists; that is, the memories are false (although believed to be true by the complainant). An excellent review of these issues is found in two articles by Lindsey and Read (1994, 1995).

Although the debate between these two groups has been heated and frequent, it has been characterized by little progress. Neither group can call upon any definitive research to support its position. The debate has mostly featured each side pointing out the weakness of the other's views, rather than providing insight into the nature of the problem.

There is evidence, however, that experiencing a traumatic event can lead to amnesia (as indicated by the diagnosis in the DSM–IV; see also Christianson & Nilsson, 1989; Schacter & Kihlstrom, 1989), although little is known about the mechanism by which such amnesia occurs. Similarly, little is known about how frequent or rare such amnesia is or the circumstances under which it is likely to occur. The problem for many critics is that the evidence that does exist for trauma-induced amnesia is anecdotal rather than experimental. However, this criticism may be irrelevant, as an experimental demonstration of trauma-induced amnesia may be impossible (for obvious ethical reasons). Also, many of the anecdotal reports are quite compelling.

An example from our practice provides an illustration (see also Christianson & Nilsson, 1989; Schacter & Kihlstrom, 1989, for other examples). A woman in her 20s was visiting a city in a foreign country. She visited a night club with a female friend one night. While there she met a man from her home state whom she had not known previously. They danced together, but she developed an uneasy feeling about him. She attempted to avoid him, but he was persistent. Finally, she went to the ladies' room in the hope that he would leave her alone. However, he waited for her by the door of the ladies' room, which happened to be next to the rear exit of the club. As she left the ladies' room, he grabbed her and dragged her outside the club. He pulled her into an alley behind the night club where he sexually assaulted her. Three strangers happened upon this assault as they were walking down the alley, and they chased the rapist away. The victim was able to tell the ambulance attendants and the police what had occurred. She gave a description of her assailant, as did the other witnesses, and he was subsequently arrested. After a stay in hospital she was able to tell several other people the details of the event. However, 5 months later, when we met with her, she no longer had any memory for the sexual assault. She remembered the events preceding it and those that followed it, but she had developed localized amnesia for the assault itself. Her amnesia was not due to alcohol or drugs; she had consumed little alcohol at the time and, in any event, had good memory for those aspects of the event both preceding and following the sexual assault. She had a good memory for the sexual assault itself at one time (as detailed in her account to the police), and she was able to reconstruct it for several days after the event. We had been retained by the prosecution to assist her in recalling as much detail as possible. She expressed a desire to recall the assault in order to assist in the prosecution of her assailant. However, her best efforts, as well as ours, met with no success.

This anecdote outlines a pattern of memory that requires a concerted research effort. We need to explore the frequency of occurrence of such trauma-induced amnesia. We need to understand when and how recovery from such amnesia can occur. We also need to know if such recovered memories can be distinguished from those that may be created through the use of misleading therapeutic techniques. Researchers such as Daniel L. Schacter and John F. Kihlstrom (formerly at the Amnesia and Cognition Unit at the University of Arizona) have explored these phenomena in some detail. Hopefully, researchers interested in eyewitness memory will join in this research effort. It is clear that this has increasingly become an area of interest in the forensic context. Memory disturbances (e.g., reported amnesia, dissociation, flashbacks) in individuals who have experienced traumatic events are increasingly the subject of scrutiny within the criminal justice system, in relation to the memories or lack of memories reported by both victims and alleged perpetrators. Findings from cognitive psychology and eyewitness research are being applied to this arena with or without our participation. When applications of psychological research are made from areas outside of psychology, gross misinterpretation and misapplication can occur (e.g., Siegel, 1995). Therefore, we recommend that eyewitness researchers become more active participants in this difficult, but intriguing aspect of eyewitness memory.

THE QUALITY OF EYEWITNESS RECALL

The two previous sections of this chapter have outlined a framework for understanding how the nature of the initial event and the changes in memory over time can affect memory for traumatic and nontraumatic events. This section outlines our taxonomy of the different patterns of eyewitness recall that may occur, taking into account the factors described earlier in this chapter. Figure 8.3 provides a synopsis of the patterns of eyewitness recall that we are proposing. The contents of the figure emphasize that eyewitness recall can vary from a vivid, detailed account to little or no memory. Recall can also occur with ease or only with great difficulty. The quality of recall can vary from providing a detailed account of the event itself to only being able to report subjective aspects of the event.

Throughout the following discussion of patterns of recall, no assumptions are made about the accuracy of the recall. Although accuracy may

PATTERNS OF RECALL

1. REMARKABLE MEMORIES: Detailed recall of an event, long-term retention (months or years).

2. DISSOCIATION DURING EVENT:
   A. External focus; detailed recall from unusual focus.
   B. Internal focus; little detail, unusual qualities.

3. STATE-DEPENDENT AMNESIA: Amnesia for core element of a traumatic event.

4. NORMAL FORGETTING: Detailed recall immediately after the event followed by rapid forgetting; the focus of most eyewitness research.

5. SCRIPT MEMORY: A blended memory for a series of events.

6. DISSOCIATIVE AMNESIA: Inability to recall part or all of a traumatic event.

7. ACTIVE FORGETTING: Loss of detail due to conscious attempts not to recall event.

FIG. 8.3.   Patterns of recall.

vary from one pattern to another it is assumed that individual differences in recall accuracy within a particular pattern can be considerable. In situ research has indicated that, on the average, eyewitness recall tends to be accurate (e.g., Tollestrup et al., 1994), however, many factors can influence the willingness or ability of witnesses to be accurate in their recall (Porter & Yuille, 1995).

Pattern 1

Some witnesses may provide a detailed account of an event and they may be able to provide this recall with ease. For many of these witnesses, the memory may remain detailed over months or even years. This occurs when the memory is for an event of impact on the witness, and it is a remarkable memory. For example, this may be the pattern for a first-time victim of a robbery or a single sexual assault. Non-victim witnesses of remarkable events may also display this pattern. In addition, this pattern of recall may be observed in the case of a disturbing event that results in uncontrolled, intrusive, or recurring recall. An example of this pattern of recall may be a witness to a shooting incident who can provide a vivid and detailed account months after the event occurred (Yuille & Cutshall, 1986).

Pattern 2

A second pattern of eyewitness recall is much like Pattern 1, in the sense of a detailed, persistent memory, but is distinguished from the above by the unusual or different nature of the content that the witness can readily recall. This type of recall occurs when the witness dissociated during a traumatic event and had the subjective experience of witnessing the event from an unusual perspective (e.g., outside of the body). Here the witness has maintained an external focus so that the content of recall is largely concerned with external details, but the details would be reported as if witnessed from a different perspective than that of the witness's actual physical location. For example, one child that we interviewed habitually "watched" her abuse from the position of a plant in her bedroom. She was able to provide a detailed account, but from an external perspective.

A witness who dissociated during a traumatic event but focused on something other than the event would be able to recall little, if anything, about the event. For example, a victim of repeated child abuse that we interviewed reported that she went to a "platform in the sky" during her assaults. She could describe the subjective experience of the place she went to psychologically but could not describe the assaults. This pattern can be seen as a subtype of Pattern 2. There are obvious problems in assessing the accuracy of a witness's memory when there is no reference to external reality.

Pattern 3

During the course of a traumatic event, a participant in the event may enter a different state of consciousness, for example, a rage state, that makes it impossible for the person to recall the event from his or her normal psychological state. This pattern has been studied most extensively in murderers (e.g., Schacter, 1986a). This pattern is typically associated with crimes of passion and is characterized by amnesia for some core part of the event, usually the murder itself. It must be emphasized that it is difficult to distinguish between genuine cases of state-dependent amnesia and malingering (e.g., Schacter, 1986b).

Pattern 4

If the event is routine, then recall will most likely follow the pattern of normal forgetting. That is, there would be relatively rapid loss of information with the passage of time. This witness context may be one in which the individual's memory is the most susceptible to the effects of suggestion. This has been the most frequently studied pattern of eyewitness recall. For example, a victim of fraud may be able to recall the perpetrator if interviewed immediately after the event, but the victim would likely experience rapid loss of information over time.

Pattern 5

As noted earlier, there are circumstances in which a person may be the victim of repeated criminal acts. Child sexual abuse in particular may involve repeated victimization. Sometimes a child may be the victim of hundreds of sexual assaults over a period of months or years. Although it has been suggested that repeated exposure to abuse may lead to amnesia, a more likely memory outcome is the report of a script memory. With this pattern the witness can most easily recall an abstracted pattern of how the assaults usually or typically occurred. This memory is likely to contain elements blended from several or many specific events. This pattern may be linked with Pattern 1 memories. That is, a specific episode of assault may become a remarkable memory (Pattern 1) if it departs in some significant manner from the script (Yuille, Hunter, Joffe, & Zaparniuk, 1993).

Pattern 6

This pattern of recall may occur when a witness experiences a traumatic event that continues to be a source of extraordinary emotional disturbance for that individual. This pattern occurs when, through mechanisms not currently understood, the victim develops dissociative or psychologically based amnesia. It is assumed that this is a relatively rare occurrence and that when it does occur it is most likely to involve amnesia for a single event or part of a single event. In rarer contexts a witness may have amnesia for repeated events. For example, Dissociative Identity Disorder will result in significant gaps in memory. Some anecdotal reports suggest that if a witness recovers from trauma-induced amnesia the recovery will occur suddenly (e.g., Terr, 1994). Others have reported that the recovery from amnesia may be more gradual (e.g., Christianson & Nilsson, 1989). More research is needed to clarify how recovery from amnesia occurs. We assume that the content in this pattern of recall will be detailed if recovery from amnesia does occur.

Pattern 7

This pattern is discussed last because it is the least understood. This pattern is assumed to occur when a person experiences a traumatic event and subsequently actively tries not to remember it. For example, a victim of a sexual assault may consciously avoid thinking about the assault each time it comes to mind. Presumably, such active avoidance has some consequences on memory for the event. However, the nature of the impact of active forgetting on memory for a traumatic event is not known. It is postulated here that active forgetting will lead to some loss of detail and to difficulty recalling the event. However, this is purely speculative.

IMPLICATIONS

We have suggested that there are at least seven different patterns of recall that may be found with eyewitnesses to criminal events (or indeed to a variety of other trauma-inducing situations). The patterns vary in terms of the quality and quantity of information recalled, as well as in terms of the focus of attention and the ease of recall. There is a need for research to better understand all of these patterns. The field of eyewitness memory has suffered from a primary focus on only one of these patterns, Pattern 4. This pattern is important, but it is neither typical nor representative of eyewitness recall of criminal events. We need to redress this by generating research on the other five patterns. As all of the other patterns are likely to involve some degree of stress or trauma for the witness, it is obvious that they can only be studied in situ. Research in the forensic context, or with victims of natural disasters, is much more difficult to conduct than research on Pattern 4. However, if we wish to understand the complexities of eyewitness memory, we have no alternative than to pursue the study of memory for naturally occurring traumatic events. One route may be to join forces with the large number of researchers interested in the development of PTSD who directly study individual's responses to criminal events (e.g., Kilpatrick & Resnic, 1993; Kilpatrick et al., 1989), disasters (e.g., Green, 1991; McFarlane, 1988), and other traumatic events (for an overview, see Davidson & Foa, 1993; Figley, 1985; Horowitz, 1986; Peterson et al., 1991). Increased collaboration between eyewitness researchers and clinical psychologists could also lead to enhanced understanding of the memorial consequences of experiencing traumatic events. It has been our experience with this type of collaborative effort that both parties benefit from the perspective of the other.

The psychologist in the role of court expert may also be assisted by the framework presented in this chapter. The task of educating the triers of fact in criminal and civil cases is daunting. Each case calls for an evaluation of the type of memory pattern that one should apply in assessing the case. Psychologists have done a disservice to the courts by trying to impose findings relative to Pattern 4 onto every eyewitness context. Perhaps we can begin to redress this by acknowledging the complexity of memory and the differing impact that trauma may have on it.

ACKNOWLEDGMENT

Preparation of this chapter was supported by a grant to the first author from the Social Sciences and Humanities Research Council of Canada.

REFERENCES

American Psychiatric Association. (1994). *Diagnostic and statistical manual of mental disorders* (4th ed.). Washington, DC: Author.

Bass, E., & Davis, L. (1988). *The courage to heal*. New York: Harper Collins.

Breslau, N., & Davis, G. C. (1987). Posttraumatic stress disorder: The stressor criterion. *Journal of Nervous and Mental Disease, 175*, 255–264.

Brigham, J., Maass, P., Martinez, D., & Whittenberger, G. (1983). The effect of arousal on facial recognition. *Basic and Applied Social Psychology, 4*(3), 279–293.

Christianson, S.-A. (1992a). Remembering emotional events: Potential mechanisms. In S.-A. Christianson (Ed.), *The handbook of emotion and memory: Research and theory* (pp. 307–340). Hillsdale, NJ: Lawrence Erlbaum Associates.

Christianson, S.-A. (1992b). Emotional stress and memory: A critical review. *Psychological Bulletin, 112*, 284–309.

Christianson, S.-A, & Nilsson, L.-G. (1989). Hysterical amnesia: A case of aversively motivated isolation of memory. In T. Archer & L.-G. Nilsson (Eds.), *Aversion, avoidance and anxiety: Perspectives on aversively motivated behavior* (pp. 289–310). Hillsdale, NJ: Lawrence Erlbaum Associates.

Clifford, B. R., & Hollin, C. R. (1981). Effects of the type of incident and the number of perpetrators on eyewitness memory. *Journal of Applied Psychology, 66*, 364–370.

Clifford, B. R., & Scott, J. (1978). Individual and situational factors in eyewitness testimony. *Journal of Applied Psychology, 63*, 352–359.

Cutshall, J. L. (1985). *Eyewitness characteristics and memory: An in situ analysis*. Unpublished master's thesis, University of British Columbia, Vancouver, Canada.

Cutshall, J. L., & Yuille, J. C. (1989). Field studies of eyewitness memory of actual crimes. In D. C. Raskin (Ed.), *Psychological methods in criminal investigation and evidence* (pp. 97–124). New York: Springer.

Davidson, J. R. T., & Foa, E. B. (Ed.). (1993). *Posttraumatic stress disorder: DSM–IV and beyond*. Washington, DC: American Psychiatric Association.

Deffenbacher, K. A. (1983). The influence of arousal on reliability of testimony. In S. M. A. Lloyd-Bostock & B. R. Clifford (Eds.), *Evaluating witness evidence* (pp. 235–251). New York: Wiley.

Dohrenwend, B. P., & Shrout, P. E. (1985). "Hassles" in the conceptualization and measurement of life stress variables. *American Psychologist, 40*(7), 780–785.

Easterbrook, J. A. (1959). The effect of emotion on cue utilization and the organization of behavior. *Psychological Review, 66*, 183–201.

Eysenck, M. W. (1982). *Attention and arousal: Cognition and performance.* Berlin: Springer-Verlag.

Figley, C. R. (Ed.). (1985). *Trauma and its wake: The study and treatment of post-traumatic stress disorder.* New York: Brunner/Mazel.

Green, B. L. (1990). Defining trauma: Terminology and generic stressor dimensions. *Journal of Applied Social Psychology, 20*, 1632–1642.

Green, B. L. (1991). Evaluating the effects of disasters. *Psychological Assessment, 3*, 538–546.

Holmes, T. H., & Rahe, R. H. (1967). The social readjustment rating scale. *Journal of Psychosomatic Research, 11*, 213–218.

Horowitz, M. J. (1986). *Stress response syndromes* (2nd ed.). Northvale, NJ: Jason Aronson.

Horowitz, M. J., Wilner, N., & Alvarez, W. (1979). Impact of event scale: A measure of subjective stress. *Psychosomatic Medicine, 41*, 209–218.

Kerle, R. H., & Bialek, H. M. (1958). *The construction, validation and application of a subjective stress scale* (Staff memorandum). Monterey, CA: United States Army Human Leadership Resources Unit.

Kihlstrom, J. F., Tataryn, D. J., & Hoyt, I. P. (1993). Dissociative disorders. In P. B. Sutker, & H. E. Adams (Eds.), *Comprehensive handbook of psychopathology.* New York: Plenum Press.

Kilpatrick, D. G., & Resnick, H. S. (1993). Posttraumatic stress disorder associated with exposure to criminal victimization in clinical and community populations. In J. R. T. Davidson & E. B. Foa (Eds.), *Posttraumatic stress disorder: DSM–IV and beyond* (pp. 113–146). Washington, DC: American Psychiatric Association.

Kilpatrick, D. G., Saunders, B. E., Amick-McMullan, A., Best, C. L., Veronen, L. J., & Resnick, H. S. (1989). Victim and crime factors associated with the development of crime-related post-traumatic stress disorder. *Behavior Therapy, 20*, 199–214.

Lazarus, R. S. (1966). *Psychological stress and the coping process.* New York: McGraw-Hill.

Lazarus, R. S., & Folkman, S. (1984). *Stress, appraisal, and coping.* New York: Springer.

Lindsey, D. S., & Read, J. D. (1994). Psychotherapy and memories of childhood sexual abuse: A cognitive perspective. *Applied Cognitive Psychology, 8*, 281–338.

Lindsey, D. S., & Read, J. D. (1995). "Memory work" and recovered memories of childhood sexual abuse. *Psychology, Public Policy, and Law, 1*(4), 846–908.

Loftus, E. F. (1979). *Eyewitness testimony.* Cambridge, MA: Harvard University Press.

Loftus, E. F. (1983). Silence is not golden. *American Psychologist, 38*, 564–572.

Loftus, E. F. (1986). Ten years in the life of an expert witness. *Law and Human Behavior, 10*, 241–264.

Loftus, E. F., & Burns, T. (1982). Mental shock can produce retrograde amnesia. *Memory and Cognition, 10*, 318–323.

Loftus, E. F., & Ketcham, K. (1994). *The myth of repressed memory.*

Lynn, S. J., & Rhue, J. W. (1994). (Eds.). *Dissociation: Clinical and theoretical perspectives.* New York: Guilford.

Mandler, G. (1975). *Mind and emotion.* New York: Wiley.

Mandler, G. (1992). Memory, arousal and mood: A theoretical integration. In S.-A. Christianson (Ed.), *The handbook of emotion and memory: Research and theory* (pp. 93–110). Hillsdale, NJ: Lawrence Erlbaum Associates.

March, J. S. (1993). What constitutes a stressor? The "Criterion A" issue. In J. R. T. Davidson, & E. B. Foa (Ed.), *Posttraumatic stress disorder: DSM–IV and beyond* (pp. 37–54). Washington, DC: American Psychiatric Association.

McFarlane, A. C. (1988). The phenomenology of posttraumatic stress disorders following a natural disaster. *Journal of Nervous and Mental Disease, 176*, 22–29.

Munsterberg, H. (1908). *On the witness stand: Essays on psychology and crime*. New York: Clark, Boardman.

Myers, D. G. (1990). *Social psychology* (3rd ed.). New York: McGraw-Hill.

Nelson, K. (1986). *Event knowledge: Structure and function in development*. Hillsdale, NJ: Lawrence Erlbaum Associates.

Peterson, K. C., Prout, M. F., & Schwarz, R. A. (1991). *Post-traumatic stress disorder: A clinician's guide*. New York: Plenum Press.

Porter, S., & Yuille, J. C. (1995). Credibility assessment of criminal suspects through statement analysis. *Psychology, Crime and Law, 1*, 1–13.

Rothbaum, B. O., Foa, E. B., Riggs, D. S., Murdock, T., & Walsh, W. (1992). A prospective examination of post-traumatic stress disorder in rape victims. *Journal of Traumatic Stress, 5*(3), 455–464.

Schacter, D. L. (1986a). Amnesia and crime. *American Psychologist, 41*, 286–296.

Schacter, D. L. (1986b). On the relation between genuine and simulated amnesia. *Behavioral Sciences and the Law, 4*, 47–64.

Schacter, D. L., & Kihlstrom, J. F. (1989). Functional amnesia. In F. Boller & J. Grafman (Eds.), *Handbook of neuropsychology* (Vol. 3, pp. 209–231). New York: Elsevier Science Publishers.

Siegel, D. J. (1995). Memory, trauma, and psychotherapy. *Journal of Psychotherapy Practice and Research, 4*(2), 93–122.

Steblay, N. M. (1992). A meta-analytic review of the weapon focus effect. *Law and Human Behavior, 16*(4), 413–424.

Steinberg, M. (1995). *Handbook for the assessment of dissociation: A clinical guide*. Washington, DC: American Psychiatric Association.

Terr, L. (1994). *Unchained memories: Trues stories of traumatic memories, lost and found*. New York: Basic Books.

Tollestrup, P., Turtle, J., & Yuille, J. C. (1994). Eyewitness characteristics and memory: A survey of actual police cases. In D. Ross, D. Read, & M. Toglia (Eds.), *Adult eyewitness testimony: Current trends and developments* (pp. 144–160). New York: Cambridge University Press.

Whipple, G. M. (1915). Psychology of testimony. *Psychological Bulletin, 12*, 221–224.

Yerkes, R. M., & Dodson, J. D. (1908). The relation of strength of stimulus to rapidity of habit-information. *Journal of Comparative Neurology and Psychology, 18*, 459–482.

Yuille, J. C. (1984). Research and teaching with police: A Canadian example. *International Review of Applied Psychology, 33*, 5–23.

Yuille, J. C., & Cutshall, J. L. (1986). A case study of eyewitness memory of a crime. *Journal of Applied Psychology, 71*(2), 291–301.

Yuille, J. C., Hunter, R., Joffe, R., & Zaparniuk, J. (1993). Interviewing children in sexual abuse cases. In G. Goodman & B. Bottoms (Eds.), *Child victims, child witnesses: Understanding and improving testimony: Clinical, developmental and legal implications* (pp. 99–115). New York: Guilford Press.

Yuille, J. C., & Tollestrup, P. (1992). A model of the diverse effects of emotion on eyewitness memory. In S.-A. Christianson (Ed.), *The handbook of emotion and memory: Research and theory* (pp. 201–215). Hillsdale, NJ: Lawrence Erlbaum Associates.

Author Index

179

Silverman, W. K., 32, 54
Singletary v. United States, 136, 153
Slomovits, M., 147, 151
Smith, E., 19, 30, 31, 52, 136
Smith, S., 153
Smith, V. L.,107, 110, 119, 128, 130, 152
Snyder, L. D., 57, 108, 127
Spaulding, K., 108, 127
Spicker, B., 34, 53
Sporer, S. L., 107–110, 112, 113, 116, 129, 130, 132, 153
Steblay, N. M., 161, 178
Stein, N. L., 37, 54
Steinberg, M., 178
Stephenson, G. M., 146, 150, 151, 153
Stern, L. W., 132, 153
Sternberg, K. J., 86
Swartwood, J. N., 38, 54
Sykes, R. N., 85, 112, 128
Synder, L., 87

T

Tam, P., 55, 86
Tataryn, D. J., 177
Taylor, C. M., 31, 53
Taylor, S. E., 93, 106
Tenney, Y. J., 38, 43, 54
Teply, L., 68, 86
Terr, L. C., 32, 54, 174, 178
Thomson, D. M., 92, 106, 109, 128, 130
Thürer, C., 93, 106
Tobey, A., 60, 87
Todd, C., 38, 39, 54
Todd, F., 142, 152
Tollestrup, P., 109, 113, 130, 160, 167, 172, 178
Trabasso, T., 37, 54
Tulving, E., 92, 106, 109, 128, 130
Turtle, J., 160, 167, 172, 178
Tversky, A., 54, 108, 129, 130

U–V

Underwood, B. J., 143, 153
Underwood, G., 147, 153
Valentine, T., 115, 130
Vandermaas, M. O., 32, 34, 35, 37, 54
Vaughan, C. L., 142, 154
Veefkind, N., 136, 154
Vernberg, E. M., 32, 54
Veronen, L. J., 177

W

Wade, G. S., 146, 153
Wagenaar, W. A., 136, 154
Wagner, W., 146, 153
Wagstaff, G. F., 109, 129
Walker, A. G., 6, 9–11, 55, 62, 67, 68, 74, 78, 81, 87, 142, 144
Wallbridge, H., 137, 152
Walsh, W., 162, 178
Wark, L., 66, 86, 94, 106
Warnick, D. H., 147, 150, 154
Warren, A. R., 38, 54, 57, 60, 62, 70, 78, 80, 86, 87
Watson, E. L., 109, 129
Weaver, C. A. III, 38, 54
Webber, L., 132, 152
Weinstein, D., 34, 53
Weisz, J. R., 36, 53
Wells, G. L., 107–113, 116, 119, 126, 129, 130, 132, 139, 144, 148, 151, 152, 154
Wells, K. B., 89, 106
Whipple, G. M., 156, 178
White, L. T., 62, 87
White, S. H., 40, 44, 46, 54
White, T., 26, 30
Whittenberger, G., 158, 176
Whittlesea, B. W. A., 111, 130
Wickens, D. D., 143, 154
Wilner, N., 162, 177
Winograd, E., 38, 54
Wolfner, G., 70, 87
Wolfskeil, M. P., 107, 127
Woody, P., 36, 52
Wrightsman, L. S., 57, 62, 67, 70, 80, 86

Y

Yarmey, A. D., 107, 115, 118, 125, 130–133, 135, 136, 142, 145–147, 150, 153, 154
Yarmey, A. L., 132, 135, 136, 154
Yarmey, M. J., 135, 136, 154
Yerkes, R. M., 7, 34, 35, 39, 54, 160, 178
Yudilevitch, L., 86
Yuille, J. C., 4, 7, 8, 12, 63, 65, 70, 72, 77, 80, 87, 109, 130–132, 147, 154, 155, 160, 165–168, 172, 174, 176, 178

Z

Zaparniuk, J., 174, 178
Zebrowitz-McArthur, L., 153
Zoberbier, D., 93, 106

Subject Index

For Product Safety Concerns and Information please contact our EU
representative GPSR@taylorandfrancis.com
Taylor & Francis Verlag GmbH, Kaufingerstraße 24, 80331 München, Germany

9 781138 002975